Spoiled Sport

Spoiled Sport

A FAN'S NOTES ON THE
TROUBLES OF SPECTATOR SPORTS

John Underwood

LITTLE, BROWN AND COMPANY • BOSTON • TORONTO

FIRST EDITION

LIBRARY OF CONGRESS CATALOGING IN PUBLICATION DATA

Underwood, John, 1934–
  Spoiled sport.

  1. Sports—United States—Moral and ethical aspects.
  2. Sports—Economic aspects—United States. I. Title.
  GV706.3.U53 1984   796'.0973   84-17182
  ISBN 0-316-88733-1

BP

DESIGNED BY JEANNE F. ABBOUD

*Published simultaneously in Canada
by Little, Brown & Company (Canada) Limited*

PRINTED IN THE UNITED STATES OF AMERICA

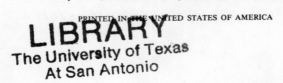

*For Donna, who saw it through and
made it all worthwhile.*

Acknowledgments

Writers, ever-relieved at seeing their creations alive and in print, are prone to praise editors far out of proportion to their worth. Having been in the writing dodge for more than half my life, I can say with some authority that more than a few of those editors to whom I have entrusted my blood were about as sensitive to the written word as slugs on a plate, and were too often cursed with ears of purest tin. I shudder to think of the damage. Having said that, I feel qualified to sincerely thank God and Little, Brown for Bill Phillips. This is our second time around, Editor Phillips and me, and if it wasn't better, it was certainly as good, because *he* is so good. Not just because he understands that writing is as much rhythm as it is words hammered out in sequence, but because he examines the content with such painstaking care. This book was a far tougher task than *Death of an American Game,* for him as well as me, and the snags we hit in piecing it together — including one at the end that was too absurd to imagine — became his campaign as much as mine. That was clear to me (writers are very sensitive to the resolve of editors) and I just wanted to thank him for it.

Others who contributed, wittingly or not, might be surprised to find their names here. Ted Williams is one; after all these years, he continues to amaze me with his interest and insight into what goes on in sport, and what hurts it. Jim Lynch, the old Notre Damer and former Kansas City

Chief, is another. And Marty Dardis, the cop, and Joe Paterno, the coach. And Father Joyce, John McKay, Bud Wilkinson, Father Thomas James of the Verbun Dei school in Los Angeles (you'll have to read on to know why; no shortcuts are provided in acknowledgments), and Charles Wright, a worthy anchorman, dean of the law school at the University of Texas and former head of the NCAA's infractions committee. I will think of others just before this goes to print and then, of course, it will be too late.

"Sport is religion, in the full, sacred
sense of the term. . . . It may well be America's
. . . most powerful religion."
> — *Charles Prebish,*
> *Professor of Religious Studies,*
> *Penn State University*

"They'd find room for Charles Manson if he
could hit .300."
> — *Jim Bouton,*
> *former pitcher,*
> *New York Yankees*

1.

A Question of Caring

I WAS about to say that I have lost my taste for sport. Not the sport that I do to satisfy those hidden competitive itches — the erratic tennis, the comic snow skiing — but the sport I watch. The sport that cornered much of my time as a journalist lo these many years, but whose madness, like that of the lovable but eccentric uncle who has finally gone over the line, I no longer find tolerable.

The sport we call "spectator" sport, as though we were detached from it, which could not be farther from the truth. The sport we call "organized" sport, although it is anything but (being packaged and merchandized is not the same as being organized). The sport of the professionals — the "national leagues" of our various pastimes; and the semiprofessionals — the big-time college teams and the aspiring Olympians who are paid, too, but not as much. The sport that drew me into the daily sports pages in my youth to agonize from afar over the ups and downs of teams and athletes who were dumb to my existence (did the Detroit Tigers ever wonder how *I* was doing?), but whom I adored nonetheless. The sport, I admit, that holds me still because in its purest form it is so rousing and conclusive, and therefore so appealing. A place where the enemy is plainly marked and victory is clear-cut, and no (or little) blood need be spilt.

Short of the love of a beautiful woman, I don't know

of anything more breathtaking than the recitals of great athletes performing up to snuff before large, admiring audiences; anything more thrilling, say, than a long, broken-field run, or more hair-raising than a last-second goal or a ninth-inning base hit that saves the skin of a favorite team. Such moments plucked from time become treasures as tangible as freeholdings, to cherish and pass down like heirlooms. For no better reason, "my" Tigers become my son's Tigers. It is practically a law.

I was about to say I have lost it, this taste for sport, but I haven't. It was taken from me — from all of us.

It did not fade away naturally, like a blemish on the skin. It was excised, the work of the quack surgeons we call "owners" and "administrators" and "league presidents" and "agents" and "network executives," the modern manipulators of sport.

Where once I would gladly plunk down the price of admission to see a team of skilled professionals improve on the games we learn in childhood, I am now reluctant, even resentful. I am amazed we have allowed it to happen. I would suspect a conspiracy, but I am not sure the opportunists who run sport are that smart. Duplicity is more their style. And bullying. And greed, of course, is their incentive. I am not sure but what they have taken the heart right out of sport. I *am* sure that it is no longer the same.

It takes no special insight to see that sport is important stuff in America, whatever the manner it is perceived or utilized — as healthy diversion for vast numbers of people, as a refuge from social demons for others, etc. etc. To each his own, and no matter. It is obviously too good to be left to the publicists and bottom-line mentalities who run it (and play it) now.

If it could speak on its own behalf, the real complaining party at the bar would be sport itself. It has been transformed into economic snakeoil. From something wonderful, it has been made grotesque by commerce. It has been distorted and polluted by money, and the never-ending quest for more. It has been appropriated by a growing army of owner-entrepreneurs who made a remarkable discovery after the 1950s: that sport was not sport at all but a tool for extracting incredible riches from the sports-hungry populace.

It is easy to follow the subversions since then. The fingerprints are everywhere. Mainly they can be traced to the two major influences that caught us up in the glamor and beguiled us into believing just the opposite as they suborned sport and altered its face. Grown to full maturity, those two influences now work as an axis, usually with their names on the same gaudy contracts. They are: (1) the rise and spread of professional sport as the *ne plus ultra* and role model (and, conversely, the decline of amateur sport in those capacities), and (2) television.

Sport has become the shill of television. The failure to recognize the contaminating power of television — not in and of itself, because television is no better or worse than we allow it to be, but by permitting it to dominate sport: *that* failure is shocking. Instead of harnessing the good of television for the good of sport, sport has been swept up by it. The irony is that the custodians of sport think it is the other way around. They think they have made television pay (those huge, happy sums) when actually they have just been bought off.

The shameless grafting of Big Sport to Big Television to produce Big Dollars has yielded a harvest of aberrations, from the monstrous brutality and drug abuse infecting the pros to the abysmal disclosures of recruiting bribery and coast-to-coast academic cheating among the major colleges. The former is still being unfolded (but no longer denied) in daily headlines. The true depths are still

being plumbed as the emerging stars of the 1980s turned
out to be the chemicals athletes use to build themselves
up and turn themselves on and tune themselves out. Much
of the violence that now saturates Big Sport is little more
than that — a form of chemical warfare.

Sport's leadership threw in to this madness by placing
such an oppressive burden on winning that it made desperate men out of its coaches and better athletes. Winning
pays the bills. Winning assures the television deals, and
the outlandish contracts and salaries. The desperate athlete resorts to almost anything — to cheating, to brutality,
even to poisoning his body with drugs — to stay in the
money.

The desperate coach becomes traumatized by the need
to win. He is not blind or deaf to the demands. He knows
that by the time he gets his ear to the ground to pick up
the negative vibrations he is liable to be out on it. In the
Big Sports marketplace, there is no such thing as security
for a coach. When he starts out, the one thing he can be
certain of is that he will be fired, sooner more often than
later. The annual turnover is awesome. The National
Football League began the 1983 season with new head
coaches for eight of its twenty-six teams — a turnover of
almost a third. The National Basketball Association had
nine new coaches out of twenty-three — *more* than a third.

The joy is swept from sport when the market relegates
everything to the bottom line. "The score" becomes its
own reward — and the market doesn't much care how it
scores. It glorifies brutes and clowns and brats, and makes
heroes of the worst examples of sportsmanship instead of
the best. (Having paid to see them once, I would not pay
again to watch John McEnroe or Ilie Nastase disgrace the
game of tennis. But others do and as long as they do
McEnroe and Nastase will continue to act disgracefully.)

The process has debauched sportsmanship to the point

where winning at all costs is, indeed, costing too much.
The items sacrificed include honor and fair play. To resort
to drugs and brutality to gain a competitive edge is a bow
to a desperation run amok. To corrupt the educational
process, to make a fraud of the student-athlete in order
to win, is not to win at all.

We are so anesthetized to this insanity that we do not
realize how unsporting our spectator sports have become — how unsportsmanlike it is to cheat, either by illegal, sometimes injurious acts on the field, or the more
insidious acts of deception and rules-bending off it.

Cheating corrupts, and inspires greater corruption. Like
dry rot, money accelerates the decay. We should admit
that we have finally bought enough rope to hang ourselves
when we look up to find that illegal gambling is now an
accepted resident of the Big Sports community. Illegal
gambling on sporting events has grown to a $120 billion
mob venture, and the influence is widespread and sinister.

College coaches complain that the volume of their hate
mail rises and falls not so much with their winning or
losing, but whether they "beat the spread." Pro games
revolve around point spreads and odds. The shills of gambling now occupy the television booth and get their "lines"
printed in the daily paper. That is not just shocking, it is
heinous.

Recently, I spoke to a class of law students at the University of Miami. At one point I said the outcome of an
athletic contest must never be doubted, because if it is,
sport dies. Either that or it becomes pro wrestling. I asked
for a show of hands of those who thought what they now
see in professional sports is on the up and up. I didn't
count the hands, but I would guess no more than sixty
percent were raised. A dubious vote of confidence.

Perhaps even worse, the market has taught the young
men of sport to accept cheating as part of the process,

even as a means to an education, or as a substitute for it.
Like zombies they willingly go along as the process hastens
their dehumanization. The "pro drafts" are slave auctions
that violate every tenet of the free enterprise system. College recruiting is a ritual of bribery that too often rewards
cheaters with conference championships and television
dates. The threat of getting caught is no deterrent.

The National Collegiate Athletic Association has had
to mete out penalties against 176 of its member schools
on 264 occasions since it began a rules-enforcement program in 1952. In 1982, the fed-up president of San Francisco University, facing the school's third probation in four
years, dropped basketball. It was the only way he knew
to stop the cheating.

Both practices — recruiting and drafting — easily create in the athlete's mind a cynicism for the system and a
broad distrust of the "superiors" he must deal with. Especially if he wakes up on the other side of his athletic
experience to find he has neither money in the bank nor
an education to count on. Along this loathsome byway,
the black athlete has been especially misused, although it
is difficult to tell him that because he has been getting a
large share of the pie lately and doesn't want to let go.
His own black leaders — most of them — don't tell him.
They allow him to believe that salvation is just one more
bounce of the basketball away. From the ghetto to the
grave he believes that, and the results are often tragic.

It would be funny if it weren't so sad, but the high-
salaried athletes of sport have achieved their own Catch
22 in the marketplace. They have become the willing foils
of their own alienation. Because they go along with the
hype (the one that confuses inflated contracts with
achievement), the greatest practitioners of sport have become affluent freaks. They are now almost impossible to
identify with, the one quality they cannot afford to lose.

A sports hero is not Frank Sinatra on tour. To reduce his status to "entertainer" and to excuse his misbehavior on that basis is a popular psychology nowadays, but it is not valid. Entertainers do not wear your school's colors and carry them into battle. They do not "represent" your city. The sports hero is a product of the allegiance of his fans, and uniquely tied to it. Sports entrepreneurs extract from loyal fans great commitments in patience and funding (while they "build a winner") because of this relationship, even to getting tax-paid arenas built for their own profitable use.

In turn, the fan wants (and has every right to expect) the athlete to be loyal — to the school or to the town, and especially to him. In order to be beloved the athlete must be able to impart to that fan the illusion of caring. Caring that the name on his shirt inspires more than just a casual commitment. He *cannot* be loved when it inspires no allegiance at all, or is exposed as a fake by the demands he makes (those massive figures) to keep him happy and in town. As often as not, that is the reason he is booed and pilloried, and has himself come to show such contempt for the fans who underwrite him.

Obviously it *is* hard to love an athlete whose celebrated million-dollar salary supports a dollar-ninety-eight batting average. On those occasions, he is more likely to be despised, if only until his next home run. The tolerance level has sunk alarmingly as the fan sees the athlete in a new and bleaker light. Combine the stupid money hype with the well-publicized acrimony between management and athlete — the almost daily reminders that they are now adversaries instead of partners in sport — and you get an image of a sports hero as mercenary, as a grifter.

Baseball managers complain that it is no longer possible to inspire an athlete with traditional team values. Gene Mauch says you can't even threaten them with fines anymore because they make so much money a fine means nothing. Tony LaRussa says you can't get them to lay down sacrifice bunts because they're afraid of losing the chance to drive in a run. Runs-batted-in are worth more than sacrifice bunts at the bargaining table. A pro football coach told me of a veteran second-string player he had who balked at a trade that would have made him a starter. The player liked the money he was getting for riding the bench and did not want to risk injury "so late in his career."

But don't be too hard on the players of our games. They have merely taken their cues from owners and administrators — from those entrepreneurs who *really* know how to jerk sport around, and the loyal fans with it.

The padrones of sport are milking it dry. They have inflated ticket prices to the point where a trip to the ballpark for the average family is now an adventure in high finance. They move their clubs and players from city to city like gypsies, or threaten to if demands for a new stadium or a better lease or a few million dollars' worth of improvements are not met. They cater to the whims of television by playing games at all hours and twisting the seasons around and stretching them out so that they overlap and smother each other in the endless grubbing for money.

Professional football is now being played in the summertime, courtesy of the United States Football League and the American Broadcasting Company, which, with a $14 million contract, subsidized the USFL's first two years of business. The USFL is, in every sense, made-for-TV sport. Anticipating television windfalls of their own, pro basketball and pro hockey expanded their 1984 playoff formats so that sixteen of twenty-three teams in the NBA and sixteen of twenty-one teams in the NHL were assured places in the "championship" tournaments. That meant that hundreds of regular season games would be all but meaningless for the paying customers of thirty-two of forty-four professional teams.

Owners, as a whole, never stop crying poormouth, and as often as not blame players' agents for their fiscal problems, as if contracts were signed at gunpoint in dark alleys. Agents are a relatively new form of coercion, and undoubtedly deserve some of the credit they get for the spoiling of sport. They crawl over the games like lice, promoting conflict and helping inflate player salaries and benefits so that the average bench-rider in professional basketball makes more than the President of the United States and some seventy baseball players make *four times* that. In the process, "labor relations" and "collective bargaining" and the harsh principles they embrace have become prominent words in the lexicon of sport. Truth-bending on both sides is epidemic.

But it is a smoke screen that hardly hides the real issue — the issue of who *really* pays for such extravagance. In this, the market has truly made fools of the paying spectators of sport. We have been cuckolded. One wonders if we will ever wake up to our disgrace. That *we* are the real financiers of the whole bloody mess. It is not the owners and the networks who pay those swollen sums, it is the fans who ultimately pay.

It is the fans who pay when collective bargaining ends and fiscal realities take over. We now have unions in professional sport, and strikes and the specter of strikes, and every time a new settlement is reached it is the fans who have to dig a little deeper. It is the poor foolish fans who make millionaires out of the entrepreneurs, and keep the exalted stars in Bill Blass slacks and the uppers and downers of their choice.

It is the fans who pay when the ticket prices go up to support the massive payrolls. It is the fans who pay when the price of a hotdog jumps a buck, a parking spot rents for five, and the county commission votes a tax increase to build the entrepreneur a new stadium, complete with sky boxes and closed-circuit TV. The fans only *think* the television networks pay when the National Football League gets two billion dollars for a new contract and major league baseball gets a billion. The networks simply pass the expense along to the sponsors, who then jack up the price of their razor blades and beer and shovel it on to the fans.

Maybe it is already too late. Maybe, without realizing it, the fans are already fed up. Not long ago I was on a network talk show with a former Philadelphia Eagles line-backer, John Bunting. The subject, loosely speaking (for that is the way the host, Phil Donahue, treated it), was "fan violence." Bunting brought along his two young children to describe the nature of the beasts who attended Eagles home games. His kids said they dreaded Sundays at the ballpark because of the slurs and obscenities the fans hurled at their dad. Bunting said he wished that that was all they hurled. He said he had taken to wearing his helmet going down the tunnel to the field to ward off the flying examples of fan alienation (cups, ice, bottles, etc.).

If sport were a hospital patient it would be in intensive care. Its very form has been altered to accommodate the marketplace, a restructuring that suffocates sport at those important amateur levels, most especially the high schools. While Big Sport and Big Television combine in the glo-rious quest for one more prime-time date and one more ratings coup, high-school sport is drowning in a sea of red ink. Car washes and streetcorner pretzel sales can't keep it alive forever. No alarm has been sounded, but in recent years youngsters have been quitting organized sports in droves. Many high schools now complain of an inability to field teams because of dwindling numbers and the high costs.

I have notes, pinned to other notes like pilot fish, measuring the withering away. Twenty-five high-school coaches in Moxee City, Washington, are coaching at half-pay. Entire little league programs across the country have caved in. Minor league and semipro sports are all but things of the past. In Miami, high-school football attendance is on a twenty-seven-year decline. Philadelphia, and the entire state of California, came close to giving up school football. Calumet (Michigan) High School, home of George Gipp, *did* give it up. It could no longer afford it. When tryouts were held for the 1984 football season at St. Cecelia's High School in Englewood, N.J., twelve candidates showed up. The school announced it was dropping the sport. St. Cecelia's is where Vince Lombardi started his coaching career in 1939.

The dying off of sport at the grassroots level does not happen all at once. It is not the quick carnage from some kind of economic cyclone. It happens gradually; a steadily squeezing hand on the throat. The reckless proliferation of Big Sport, with its seasons twining together like noodles on a plate, and its endless hype, and its deadly coalition with Big Television, makes us want to believe a myth: that Big Sport is the only sport worth watching.

It may have achieved the opposite of that: it may be the sport we should *stop* watching. At least until we realize that, on its present course, it will not cross us over into Jordan.

As with all matters of the heart, the passion we give to sport is mostly an involuntary thing. It is not required that we fall in love with the local team or its star players or give them our devotion, and the sense in it is not always easy to find. We do it anyway, probably before our powers

of ratiocination are developed. But it is fun, and it is done,
and as I have done it myself I accept it without always
understanding it. I loved the Detroit Tigers years before
I ever saw one in the flesh, or even knew for sure where
Detroit was, and I didn't even question that love until I
was in my thirties. I figured it was something I would
outgrow. I had better luck with asthma.

What follows, therefore, are not the bleatings of a de-
tractor, but the honest concern of a lover of sport who
just can't stand the unsightliness of it any more. Or, closer
to the point, the meanness of it. Sport is such a personal
thing and much of the passion for it so personally felt that
one would be lacking good judgment to attack on too
broad a front, however. So if I miss some of the more
popular areas of complaint, or have not proffered solutions for every single example of mismanagement, it is
because these *are* personal feelings that do not naturally
stretch out to cover the landscape, and because I simply
don't have all the answers. I wish I did.

I said earlier that it is not the same, sport isn't. Clearly
this is so. But to understand the difference, I think it is
important first to appreciate what we had. Not for nostalgia, although I am a sucker for that, but for reference.
Not because sport was all that cleaner "back when," but
because it was more positively perceived, and less confused by labor relations and marketplace ethics, and better
administered (because it was *less* valuable to manipulators), and therefore infinitely more appealing.

My own appreciation was updated, rather excitingly, I
thought, on a recent duck hunt with Ted Williams, the
old ball player. I undoubtedly derived more from the experience than Ted did, he not being in the analysis business, but I don't think he would be offended if I used him
to make the point. He will be offended by my calling him

"the old ball player" because that's a little like calling Jascha Heifitz "the old fiddler," but this is my book, not his.

We had hunted early, but futilely. The Arkansas floods had scattered the ducks and Stuttgart was crawling with frustrated gunmen, their trigger fingers itching perceptibly. Ted was not one of them. Frustrated, I mean. At such times my own tolerance for the job goes quickly, like bathwater down an opened drain, but his never wanes. For such a chronically impatient man he is maddeningly patient on a hunt.

Since before the predawn mist had lifted he had stood like a sentinel beside a huge but deformed pin oak, its grotesque limbs reaching up in desperate prayer. Only occasionally did he shift in his waders, then doing it deliberately to ruffle the gelid water around the decoys. If I were not used to it, I would have sworn he was napping. My own prayer was that we go home.

I watched out of the corner of my eye from my place in the frigid blind, and silently berated him for his staying power. I imagined him finally coming unglued and with a cry hurling his shotgun into that grieving Arkansas sky, the way he once threw baseball bats (and the way he now sometimes throws tennis racquets), and the two of us, amazed, watching it spiral comically into the air and splash down, and him wading out to retrieve it, embarrassed. But I knew he wouldn't do it.

A single mallard flew over then, flying high and fast and ignoring the decoys. Ted gave it the dispassionate glance it deserved and didn't move. With my less-practiced eye and more advanced ardor, I jerked up my 12-gauge and lobbed a single shot, aiming well ahead. To my surprise, and undoubtedly to his, the duck flinched massively, and fell. It took forever getting down, fluttering dramatically. A hotdog wrapper on the wind.

Ted was closest to the landing spot and volunteered to wade out after it, muttering aloud as he went that the duck probably hadn't been hit at all. That upon seeing pellets at that altitude it had probably suffered a heart attack. Later, when we had returned to the lodge and were sealed comfortably in its warmth, he renewed his rationalizing against "circus shots" (I refused to recognize it as a "throwaway"). He said if more were forthcoming the next day, when conditions were forecast to be no better, he'd just as soon go into town and watch the local artists make duck callers. We were interrupted by a knock on the door.

Again Ted was closest. He opened to an angular, gray-haired man in his seventies, with the limby, loose-jointed look of a born athlete. A guest Ted obviously would have welcomed under any circumstance. It was galvanic.

"Ted, how are you? How's the hunting?" the older man said, grinning.

"Bill Dickey!" Ted shouted. "Geez, Bill, you look terrific. Doesn't he look terrific? Come in, come in. We're gonna eat soon. Fried chicken. No duck." He gave me a look. "Geez, this is great."

Understand, I am not a hero worshipper. I have my heroes, but most of them are alive only in books, and I am not even sure what my requirements are.

But that night in Stuttgart in the company of those two Hall of Famers, catcher Dickey of the Yankees and out-fielder Williams of the Red Sox (it is important to note that they are identified only with a single team), their baseball lives spanning the decades like golden arches from the 1920s when Dickey started to 1960 when Williams retired, I experienced a high I would not ordinarily expect in matters removed from the heart.

I was, in a word, captivated. Once a fan always a fan. A couple more tonics laced with the good gin Williams had freighted in for the week and I think I would have achieved levitation.

They talked about many things, ricocheting material off their tiny audience. It was as if they had been hired for the evening, like a song-and-dance team from Western Union. I knew better. They did it to satisfy each other, the way veterans of some past worthwhile endeavor always do: to review the battles, to compare priceless notes, to reminisce.

They talked about Ruth and Gehrig. (Their feuding was a myth, Dickey said. "Only their wives were rivals. Their wives didn't get along worth a damn.")

They talked about managing — Williams had been lured into it in the 1970s ("what a lousy job *that* was") — and of the great managers they had known, Joe McCarthy and Joe Cronin and Casey Stengel, and of the great modern players, Mantle and Mays and Aaron, and the ones who will be great. Williams said McCarthy once told him if he could have hit like Ted he'da "played for nothing." "So would I," Dickey laughed.

They talked about how pitching styles changed overnight when Don Larsen pitched his perfect game in the 1954 World Series, without ever using a wind-up. And about how catchers no longer catch with "two hands." Dickey held up his own misshapen right hand, splaying out the twisted fingers to form what resembled a bouquet of crullers. Every one had been broken at least once, Dickey said. "It was dumb for coaches to insist on sticking that free hand up there," he said. "Put it behind your back where it's safe."

They talked about the consequences of big league expansion, first to the West Coast, then in all directions, forever changing the map of baseball, and the lingering death of the minor leagues. How those two happenings coincided with the irresistible growth of televised sport. And they talked about the advent of the millionaire ball-player who couldn't hit his weight. And the new breed of owners with their bizarre ways. They agreed that no one was more bizarre than George Steinbrenner.

Dickey apparently had done well since he left the game. There were investments, and he had worked to a position of prominence for a stockbroker in Little Rock until his retirement the year before. Williams, of course, had never lost his popularity. By his own unsophisticated marketing of that attraction (I have never been with him that he was not hounded for autographs) he had achieved a considerable affluence, one that had never fully dawned on him. Doubting he would ever "have it made," and without an agent to run his interference, he kept plugging away.

My own mind wandered then to a portion of the research I had done for this book. Specifically, how the money glut had altered the priorities of professional athletes since television gained control. In the decade of the seventies alone, major league baseball salaries had gone up 500 percent. After that they *really* soared. Dave Winfield, an outfielder who had batted .300 only one time in his entire career, had been the beneficiary of a Steinbrenner windfall that figured out to more than $1.8 million a year. Steve Garvey had signed a five-year contract to play in San Diego for $6.6 million. Dale Murphy got $8 million for a five-year deal in Atlanta. George Foster of the Reds presumably would be getting $2 million a year into middle age.

The *New York Times* averaged out the capital gain of a ball player named Ronnie Stennet — I couldn't even place the name — to demonstrate precisely how much was being paid for how little. Stennet averaged $6,896 per trip every time he went to the plate for the Pittsburgh club in 1981. Carrying the computation a step farther, and taking into consideration that he made outs at least two out of three trips, Stennet's "earnings" figured out to about $20,000 per hit.

And I remembered something Williams himself had told me years ago: that before his last season with the Red Sox he had actually asked for a pay *cut*. He had come off his only sub-.300 season and had refused Tom Yawkey's offer to play one more year at $125,000. He went to Yawkey, a man he loved like a father, and said he would play, but for $90,000.

I brought up the incident for Dickey, and Williams nodded.

"That's right. It was all I deserved."

"I doubt you'd find many players knocking down an owner's door to do that today," Dickey said, and laughed softly. "The most I ever made was $30,000. But, of course, $30,000 was a lot more money then." He said he did not begrudge the modern players' affluence. To the contrary. He thought it was just great.

"You're damn right," Williams said. "I'm all for 'em. Let 'em get whatever they can while they can. The owners will never pay more they can afford anyway."

"But you know, Ted," Dickey said, "I think we really had it better. I mean even back when I played."

Williams agreed. "I know I've always said that the best time for me was right after the war, the way the game was played, the way it was received. I used to say all I cared about was my next turn at bat, and I probably acted that way, too. But I was *so* gung-ho. So eager and full of vinegar. I couldn't *wait* to get to the ballpark."

"I enjoyed it so much, even during the Depression," Dickey said. "The Yankee teams were as close as any group I've ever been around. Even the train rides were fun."

He said he could remember very few hassles with man-

agement. Once, in 1939, the great DiMaggio had held out
for $40,000, refusing to go to camp until he got it. When
he didn't — he got the $25,000 he had been offered —
he went to camp anyway.

"We were family," Dickey said. "Like we were all in
it together. The fans were great. They couldn't have been
more supportive. It's a different game now. I don't think
I would enjoy it as much now as I did then. I wouldn't
trade, not even for all that money."

"No," Williams said. "Not for anything." He grinned.
"And I didn't always think the Boston fans were so wonderful, either. I do now. I must really be getting old."

It dawned on me then why I was so charmed by all this.

These giants of sport were heroes not just because they
were such great athletes, although they were. And not
because they blazed across the heavens of my memory
from an earlier time, when everything seemed better. I
scarcely knew Dickey; he was a name that descended before baseball captivated me. And, as a kid, I remembered
the infernal Williams more for the wreckage he caused
whenever the Red Sox took on my beloved Tigers. He
seemed always to be going three-for-four.

No, they were special to me at that moment — instant
heroes, I suppose — because they so obviously cared about
the sport they had played, and that had been so good to
them. Cared about the people they played it with, and
the men they played it for, and the patrons who funded
it. Cared, without having to say so, about the way it was
treated. They seemed to know instinctively how important
all this was. And it dawned on me that so simple an expression evoked so warm a response because caring was now
in such short supply in sport. And that sport had been
spoiled terribly because of it.

I wondered who if any in that seemingly endless parade
of modern athletes who were making the police blotter

instead of the Wheaties box knew about caring. I wondered if the Chicago Cubs pitcher arrested for assaulting the police officer cared.

Or Art Schlichter, the Baltimore Colt quarterback with the $300,000 illegal gambling debt.

Or the three Kansas City Royals sentenced to prison for drug buys.

Or Mercury Morris, the former All-Pro halfback, imprisoned for dealing.

Or Steve Howe, the Dodger pitcher who lived in a perpetual cocaine cloud.

Or Billy Cannon, the dentist-turned-counterfeiter with the most dolorous distinction I could imagine: the only Heisman Trophy winner ever to serve time.

One after another they had marched across the sports pages of America, a shabby, tacky group making their mark not for dramatic home runs or touchdown passes, but for sexual assault, and drug running, and urinating in public places.

And I wondered, too, if a poor, confused, embittered young black man named Don Reese knew any more about caring than he had when I first met him. Certainly Don Reese knew about the spoiling of sport.

Chaos can have gentle beginnings. The evolutionary process that leads to the manipulation and dehumanization of today's athlete is hatched more often than not by caring people who love him. But once in motion it moves him as remorselessly as an assembly line, often under the control of *un*caring people who use him. When he emerges on the far side, himself a user bereft of gratitude or grace, and sometimes dangerously antisocial as well, it is easy to forget that it may have begun with the best of intentions.

I have a tape that Bill Walsh made for me just after he defected from Stanford to coach the 49ers in the National

Football League. I met Walsh on that tape, but I felt I had known him for years. We could have sung duets.

The process starts, Walsh said, with that first day the youth league coach takes the youngster under his wing and tells him he can be a "great player." To do it, he tells the boy to specialize, to "forgo all the other sports — no tennis, no swimming. 'Never mind the piano, practice your baseball.' The coach cares. He enjoys his work and, naturally, he'd like to develop a star player.

"The boy enrolls in high school, and the coach there sees his potential. He wants him to have the 'opportunity to excel.' Whether he realizes it or not, the coach starts directing his life — telling him what courses to take, giving him a study program that does not challenge him in the classroom or develop the disciplines of the mind that will best serve him in society.

"The parents fall into the trap. They're happy their son is being 'taken care of.' If he is really exceptional, the local townspeople get involved, from the mayor on down. They treat him specially, to the point where he does not have a real perspective on life. 'Things' are done for him. Grades are 'given.' No one wants to spoil his chances to make it big.

"The college recruiter visits. He tells the parents he will 'take care' of their boy. That he'll have the 'best of everything.' The young man still has not had to deal with the day-to-day frustrations others feel. Subconsciously, he is quite willing to accept this attention — his name in the paper, a suit of clothes, being steered away from classes he 'won't need.' After all, he's going to be a pro."

Walsh said that such a boy goes through his entire academic career "protected." He lives in special dormitories, eats special food, takes carefully chosen courses. He lives and moves with youngsters of the same narrow, selfish interests. The coaches try "harder and harder to segregate him because that's what the competition does, and he goes along willingly, and so do his parents. We do everything but educate him. We're afraid he'll fail, so we look for ways of making it easier. Soon his entire outlook is distorted."

The climb leads to more and larger distortions. "To fast money, and faster friends. To 'deals,' and maybe to drugs and shady people. He's like the beautiful woman who has been 'taken care of,' until her beauty wanes or her dumbness manifests itself. Then comes reality. Suddenly he can't handle the things he has been sheltered from. He wakes up at twenty-five or so with no education and nothing to grab hold of. Resenting everything, unhappy with himself. And if he's black, he'll say it was a racial thing. 'I was taken advantage of because I was black,' or because 'I was poor.'

"It can be devastating."

Don Reese is black. He knows about distortions. About being given things, and having them taken away. He knows about life in the fast lane, and the realities to be found in the vast and soulless empire of professional sport. He woke up at thirty, just in time. Maybe.

By all reckoning, Don Reese did not figure — not as the typical exploited black athlete. He was not raised in a ghetto. He knew neither poverty nor hunger growing up. His large, tight-knit family was a model of decorum in Pritchard, Alabama, a town of eighty-five hundred "a skip and a hop" from Mobile. The Reeses worked hard. They had "influence." They exhibited character. Don knew the inside of the Baptist church from a regular association.

He had been the fourth of eleven children born to Albert and Osie Dean Reese. His father owned a funeral home and had a grave-digging business in Pritchard, and pushed discipline and education. An older sister and two older brothers went to college ahead of Don, one to play football at Grambling, and others coming up behind were pointed in that direction. Don knew he'd go to college, too, because "Daddy had me digging graves with a pick and shovel at fifteen, and I didn't want to do *that* the rest of my life." Sometimes, he told me when we discussed his story for *Sports Illustrated*, "the funeral procession would be coming down the road and I'd still be digging."

He said he wished he had "never played football after high school." But how much he wanted to play even then is a moot point. He was very big, and very strong, and he got "good" despite himself. His father, he said, pushed him hard. "If I didn't play, Daddy said I couldn't use the car. He had a pink 'seventy-three Brougham. That was a good argument."

In high school, the only thing he knew about drugs was what he heard. He tried wine, but it made him sick. There were, however, other forms of permissiveness. "I wasn't the best student. I didn't try." He passed anyway — until the end of his senior year when he got suspended after a fight with a white player. To get his diploma he was made to finish his last four months at a trade school, at night. By then, of course, the football season was over. There were no more games to play. He was expendable.

His indifference toward playing big-time college football (there had been "many offers," including one from Alabama) irritated his father, Reese said. So he agreed to go to Jackson State, a predominantly black school across the border in Mississippi.

"Why Jackson State?" I asked.

"Because it was close to home. Only a hundred and eighty miles away."

"You'd still need wheels to get back and forth."

"Yeah. My dad gave me a 'sixty-seven Chevrolet Impala, SS 396. The slickest car on campus."

On hearing of Don's interest, Jackson State offered him a scholarship. It was that easy. He was a "property." He said the assistant coach who talked to him said he could "look in my eyes and tell I was going to be a great player." Great players, he found, didn't have to study much at Jackson State, either. He "got by," but he wasn't "into" school. He was into "other things."

He wore a diamond in one pierced ear, and his hair piled up on his head "like the punk I was," and he enjoyed life as a privileged athlete. He tried pot for the first time. It made him sick. But he tried it again. After a while it didn't make him sick anymore. He "never had to pay for it," it was something he took for granted. "No big deal." Only much later would he realize that you *always* pay.

The learning process accelerated. Reese had frequent run-ins with his coach, Bob Hill. He broke curfew. He jumped the wall to visit a coed, his wife-to-be. He used pot when he had the chance. After his last game, on a Thanksgiving night, he and a few of his teammates "sneaked a couple of majorettes up to my room at the dorm to smoke some reefers. We had barely lit up when there was a banging on the door. 'Reese!' It was Coach Hill. '. . . Pack your bags, Reese, and get the hell out of here. We don't want you here anymore.' I packed up and left the next day."

"In the Chevy?"

"No, on a 750 Yamaha I just bought. My father had sent me eight hundred dollars for it."

It is important to note that as in high school he was suspended *after* he had used up his eligibility. It was also interesting that in the days that followed he was invited to play in the Senior Bowl, and did, and was subsequently drafted in the first round by the Miami Dolphins — and then received another message from Coach Hill, quite different from a pounding on the door. Hill called "as if nothing had happened" and invited him *back* to the Jackson State campus. To be "honored." To get his picture taken shaking hands with the governor.

I asked Reese if he ever got his degree, but knew the answer before he gave it. "No."

It would be nice to say that in his account of the years that followed — the precipitous decline into drugs, the disgrace of a jail term in Miami, the further degradations in New Orleans and San Diego — Reese exhibited a keenness for pinpointing causes. He did not. Not because the accumulation was so vast, I think, but because it had grown into something much more chilling. Excess begot excess. It was all around him. It had become a way of life.

He remembered that a Dolphin scout had come to Mobile to escort him down to Miami for his contract talk with the Dolphins. "We were the only two in first class, in a big Delta jet. He said, 'You in the big time now, baby, order anything you want.' I just laid back, and I ordered a vodka and orange juice, a gin and orange juice, a *bourbon* and orange juice. I was flying high."

He remembered going to the Dolphins' owner's house, "and seeing booze and dirty glasses all over the place, looked like from two or three weeks." And after signing, being taken back to Dallas by his agent, Abner Haynes, "to celebrate." He sat in a room at the Holiday Inn and watched some of the celebrants "take out those little brown vials of white powder . . . and sniff it up their noses. My first look at cocaine."

He said he didn't try it then. "I wanted to, but I held back."

When a defensive back named Lloyd Mumphord brought some to his room the first week of camp, he held back no longer. He said "a lot of the guys were doing it, and if they were doing it, why shouldn't I?" It burned his nose, but he got a powerful "zing," and a sudden urge to go to the bathroom. "I remember sitting there thinking, 'Dang, this is the best shit I ever had.' "

He estimated "about half" the Dolphins were using, in "recreational" doses. He said some of them had "hot plates in their rooms at camp to prepare it." On team charters coming home from road games, he said, they clustered in the back where it was dark and sniffed from little brown bottles. He said he knew because he was one of them.

He remembered how easy it was to get. How it "didn't cost anything for a while, and even after it did the players could get it cheap." Didn't he consider the consequences? "I wasn't thinking about no consequences. I was thinking about enjoying myself, just like everybody else." He said "most of the black guys were on it. There were some white guys on it too, but I didn't know how many." By his third year, he was up to four or five grams a week.

I asked where he got it. He said he had "about twelve connections." In New Orleans, there were "more than that. You could 'beep' 'em and they'd bring it to you." I asked him who, where, how. For the first time he grew reticent. "It wasn't my concern at the time," he said. "It's people, man. And they're not good people. It's people you don't play with. People who have a lot at stake. I'm not going to say where I got it."

Reese said they were well known by the players. That they even came to practice, "right to the edge of the field." That they were "into things" besides drugs.

On May 4, 1977, set up by an airline stewardess they had "tooted with" previously and who claimed she needed money for her mother's hospital bills and could arrange a deal, Reese and teammate Randy Crowder were arrested in a Miami motel room for attempting to sell a pound of cocaine to two Miami undercover cops.

Judge Joe Durant sentenced Reese and Crowder to a

year in the Miami stockade, a reasonable punishment for first-time offenders but criticized as "lenient" by the local press. They were, after all, big-time athletes who should have set better examples. For his part, Durant acquired a nickname that would haunt him and eventually ruin his career: "Let 'Em Go Joe."

What did the brush with disaster teach him? Reese said: "For five hundred bucks I threw my career in the toilet." But it didn't turn out that way. Not at all. If it taught him anything, it taught him how far beyond the pale a big-time athlete could operate. If anything, it reaffirmed how much he could get away with.

Prison did not cure his drug lust. Just the opposite. In the Miami stockade he found "as many drugs inside as out. We used marijuana freely." He even sniffed coke once, "although I was wary." And if the Miami press was unforgiving, the football establishment was not. He was still in his prime. He was still a "property."

The day Reese was released from jail, he got a call from none other than Bob Hill, his old coach. Hill had gone to work for the New Orleans Saints. The man who kicked him out of school for sinning was "eager" to usher him back into football as a Saint. Reese drove to Vero Beach, where the Saints trained, and met the owner, John Mecom. He liked Mecom. Mecom hugged him and pushed money on him and said, "I don't care what's happened before, you're a Saint now." Reese signed on. A new start.

By 1980, Reese was making $150,000 a year, plus bonuses. He was the Saints leading tackler, and their 1979 Most Valuable Player on defense. Certainly it must be true: he was invincible. He could get away with anything. He had been doing it all his life. Cocaine? Bring it on.

New Orleans turned out to be a coke-head's paradise. Saints players even snorted in the locker room before games, and sometimes at halftime. Reese learned "to free-base" — to cook a large amount of coke down to a gummy rock, freeing up the base, then with a glass pipe inhaling the fumes from the reheated scrapings, "the ultimate high."

The very best Saints players were on it, he said. "Chuck Muncie, a superman. And George Rogers, the Heisman Trophy winner." Rogers had been the Saints' number one draft choice in 1981. Reese said Rogers approached him in the locker room shortly after camp opened.

"I didn't even know him. Never met him. Never even seen him play. But we were in the dressing room and he and another dude came over to where I was standing. He said, 'Hey, man, I understand you're the one can put us on to a little coke.' I couldn't believe it. I said, 'Get your ass away from me.' " (Rogers implicated himself to police later, admitting to a $10,000 cocaine habit.)

From the edge of All-Pro in 1979, Reese was to the edge of oblivion in 1981. His growing addiction alienated his family and wasted his fortune. He told of experiencing the humiliation of having checks bounce and cars repossessed. He told of discovering the dark side of the drug world. Of twice being threatened by "creditors" with loaded guns. And how in his despair he had put his own gun into his mouth and "practiced" pulling the trigger. He said if he had had the guts, he would have. One night in Miami, he roamed the streets for hours trying to buy enough heroin to do the job.

By the time he was traded to San Diego in 1981, Reese's cocaine habit was costing him $1,500 to $1,800 a month. In San Diego, "the only difference in the drug abuse . . . was that more and bigger names were involved." A Chargers wide receiver met him at the training camp the minute he arrived, and within hours they were "cooking." They cooked until two in the morning, and the next day Reese passed the team physical — to his everlasting amazement. But by then he was on borrowed time. His descent was irre-

versible. Less than a year later, Reese walked into a re-
habilitation clinic in Orange County, California, to give
himself over to treatment. The fact that he could walk at
all was something he no longer took for granted. At thirty,
his mind and body were in ruin, his football career over.
He was lucky to be alive. And he knew it.

The story ran in the June 14, 1982 issue of *Sports Illustrated.*

The criticism came in a torrent before the magazine was
comfortably in place on the nation's newsracks. I expected
that. But I also expected something better than that. I
knew the injured words that came from the commissioner's office — charges of "sensationalism" and "exagger-
ation" — would have to be eaten sooner or later. (They
were. Sooner, I am sure, than Pete Rozelle would have
liked.)

I knew, too, that the players Reese had named, and a
vast number he *didn't* name but who nevertheless felt it
necessary to make disclaimers, would call him a liar, or
worse. And then, in time, be made to realize how foolish
they were to do so. And that those journalists who followed Rozelle and the indignant players into the breach
would, themselves, be caught in the crossfire.

But mainly I expected better, and was disappointed,
because somewhere along the line the larger issue had
been missed: that it was not just a matter of who does or
who doesn't, or what the percentages were, but how dangerous the implications were, and how clearly that danger
was reflected in the tragic figure of Reese himself.

Had they, after all, failed to see that Reese had cast a
light into the bitter inner landscape of professional sport?

Alex Karras called the story "silly." Gene Upshaw, the
president of the NFL Players Association, called it "stupid." The NFLPA's director, Ed Garvey, hinted darkly

of a plot between *Sports Illustrated* and the NFL to discredit the union. This, of course, was news to the NFL because *its* leaders were debunking the story, too. Don Shula, a favorite of mine, alas, dismissed it as an attempt to "sell magazines."

Former teammates railed against Reese. Ed Newman of the Dolphins called him a "rat fink," and Bob Griese said those who took him seriously "should consider the source." Mercury Morris called him "a big dumb farm kid . . . a stupid punk." Dan Fouts said he knew "nothing" about drug use on the Chargers. Etc., etc., etc. One publication called me *SI*'s "hatchet man."

But even in that sea of first doubts, there were a gratifying number of athletes and journalists who knew better. Bob Trumpy, a former tight end with the Bengals who had a radio talk show in Cincinnati, called on the air to say that he knew years ago the league was heading for this embarrassment. That drug use among its athletes had become "very fashionable."

Trumpy asked why I thought more players didn't go to the league for help. Only seventeen had come forward in the years the NFL had offered its counsel. "Because they're afraid for their jobs," I said. "They know owners and general managers and coaches won't suffer a player who can't perform up to par, no matter what the reason."

Joe Robbie, the Dolphins owner, provided a chilling example. When the story came out Robbie said he "wouldn't think twice" about turning his own players over to the law if they were caught with drugs. Then he admitted he "shipped out" drug users after the Dolphins went 6–8 in 1976. He *conceded* his team had a drug problem that apparently nobody knew about. So how did he solve it? He shipped it someplace else. The cancer wasn't cured, it was traded.

Bob Griese criticized Reese, and I know Griese. He is

a smart young man. But he is also a white ex-quarterback. You don't get much more establishment than that. Reese hardly knew him. Few of the black players did.

But what bothered me about Griese was that he quibbled over the percentages of alleged users. He "doubted" Reese's estimates. He missed the main point. If I were a "straight" player, especially a quarterback who had to rely on other players to keep 250-pound linebackers off my neck, I'd certainly want my teammates to be straight, too. Never mind whether it's fifty percent or ten percent of the team on drugs. If *one guy* is on the field in a semistupor, it is too great a risk.

The tide turned overnight. A week after the story broke, former All-Pro Carl Eller, a paid spokesman for the NFL and himself a one-time coke addict, said that "forty percent" of the players in the league probably used the drug, and as much as twenty-five percent could be "problem users." Braced with this information, Rozelle, to his credit, made an about-face. He said the NFL's drug problem "may be a bigger one than society as a whole."

When I approached him before the story appeared, Don Shula had told me he "knew nothing" about Dolphin players using coke, that he had only heard an occasional "rumor." Pot, yes, but not cocaine. At that point — even though the investigation was not complete — I could have given him a substantial list of Dolphin players I had reason to believe used coke, but I decided not to. He was a friend.

A few weeks later, I went to San Francisco to see Delvin Williams, a former Dolphin halfback who had led the team in rushing in 1980 and was an All-Pro with the 49ers before that. Williams said his habit got so bad in Miami "I was falling asleep in team meetings." He said he had gone to Shula twice about his own coke addiction. "What did he

tell you?" I asked. "He told me to 'straighten myself out.' "
The Dolphins traded Williams in 1981.

Seven months later, ex-Dolphin Mercury Morris, who
had called Reese "stupid" and "a punk," was sentenced
to fifteen years in prison for dealing. He said he had been
using cocaine for years, "as a pain killer" for the injuries
he suffered. Leroy Harris, another former Dolphin back,
confessed that he spent $21,000 of the $38,000 bonus he
got to sign with the Eagles in 1982 on cocaine.

By early 1983, there were so many name athletes trying
to get into the confessional that Reese couldn't have backed
out if he tried. What wasn't admitted to was revealed.
Some of those who were revealed were also arrested. Or
convicted. Baseball players Alan Wiggins of San Diego
and Ferguson Jenkins of the Texas Rangers were arrested.
E. J. Junior of the football Cardinals pleaded guilty to
possession. Mike Strachan of the Saints got three years
for dealing.

Darrell Porter, a $700,000-a-year catcher for the base-
ball Cardinals, admitted he had undergone extensive treatment. Porter said he was a walking drugstore. He used
cocaine. He used Quaaludes. He used marijuana, am-
phetamines, and depressants. He drew the line only at
heroin because he was afraid of the needle. Montreal outfielder Tim Raines said he consumed $40,000 worth of
cocaine the first nine months of 1982. Dodger relief pitcher
Steve Howe, the 1980 National League rookie of the year,
said the "pressures" got so bad that he was snorting coke
between innings in 1982. He finally checked into an Arizona drug recovery center.

A *Miami News* writer asked me what I thought the
solution was. I said it was simple. Urine tests, either on
a regular basis or by spot checks before or after a game.
Such testing has been suggested, but the players resist.
They say urine tests are demeaning. They say athletes are

not dogs or horses. They say tests are an invasion of privacy.

Are they? Maybe. But Olympic athletes endure drug tests, for a very good reason. They got caught cheating so many times they were forced to do it to protect the Games. Are football players better than Olympic athletes? Are football games better than Olympiads?

And what *is* an invasion of privacy? Is a blood test an invasion of privacy? You cannot get married without one. Is an eye test? You can't get a driver's license if you don't submit to an eye test. If you can't see, you are a menace on the highway. Same thing on the football field. If you're on drugs, you're a menace.

It's wacky when you think about it. The players object to something that will prove they might be doing something wrong, and get carte blanche to keep on doing it. Cocaine is a $30 billion business in this country. If I were in the football business, I would want to make sure the two enterprises did not overlap.

Hardly a week went by that some new recalcitrant didn't stumble forward. By the fall of 1983, no pro sport had escaped scandal. Howe was docked thirty days' pay for his continuing drug dependency. Three Kansas City Royals, Willie Aikens, Willie Wilson, and Jerry Martin, drew jail sentences and fines for "attempting" to possess cocaine. Three National Basketball Association All-Stars, David Thompson, Michael Ray Richardson, and John Drew, were revealed as users, and the NBA Players Association announced that it would bar for life any player convicted of or pleading guilty to a crime involving heroin or cocaine. They gave users an amnesty period to the end of the year to seek treatment.

In the NFL, Washington safetyman Tony Peters was indicted for coke trafficking. America's team, the Dallas

Cowboys, admitted that Tony Dorsett, Harvey Martin, Tony Hill, Ron Springs, and Larry Bethea had been called as "witnesses" in a federal drug investigation. Cleveland's Charles White and Minnesota's Dennis Johnson admitted their dependency. Finally, just before the season started, a fed-up Pete Rozelle suspended four players for four games for their drug involvement: E. J. Junior and Greg Stemrick of the Oilers, and Pete Johnson and Ross Browner of the Bengals. He said enough was enough. He said the "integrity of the game" was at stake.

Reese, at the very least, had been exonerated by the actions of his peers. In time, even those dowagers of the media who had such trouble accepting the evidence against their heroes relented.

Shortly after that, I read what to anyone else would have seemed an unrelated story. Bill Walsh, apparently disheartened by a losing season after his Super Bowl victory in 1982, was quitting as coach of the San Francisco 49ers. He indicated a growing disenchantment for the game that he loved. A San Francisco paper revealed that among the problems the 49ers had that season was "several key players" being heavily into drugs, "mostly cocaine."

Later, I read that Walsh had chosen not to quit after all. That still small hope we all carry for a better day had apparently survived in him. He was going to give it one more shot. I didn't know to be glad or sorry.

2.

Television: The Aerial Pollutant

M ANY things have happened to sport since television gained a stranglehold, and some of them are good.

For example, television has blessed sport with the very best of its technology. We would all find it difficult now to live without instant replays. Or, for that matter, split screens, stop action, slow motion, or the Prudential College Scoreboard. I am in awe, and grateful, that television can bounce an Olympiad off a whirling metal pumpkin in space and carom it into my living room.

It is also wonderful that invalids and recluses can watch the World Series, and whole generations of women can discover for themselves the things that siphon off a man's interests, even to the point of getting interested, too. Maybe even learning something, as I do watching *The American Sportsman* or *Wide World of Sports,* the best of sports programming.

It is also commendable that television has given work to talented men like Keith Jackson, Jim McKay, and Jack Whitaker, and good and interesting men like Ara Parseghian, Joe Garagiola, Don Meredith and Bill Russell, men whose lives in sport might have otherwise been over. Say what you will about Howard Cosell, he makes television sports commentary a legitimate journalistic expression.

Sport has been glorified by television. It is the best that television does.

But it is also the worst.

Television is at once the strongest ally and the greatest despoiler of Big Sport. It is sport's flashiest expression, and its most baleful influence. It probably didn't intend to be, but that's the way it turned out.

Years ago television made sport an offer it couldn't refuse — a chance to achieve a standard of living beyond its wildest dreams. Itself a slave to profit, no greedier nor more malevolent than, say, the United Fruit Company, television saw its own good fortune mirrored in sport's market potential and bought in.

And it bought and it bought, steadily expanding its investment until it became the principal financier of Big Sport's rocket ride to affluence. It showered millions of dollars on sport. And the shower was, for all appearances, benign. More than one league or program was saved from fiscal ruin by a television contract. More than one worthwhile sports enterprise owed its success to television exposure.

Big Sport refused to alter this course while it still had the chance because in its own lust for gold it welcomed television money with open arms, accepting it gladly and virtually without restrictions, to be counted and counted on. Big Sport woke up — or at least lifted an eyebrow — one day to find that the television money was no longer a dividend, it was a necessity. No matter how much came in, it was never enough to support a growing dependency. Big Sport was hooked.

Television protects its investment in sport any and every way it can. Not out of any evil intent but simply because it is what it is; television manipulates sport and extracts great concessions from its operation. It bribes and bullies and makes whores of the administrators of sport, and helps make money-grubbing freaks of its heroes. It even modifies and distorts the way sports are played.

How much money does television shell out for this control? So much that everything else pales by comparison, but the real issue is how quickly sport assimilates it.

Two years ago the networks struck an agreement with the National Football League to pay more than $2 billion for five years of television rights. Salaries and expenses presumably went up throughout the league, the bidding for new talent soared to new heights (e.g., quarterback John Elway's five-year, $5 million deal with the Denver Broncos), and, one can assume, new desks and carpeting were ordered all around. Because not one — not a single one — of the twenty-eight clubs lowered ticket prices. (The paying fan, you must always remember, *never* stops paying.)

At about the same time, major league baseball made a network deal for more than a billion dollars. ABC and CBS paid the National Collegiate Athletic Association $280 million for the rights to college football, making a national appearance on television worth $660,000 to each participating school. That amount would have satisfied most schools' entire football budget a decade or so ago. None of the recipients bragged that they had made it to Easy Street, however. Instead, they complained how rocky the road was and that the money wouldn't be enough.

Big Sport's budgets grow like viruses, and with each new television contract the figures reach ever more absurd heights. Boston's Larry Bird signed a basketball contract calling for a salary of more than $2 million a year for seven years. There was, of course, no way the Celtics could have afforded such an extravagance without television. During his entire Hall of Fame career that included eight World Series appearances, Lou Gehrig earned $405,900 from the

New York Yankees. Today the Yankees would gladly pay
Dave Winfield that to play half a season.

The tremendous infusions of television money in other
sports where fan interest is more parochial has led to
incredible purses, and a new phenomenon: the high-paid
misanthrope. Tennis' leading money winners went from
scavengers playing exhibitions in parking lots in the 1960s
to crude, rude, sour-faced millionaires flipping indecent
remarks and gestures into television lenses in the 1980s.
Tournament directors cannot control their boorish behavior because they are television "draws," essential for
the ratings. One, John McEnroe, even exploits his brat-
tiness in a commercial.

In 1940, the Professional Golf Association's average
tournament purse was $4,333. By 1960, it was $32,567.
By 1980 it was seven times that, and now, thanks primarily
to television, the average purse on the PGA tour is $423,913,
from prize money totaling $19 million. Sam Snead laughed
when we talked about the differences a few years had
made. As the leading money winner on the tour in 1950,
Sam collected $35,000, and pro golfers drove "jalopies"
instead of Lear jets and scrounged for their pennies like
gypsies. Sam said it was not uncommon to play an entire
round with the same ball, "until it got so soft you could
squeeze it."

Television money is now the only reason many sports
enterprises get started in the first place. Television staked
the United States Football League to a beginning (in 1983),
even though the USFL was going to play a cold-weather
sport in the summertime and televised football was already
dangerously close to a saturation point. The USFL has
been an economic flop. Each USFL club admitted to losses
of from $1 million to $2.5 million the first year. The Niel-
son ratings dropped steadily from the first week of the
season to the last. But the USFL had its plasma hooked

up and feeding into the veins even before the first ball was teed up: a $14.5 million contract with ABC and ESPN. It survived to live another year.

For television, of course, this is not largesse, this is business. These are not gifts, they are endowments. The networks recoup, and profit in a big way, when they invest in sport. Advertising revenue from football alone accounts for almost an eighth of the total ad revenue of the networks. The cost of a thirty-second commercial for Monday night football has risen at a rate of ten to fifteen percent a year, going from $32,500 in 1970 to $185,000.

(Do not doubt where the body is buried, however. The commercial sponsors pay, but not in the end. In the end, remember, *they* recoup by raising the price of their insurance and their beer and their Japanese automobiles. As always, the real sponsor of the whole process is the fan. The fan *always* pays.)

When you make a pact with the Devil you have to give the Devil his due, of course, and the dues television extracts extend even to the structure of sports. When networks say jump, sports administrators say how high. Games are begun at ten o'clock in the morning on the West Coast to accommodate television audiences in the East, or moved from day to night, or from the beginning of the season to the end, and never mind how these things might inconvenience ticket-buying customers or affect the performance of the athletes.

Colleges move football and basketball dates into the heart of their athletes' examination periods to get television exposure. Teams change starting times at the last minute ("We'd play at two A.M. if they wanted us to," said FSU coach Bobby Bowden when one of his games got a network spot), play baseball on wintry nights and football on torrid summer days, all for television. When outright bribery is required, the networks come through.

ABC sweetened the pot of the Sugar Bowl by $100,000 one year to help it land a highly ranked Pittsburgh team, and could see no wrong in it. Given the state of the art, I doubt you could convince anyone otherwise.

Bowl sponsors themselves are wed to television money, and so are not reluctant to go to the networks for "counsel" before they make a pairing. The grubby practice invariably embarrasses the bowls and diminishes their significance. SMU, despite an outstanding record, got x'ed out of a major bowl in 1983–84 when a deal was struck between the Big Ten Conference and the Sugar and Fiesta bowls. The Michigan–Ohio State winner (Michigan) was earmarked for the Sugar Bowl, the loser for the Fiesta, and SMU, whose rank and record were better than both those teams, had to settle for the Sun. SMU coach Bobby Collins was justifiably enraged.

The administrators of sport do not always wait for television to come to them for manipulation. To make themselves more salable to television, teams and leagues and organizers of special events twist programs around and alter playoff formats to find ways to attract the cameras. The NFL originated Monday night football and major league baseball began playing World Series games at night just for television. The NBA expanded its playoff field to sixteen teams in order to increase revenues. Tennis and golf pairings for even the most prestigious tournaments are lined up to accommodate network airtime.

Television ratings have thus become as crucial to sports enterprises as they are to the networks. The National Football League is quaking just now because of a nosedive in its ratings. Pro football's popularity has suffered grievously since the strike and the revelations of players' drug abuse in 1982. The fear, naturally, is that if ratings continue to drop, sponsors will have to be charged less for airtime — and the networks will pass on their losses to the league when the contracts come up for renewal.

Concern for the demographics of television viewing is also shared by the leagues, because the networks have demanded it be so — in no uncertain terms. When the Jets left New York for the nearby New Jersey Meadowlands in 1983, the nation's most important city was, for the first time in NFL history, bereft of a professional football team (the Giants departed in 1977). Mayor Koch tried to lure in another franchise, but when he got nowhere the NFL hinted he should quit trying because New York wasn't going to be allowed one anyway. An NFL spokesman said the television market couldn't stand a third franchise in the area.

But the greater sins television must answer for are the manipulations that led to the disfiguring of the sports themselves. By becoming creatures of television, Big Sports are changed for the players and spoiled for the fans. They have become mutations, not just in the way television covers them (the games are always better in person, especially baseball, whose essential breadth and vital angles are lost on a nineteen-inch screen), but in the way they are conducted.

In order to get their twenty-four commercial breaks into a pro football game, networks expand dead time so that it disrupts the natural flow of play. Television "engineers," stationed on the sidelines, signal the stops and starts, granting time-outs where time-outs are not warranted. Games are not only stretched to boring lengths by this practice (I quit going to Dolphin games in Miami primarily for that reason), but they reduce the importance of conditioning as a key element of sport.

The number of time-outs allowed by the rules in a basketball or football game are set because conditioning is *supposed* to be a factor in sport, and even part of its strategy. It is not when breathers are allowed just so a sponsor can sell his electric shavers or his California Chablis. In baseball, a game that already has plenty of dead time, the rhythm of a contest is critical, especially to pitchers and fans. Lengthy interruptions do it no good. ABC wanted 120 seconds — a full two minutes — between innings for its latest contract with major league baseball. It didn't get it, but baseball continues to lose ground to such incursions. The average San Francisco Giants home game, as a typical example, has increased by thirty-three minutes in five years.

In the top of the eighth inning of the first game of the 1983 World Series, Baltimore pitcher Scott McGregor had completed his warmup throws and was ready to pitch when a man in the Orioles dugout waved a towel. The man was an ABC field director. The signal meant McGregor would have to hold up while (as he found out later) Howard Cosell finished interviewing President Reagan.

The interview took almost two minutes. McGregor said he "understood" where the delay was coming from ("TV runs things and puts up a lot of money"), but he thought it disrupted the game. He said he wished the networks would "take a closer look" at what they were doing.

The machinery, of course, is already in place to control television; only the will is lacking. Every professional and major college sport has the vested interest to intervene on its own behalf, for the good of its own games, if only it would dare. Both groups have special television committees answering to their leadership, formulating and managing television policies. But they formulate out of greed, and manage out of fear.

Once, in a moment of weakness not entirely influenced by his observance of the New Year's Eve ritual, a friend in the networks admitted to me that he often wondered why sports administrators did not do a better job of "insulating" their games from television's control.

I asked him what he meant by "insulating."

He said, "Protect themselves from being prostituted, from being used, by establishing firm guidelines — rules, if you will — that we would have to live by. It doesn't make sense, really. They could tell us in a minute to quit jerking them around and we'd do it. We'd have no choice.

"But for some reason they think if we make demands and they don't cater to them, we'll pull the plug. How could we? Television does not 'produce' football games and basketball tournaments and the World Series. We only say we do in the credits. Television merely sends the signals out. Television needs sport more than sport needs television. Don't ever forget it."

He said the insulation could be provided either by the authorities already extant or by the establishment of commissions, preferably free of (but not ruling out) governmental involvement. Then, for the good of their own games, such authorities should say to the networks at contract time: (1) Don't ask us to stop our games or slow them down just to cram in another commercial. We won't allow it. Work them in wherever you can. And, (2) Don't ask us to hold any event, to play any sport at any time that is inappropriate or inconsiderate of the game or the players who play it.

Would such controls mean less revenue? They might. But they might not. When the orange crop freezes and twenty percent of the fruit is lost, the surviving eighty percent soars in value. When setbacks occur, the market adjusts; it always does. But if it doesn't, you simply learn to live with less. That can be done, too.

The dependence on television money may not ever be completely broken, but it does not have to be. What it

has to be is more effectively controlled, by sports states-
men rather than pillagers of sport. Commissions *for* sport
would not necessarily be *against* television, only the vo-
racious demands television makes.

But the most crying need is to negate television's distortions of the games themselves, and to minimize television money wherever it becomes a disproportionate factor
in the success of one program or another (in itself a distortion of sport). This is not as difficult as it sounds. The
colleges, certainly, could spread the television wealth around
so that those playing a sport at the same level of involvement (e.g., Division I-A football, where the philosophical
and marketing committment is "big time") would share
television monies equally. In such an environment as now
exists, television does not enhance, it enslaves.

In all cases, sporting events should be sanctioned first
for their value to sport, not their value to television. When
television extracts the concessions that distort play, it is a
short hop to the mutations that spoil sport. Television's
worst influence is in its encouragement-by-glorification of
the clowns and bums and brutes of sport. It has created
a format that has produced one Titanic Thompson after
another, and a proving ground for the most outrageous
displays of barbaric and unsportsmanlike behavior.

Almost anything goes in Big Sport today, and not the
least of it is the pre-event braggadocio and the end zone
spikes and the flagrant, disrespectful dances over beaten
foes that we see regularly on television — the very worst
examples of sportsmanship instead of the best. I don't
know Mark Gastineau, but I would like to think he might
have second thoughts about the posturing he does over
downed quarterbacks if he were made to see how unsporting it looks and how much it caters to the worst
instincts of the idiots who applaud him. The only way that
will happen, however, is for a quarterback to preen and

gesture over *him,* and that is not likely to happen anytime soon.

In the final analysis, television's most reprehensible influence, its most egregious contribution, may be this. In the pressurized world of Big Sport, television has allowed and even encouraged the tide of bad sportsmanship that now infects all of sport: the boorish ways of star athletes, and the dishonest and sometimes savage acts that spoil it. Ironically, it has done its worst damage to the one sport that used to pride itself on its decorum.

As a greenhorn writer just starting out on the *Miami News,* I learned the difference between a volley and a rally from a star tennis player named Gardnar Mulloy. Mulloy was about forty then but he was still going strong and had, in fact, been ranked number one in the world the year before. I first met him when he materialized early one morning at the sports desk of the *News,* a vision in white tennis shorts, clutching a fistful of copy paper. He looked to be what I had imagined the classic tennis bum should look like: tall, tan, trim, handsome, gray at the temples, blue in the eyes, and dazzling white in the teeth.

Except Mulloy was no bum. In subsequent encounters I found him to be a bright, articulate, engaging guy with a law degree and a dry cleaning business, and a wonderful gift for infuriating the tennis establishment. The sainted Stanley Woodward, then the *News'* sports editor, had hired Mulloy to write inflammatory columns about the game. This was right up Mulloy's alley because he had a reputation for pointed commentary (not to say wild-eyed criticism) that was no lie. Woodward himself enjoyed such a reputation, and thus enjoyed Mulloy immensely. He worked hard to keep Mulloy's copy in the paper and out of libel court.

Weekly, the *News* copy desk would brace for Mulloy's

arrivals, ever aware that the next ox he gored might be
the one to stagger to its feet and sue. As I remember,
Mulloy never disappointed us. He was always in high
dudgeon over some new expression of silliness or injustice
by the U.S. Lawn Tennis Association (now the U.S.T.A.),
and his comments were always good for a laugh or a cocked
eyebrow. Woodward loved him.

In his playing days, Mulloy was not one to stifle his
emotions. Once in Australia he held up a match to grapple
with two hecklers who came down on the court at his
invitation. English tabloids called him "The Miami
Mouthpiece." After a particularly captious afternoon at
Wimbledon, during which Mulloy complained quite accurately that one of the linesmen was sound asleep, a
writer named Peter Wilson called him "the worst [be-
haved] player on all courts all over the world" and suggested he "throw his racquet over the cliff and forget to
let go." All this, Mulloy told me, somewhat innocently,
"because I said the officiating at Wimbledon stinks."

Mulloy won more than five hundred titles as amateur
and pro, when the line between the two was more clearly
drawn, and got into frequent tiffs with tennis poobahs over
his insistence that the former (amateur) was a sentimental
myth and the latter (pro) was what you had to be to play
in the major tournaments. Without taking "something under
the table," he said, you couldn't make it. He admitted he
did exactly that. In this respect, he was way ahead of his
time, but he wasn't exactly rewarded for it. He complained
that the best he could do was $10,000 in a single season,
peanuts by today's standards.

I had thought of him often over the years as tennis grew
to major status as a money sport, and, at the same time,
deteriorated into a snakepit of disgraceful behavior. His
name kept popping up. He still played — he was, in fact,
ranked number one in the 65-and-over class the last I

heard — and had taken a cushy job as the pro at the California Club in North Miami, still tan and fit and looking great.

I noted, too, that he had taken to writing letters to newspapers and tennis magazines. With the same clarity of expression and indignation, but with an apparent change of sides, he wrote to deplore John McEnroe's "ridiculous" behavior, blaming McEnroe's upbringing, and in a letter to the *News,* complained that sports, instead of the good influence they should be, were "becoming the most insidious corrupter of our values."

Two stories by Barry McDermott in *Sports Illustrated* made me decide to seek Mulloy out. One was about a girl named Lori Kosten who had leaped into the pressure-cooker of modern-day junior tennis as a prodigy and, after accumulating a few metric tons of plaques and trophies, quit at age fifteen "because she made one too many trips to hospital emergency rooms," and "lay awake one night too many" worrying over the fanatical need to win that had become her way of life.

McDermott painted a grim picture of the world in which Kosten and her peers lived. An awful place where fathers of bright young hopefuls (hopeful, that is, of crashing the big time and raking in all that money) got into fistfights on the edge of the court, and coaches and parents screamed at and threatened teenagers, and children cheated and argued with opponents and insulted officials and threw racquets and tantrums.

At one tournament, Kosten's mother "saw a father smash his son's head against a tree after the boy lost. She watched as parents fought. She saw children cheat. It never made sense." A boy named Howard Schoenfield "won almost every tournament he entered in 1975, including the national 18-and-under championship. Later that year he had a nervous breakdown and entered a mental hospital." At

twenty-four, Schoenfield was residing "in a halfway house
on the outskirts of Jacksonville, suffering from a mental
illness his psychiatrists have been unable to diagnose with
any certainty."

McDermott's second story was about a popular young
professional player named Johan Kriek, who could be
depicted as one who made it out of the pressure-cooker
into the money. But Kriek's portrait was no more appealing. Only grander. A South African living in Naples,
Florida, Kriek owned two Porsches, a Jeep, a Corvette
Sting Ray, and a twenty-seven-foot Chris-Craft. He had
a wife who, according to McDermott, "could have walked
off the pages of *Vogue,*" and a "big house with great white
pillars and a circular dirveway." He had all these things,
and he was twenty-four years old.

And he had something else. A reputation as an "ani-
mal," with "a chip on his shoulder that would make a
hunchback of Arnold Schwartzenegger." Kriek, reported
McDermott, was the nemesis of officials, fans, ball boys
and other players, as well as locker room walls and umpires in their chairs. He shook the latter at the U.S. Open
and put a hole in the former at Newport, and when he
went out to play, Kriek said he had "no respect for anyone."

Kriek threw tantrums, and matches. He admitted he
deliberately "tanked" when he "didn't want to play anymore." He boycotted awards ceremonies. He led the pro
tour in fines. "In many respects," said McDermott, "he
makes John McEnroe . . . and the Jimmy Connors of yes-
teryear look almost like choirboys."

But there Master Kriek was, gracing the pages of *SI,*
getting all that multicolored ink. The rich young tennis
pro, ranked twelfth in the entire world. The handsome,
smiling role model for thousands of kids who dream that
they, too, through the magic of tennis, might some day

get their hands on the wheel of a yellow Porsche or a red Corvette and a beautiful girl like Mrs. Kriek. I would have thrown up, but instead I put a call in to Gardnar Mulloy.

It was ten in the morning and he wasn't in. The boy who answered the phone at the California Club explained that "living legends tend to come in when they see fit." (It must have been a portent. A few months later, Mulloy quit and moved to Boca Grove Plantation.)

Within the hour, he called back. Across all those years, his voice sounded the same — youthful and assertive and faintly aristocratic, and smooth as buttermint. He wanted to know what I'd been up to, and if I ever learned anything about tennis that could be called firsthand knowledge. I told him I had taken up the game some years before and when I saved up enough money I was coming up to take a lesson.

"At forty dollars an hour," I said, "you're something I would have to plan for."

He laughed. "Come up anyway," he said. "I'll give you a freebee."

I asked him if he ever went out to watch the touring pros play.

"Not if I can help it," he said. "Oh, occasionally, when it's somebody I really want to see, but I don't like the actions. It's not fun for me anymore."

"I understand you don't think much of McEnroe."

"I like him *off* the court. Off the court he's a friend of mine. So're Connors and Nastase. But on the court, they're ridiculous. Kriek's the same way, and the German, Bruning. Hotheads with no class. They get away with murder. And the girls are the same. They even use the same filthy language. And none of them are good sports. They lose and they never say, 'Nice game.' Or, 'He was too good for me.' They say, 'I was off. I didn't serve well.' Always some excuse."

"I don't remember you as being such a sweetheart. Are you saying it's different now?"

"I *never* did the things they do today. I never cussed an umpire, I never used profanity. When I was sixteen, I was playing in the semifinal of the Dade County championships. I was playing Carroll Turner, the best in the area then. We were four-all in the fifth set, and we got into an argument. The umpire was inexperienced, and he let it go on. I wouldn't play, and Carroll wouldn't play. Suddenly my father came down out of the stands and picked up my racquets and told me to go home.

"I said, 'Dad, I can whip this guy.' He said, 'How can you without a racquet?' Later he lectured me for two hours. He said, 'Stand up for your rights, but don't raise your voice, and don't use profanity, and don't carry it on. When you've said your piece, end it.' Today they *never* stop. McEnroe's the worst. He's disgraceful. His father says, 'I wish he wouldn't do those things.' He shoulda stopped him from doing them a long time ago."

"You blame the parents?"

"I blame the parents, yes. And the U.S.T.A. for putting up with it. They don't have the guts to punish anybody anymore, and everybody's afraid to do anything. I was referee of the Orange Bowl juniors this year. I couldn't believe the actions. The grunting, the complaining, the *cheating*. Every time there was a close call you'd see a kid scream and walk around the net. I spent half my time settling arguments.

"A kid would lose, and he'd stomp his feet. And the coach would yell at me, and the parents would yell at me. I couldn't believe it. A coach told me, 'I can't do anything, that's the way this kid is.' I said, 'Then you're a helluva coach.' One player was raising hell, and his mother was watching with me. The rule says you warn 'em once. The second time you take a point away, then a game, then you default 'em.

"The referee took a point, then a game. I told the mother, 'One more and he's out.' She said, 'Why does he do that?' I said, 'Mother, you should know. He has no discipline. It's your fault.' "

"What would you do?" I asked.

"It's hard to say because you see it throughout sport. Nobody has any feeling at all for sportsmanship. I went to a Miami football game. The crowd *booed* the other team when it came on the field, and booed when it went off. There's no respect for the opposition in any sport. But I blame the people in charge. The association shouldn't put up with these things. They fine a McEnroe or a Nastase, but what's a couple thousand dollars when you're making all that money? Fines don't matter."

Sometimes they don't even count, I said. McEnroe had disgraced Wimbledon a couple years ago and got fined $10,000 by the international council. The council reduced it to $5,000, but McEnroe appealed. The rules at the time allowed him to choose one of the three judges who reviewed the case. The judges voted 2-to-1 against him, but he *won* the appeal because it *had to be unanimous*. Guess which judge voted in his favor?

"Ridiculous, isn't it?" Mulloy said.

I said that for me tennis as a spectator sport lost half its charm when it lost most of its decorum. (As a traditionalist, I admitted I felt the same about hockey.) All the money lavished on the game had made facsimile rock stars out of its better players, and locked the system tighter than any other into the Big Sport/Big Television axis. It was a situation made to order for such indulgence.

Promoters who could care less about decorum or sportsmanship and television ministers willing to tolerate almost

any form of boorish behavior in order to deliver the right
act to the screen on tournament day were happy teams
indeed. It did not matter that they were making monsters
of ego out of the athletes. Monsters beyond the reach of
what used to be the normal disciplines.

Under the circumstances, it was only natural that the
players' conduct got worse and worse, Mulloy said. And
until the leadership was willing to give up a few circus acts
and television dollars in order to control the sport for
good, tennis was going to keep right on fouling its own
nest.

What would Mulloy do? I asked.

"Put somebody like my father in control," he said.

What would Mulloy do with the players? I persisted.

"I guess I'd do what they did to Earl Cochell."

I asked who Earl Cochell was. Mulloy said he was a
high-ranked ("sixth or seventh") player from California
whom Mulloy had beaten in the U.S. Open at Forest Hills
in 1950. Cochell had gotten behind, and then blatantly
threw the last few points of a set, not moving at all as
Mulloy sent shots past him. Warned by the umpire, Cochell argued, then cursed the umpire, "and when we got
into the dressing room he kept it up."

"What happened to him?"

"They suspended him."

"For how long?"

"For life. He never played in a sanctioned match again."

"That would do it," I said.

"Yeah," Mulloy said. "That would do it."

3.

The Alienated Fan

THE following is a portion of a conversation I had with Rollo May, the laureate psychotherapist. Dr. May was not analyzing me at the time; I was analyzing him. At least that's what I think I was doing. You never know with psychiatrists, even when they bill you.

I had been assigned to take a hard look at the condition of competitive sport in America — its problems, its prospects — for *Sports Illustrated*. Hopefully, to find something to cheer about for inclusion in Time Inc.'s upbeat "American Renewal" project. I figured that May, as a kind of Anglo-Saxon Sigmund Freud with many credits (*Love and Will,* et al.), would help satisfy my need for an overview. I wanted all the help I could get. I especially wanted it from May because it required going to San Francisco, a place I happen to like being required to go to.

We sat on a porch on the second floor of his office-home near Sausalito, just north of the Golden Gate Bridge. I had arrived at dusk, driving in directly from the airport, jet lag be hanged. The familiar, inevitable evening chill had already come on. From what was clearly a privileged vantage point, I could steal glimpses of the ships slipping through on the far side of Alcatraz Island, pushing on toward Oakland or (more appealingly) the open sea.

A lean, dapper man in his seventies, Dr. May had included an ascot in what was otherwise informal dress, and

I thought to myself he was one of about three people I had met in my entire life who could get away with it. He looked like a man who instinctively knew the difference between "arriving" and "making an entrance." After a day of picking through the faulty wiring of other people's psyches he seemed glad to have me drop by, if only to bat around a few ideas he would not ordinarily deal with.

He poured wine, in generous portions. He said the subject "intrigued" him, and got right to it.

Even in my enchanted state, I was amazed how readily he focused in. He said that as a onetime high-school footballer and a dabbler in various sports he knew the fun of it, and as a former proud member of the Michigan State marching band who had "played" before a hundred thousand people at Ann Arbor a couple times he certainly could appreciate the thrill of it at the "gladiators' " level.

And although he had not really *followed* sport that closely in recent years, and the little he still engaged in was more to satisfy minor fitness needs, he thought it "extremely important." More important than ever now that it had gotten "all twisted around."

And that I was right when I said spectator sport had become "a catch-all for emotion and obsession," exaggerated in importance by television and media hype.

He called it a "symbol," one that had taken the place of "our other symbols that have disintegrated in one way or another" (marriage, religion, etc.), and said we were "investing too much of our emotions," not to mention our entertainment dollars, in it. He said it might be better than "spending it on motorcycles and knocking down pedestrians," but the investment was a flier because we have "conferred on sport our worst anxieties," and sport was not holding up.

"A bad investment?" I said.

"Yes. But it is the obsession to win that ruins it, not

sport itself. The good of sport has very little to do with winning or losing. For participants it should always be a win-win thing, not a win-lose.

"The same for spectators. The enjoyment should never depend on winning alone. When winning itself becomes the symbol, that's destructive If you win, you're okay. If you lose, you're not okay. The symbol becomes *very* destructive when we put so much of our emotions into it. It is like clinging to a chip of wood, hoping it will save us from drowning."

I asked if the anxieties had anything to do with threatened loyalties. If the business aspects that now dominate sport had not undermined the fans' allegiance. Fans unable to cope with mercenaries for heroes, growing alienated without even knowing it. Wanting to belong, but with no true sense of belonging. Fans unable to fathom why the obsession for winning obsesses *them*. Why spectating itself is now so often frustrating, even leading to violence. And leading, as well, to an alarming increase in gambling on the events that are watched. (Alarming because gambling interests historically have been so corruptive.)

"Isn't that just another sick way of investing in a team, a way of validating the identification?" I asked.

"You are right on target," he said. "I am cheered that you have given this some clear thought."

"Some," I said. I was glad he noticed.

"The real value of sport is driven out by the obsession," he said. "Without the old symbols to rely on, we walk around with all this emotion and no place to put it. So we put it in sports. To building gladiators, and buying teams. The Phillies are not *really* Philadelphia, but as the symbol of 'our place' they become 'us.' We are frustrated because it doesn't get us anywhere."

Then, in a language of his own, May described how he had watched "a great deal" of a recent World Series on television. "I have always enjoyed baseball," he said, "and this seemed to me to be good baseball. I especially enjoyed the play of the third baseman, Mr. Brett, of Kansas City, who seems like a wonderful fellow, and the pitcher for Philadelphia, Carlton, a great pitcher, and the other third baseman, what's his name again?"

"Schmidt."

"Yes. Mr. Schmidt was also wonderful to watch. Then the day after the Series I saw on television where a million people in Philadelphia came out to celebrate the new champions. A million people celebrating the Phillies as extensions of the town, even though it would be just sheer luck if even one of them had been born there.

"And I watched, amazed, as they cheered, and I thought to myself, 'There but for decisions made by men in smoke-filled rooms go a bunch of guys who would rather be in San Francisco.' "

Fan violence is an increasingly popular topic in sports literature. Most of it is presented with breathtaking evidence of the bestiality of spectators (e.g., three hundred people killed and five hundred injured in a Lima, Peru, soccer riot) and expert testimony from sociologists and psychologists — tons and tons of expert testimony raining down and landing everywhere but on the heart of the problem. The heart — in this country, at this time — being fan alienation:

Fans less and less able to identify with obscenely over-paid athletes who have been made to believe by their employers that it is better to be envied than respected. (It is immaterial whether Magic Johnson will still be able to play basketball at age forty-six. The question is: Can someone who is being paid a million dollars a year for twenty-five years to throw a ball in a basket be tolerated when he *misses the basket*?)

Fans unsure that the heroes they invest their affection in today will be around tomorrow — or, for that matter, whether a whole team of heroes will be around tomorrow. (Some sports psychologists believe this to be a reason for the heavy gambling done on pro sports. One thing the fan knows will be around tomorrow is his bookie. He will keep him in the game regardless. An increasingly popular way for fans to get back at their fickle heroes is to boo like hell when the heroes don't cover the point spread.)

Fans bewildered by the oafish, antisocial behavior of their heroes, some of whom have expanded their capabilities to include rape, robbery, drug-dealing, extortion, and grand and petite larceny. These revelations are said to be "overplayed" by media critics and management who expect newspapermen to overlook the oafish behavior and ignore police blotters.

Fans being jerked around by management. Abused, and even cheated by management. Fans building up hidden frustrations against management.

Fans taking out their frustrations on nearby objects.

In 1978, fans at a New York Jets game threw a security guard over a railing and cracked his skull. A Yankee Stadium fan tried to blackjack an American League umpire. At a disturbance in Madison Square Garden, two men were stabbed and one was shot. At a Rams–Bears game in Chicago in 1981, thirty-one fans were arrested during a riot.

Tethered police dogs now patrol the sidelines of many big-city ballparks. At Fenway Park in Boston, the frequency of rowdy behavior caused Red Sox management to hire twenty college football players to help control the crowds. An entire section of the stadium in Detroit was barred to paying customers because of the regularity of violence there.

Athletes in almost every arena, in every sport, now

complain about fan behavior. About curses and epithets. Racial slurs. Death threats (by wire, phone, mail, and in person). Obscene gestures. Flying objects. In Pittsburgh, Pirates outfielder Dave Parker was so regularly pelted by apple cores, radio batteries, cans and paper cups that it got to be a joke. Parker wasn't living up to his outrageous salary. Nobody threw apple cores at management for paying it, however.

Once unleashed, the passion for violence respects neither age nor amateur status. Many high-school football games are played in the daytime to avoid trouble at night. Some have been banned to spectators entirely, to avoid trouble at any time. The parents of a University of Missouri football player received death threats in Omaha after their son's jarring tackle knocked the Nebraska quarterback out of a game. A University of Miami baseball coach was knocked unconscious by a chunk of ice hurled from the stands in Tallahassee. In Gainesville, Florida, fans threw oranges *and* ice at the Miami football team.

Sports psychologist Bruce Ogilvie once told me he thought the players of sport "have every reason to hate the goddamn fans" and their "monstrous potential for antipathy." He said fans give love and take it away capriciously, "and when they get mad, they're savages. The fans in the L.A. Forum are sickening. Philadelphia is a jungle." Ogilvie said it was understandable that pro athletes treat fans "the way whores treat their clients" — secretly despising them, but smiling gamely through the experience.

Quoted in *Sports Illustrated,* sociologist Dr. Irving Goldaber blamed fan violence on a number of things. On a reaction to the violence fans see *on* the field, and on the ice and court. On being jammed in with strangers for whom they might have an aversion. On a need to be assertive that they do not express in "real" life. On booze (ninety percent of the arrests at ballparks are alcohol-

related). And, more subtly, on the fans' desire to "be in
the game," which they do not get by simply wearing the
silly hats and the lettered jackets and sweaters and by
waving the appropriate pennants.

All these I am sure are valid reasons, but nowhere in
Dr. Goldaper's analysis did he mention fan alienation.
The violence was blamed on everything but. On beer, on
drugs, on poor seat location, but not on the hundred subtle
(and not-so-subtle) ways management and athletes have
of treating the fan like an unwanted, dim-witted child.

Is it not logical that fans might eventually wise up and
resent having to pay (and pay) every time the inflated
salaries go up? That they might burn a little inside when
their well-heeled heroes willingly sacrifice the team — the
ultimate "symbol" of togetherness — for the next big stake?
(Talk about capriciously given love.) Why *shouldn't* their
resentment bubble over when the tycoons muff ground
balls or drop forward passes? Violence is, after all, a very
sincere form of expression.

I am not talking about *all* fans, of course. I cling to the
ragged hope that a majority still go to competitions to
appreciate — even be thrilled by — the skills involved.
No more, no less. I would like to think, too, that the
greater number still prefer their athletics straight, without
the need to gamble on them, but the evidence may be
against me there.

And I am not talking about *all* pro athletes. The majority, I think, would still play for the fun of it, given a
choice. Asked what he would do if the lights went out and
pro football salaries went back to the pre-television $15,000
level, Terry Bradshaw of the Steelers said, "I'd play for
$15,000." Jean Beliveau, the former Montreal Canadiens
star, said he loved hockey so much he "would have played
for nothing if I had other means to earn a living."

The true competitor will always perform up to snuff

because he *is* a competitor, not because of dubious loyalties or paycheck considerations. I have only seen Larry
Bird play a couple times, but his love for basketball is so
compelling that I think he probably wonders why he gets
paid at all. John Havlicek was that way, and I know Havlicek. He played for the Celtics all his pro life — he epitomized the Celtics — and he said he would only stop playing
"when I embarrass myself or my team." He quit before
that happened.

But long ago we conferred under the general rubric of
"character-building" many noble ideals on sport. For a
long time we were able to sustain that feeling, even though
it might not have been realistic. When Big Sport and Big
Television got their hands on the gullet, we moved away
from the consideration that competition at the highest
levels was intrinsically good and toward a different view:
that it was good mainly as a source for lifetime riches.

Big money, from the Big Sport/Big Television axis, conferred on the athlete a different set of values. Achievement alone was no longer a barometer. Trophies and records
and championships and applause were not enough. The
emphasis shifted to huge material benefits, brought about
by television's massive infusions of cold hard cash.

When packaged as high-priced entertainment, sport becomes more important as business and *less* important as
sport. When competitive athletics dance to whatever tune
the company is playing, it only appears to be good for
sport. By turning players into entertainers, sport is triv-
ialized. The strengths of their decorum and conventions,
things that bind spectators and players, are diffused.

Of course the athletes saw it. They had to because play
itself was distorted. In television's case, commercials —
incessant, interruptive — disturbed the flow of play. Football especially was distorted. Larger players, weight-trained

to abnormal sizes, did not have to worry about stamina. Commercial breaks took care of stamina. Televised professional football games now go on forever. It requires as exemplary an act of attentiveness for the viewer to sit through a Monday night game as it does the players to play one. Play is never continuous. If it were Broadway, the audience would sprint for the exits.

As a result of all this commerce, athletes came to vie tooth and nail and across the sports pages with management. Contract terms were argued in 60-point type. Entrepreneurs sensed that the more money they rained on their athletes, the more snowed the public could be, so they allowed it to go on. It is axiomatic that Sonny Werblin and his $400,000 quarterback would, less than twenty years later, seem like small potatoes in the money hype.

But the ploy backfired.

Seeing evidence of more, the athletes wanted more. And more. And more. Knowing the owners were raking in the spoils, why not join in? Greed was the name of the game and thus athletes and management became adversaries, and bitter ones at that.

And what happened to the loyal fan? The loyal fan got caught in the middle. The outrageous figures in the headlines made him aware, too. He was paying for sport, and getting the business.

What else was he to believe when, like Teamsters, baseball players went out on strike in 1981? And football players *twice* went on strike, the last time for nine weeks in 1982? How could he abide the picket lines when any student of ninth-grade economics could tell him the sums struck for would inevitably come out of his pocket? How could he even *pretend* to empathize when in 1983 the membership of the National Basketball Association, with an *average salary of $246,000 a year,* threatened to strike?

A strike its own counsel admitted could put "three or four" NBA clubs out of business. Was this any way to treat a loyal fan?

The willingness to compromise personal preferences in order to achieve a shared goal is a commitment expected in team play — even if the only one who expects it anymore is the paying fan. When there is a haughty disdain for team loyalty, when breaking contracts is a way of life, when players walk out on commitments and admit they haven't even tried their best, where does that leave the fan?

Billie Jean King now says that platitudes about winning for this or that group "were never for real — everyone was kidding themselves. They wanted their peers and the public to like them. It's just the opposite. People do whatever's in their self-interest."

Well, of course. If that isn't true, why would wide receiver Leonard Thompson of the Detroit Lions say what he did? Thompson said he did not try to score after catching a pass against San Francisco in a game a couple seasons ago because he wanted to "avoid injury." Thompson ran out of bounds instead. "I was thinking about turning in," he said, "but [as a free agent] I don't have that contract."

The fallout from such cavalier pronouncements, even if "up-to-date" and honestly expressed, could not help but alienate fans.

I was living in Miami when Larry Csonka, Jim Kiick and Paul Warfield quit the Miami Dolphins for the gold rush to the World Football League in 1974. I knew Csonka and Kiick. They seemed to be dedicated enough athletes, each with a broad following. Csonka, especially, was enormously popular. Grown men and women wore his number (39) on their chests.

How much they were making (Csonka was always in some kind of hassle with owner Robbie, so it must have been less than the price of a DC-10) and how much they would harvest by leaving was of no interest to me. The figures are always outrageous anyway. What interested me was what their defection might do to the Miami fans. How much it would damage fan loyalty.

Economist George Burman, a former NFL lineman, would argue that any talk of moral obligations to an area is "spurious" and "purely sentimental, and ignores the reality of the marketplace." He says that if a franchise shifts to a bigger market, the new location has a "greater right" to it because it can give "greater support" (i.e., more fans and more money). That view would probably not be shared by many boosters clubs, however. Probably not by *anybody* who has seen what happens when a favorite team quits an area. How it tears holes in an entire community's perception of itself.

Brooklyn was never the same after it lost the Dodgers. Washington has twice lost major league baseball teams, with much public and editorial outcry, and was so paranoid about losing its hockey team in 1982 that it agreed to demands (by the club owner) that could only be considered ransom: reduced taxes, reduced rent, double the number of season ticket sales, and a guarantee of ten sellout games.

Would just a trio of stars — Csonka, Kiick and Warfield — thumbing their noses at the community that loved them have an effect? What would all those fans do with all those number 39 T-shirts? I don't know if it was the only factor, but time did reveal *some*thing. The Dolphins averaged almost 77,000 paid attendance in 1974. They have not come close to that since. They now average less than 60,000 at home games.

Conclusion? The disenchantment probably had less to do with losing three star players than it did with the rejection fans felt, an alienation that resulted from being spurned. *I* felt rejected — I enjoyed Csonka's thundering runs — and I wasn't even a Dolphin fan.

It could be argued that we have never, as spectators, been rewarded even-up for our loyalty. Historically, pro franchises, through the somber rituals of trades and waivers, tromp all over loyalty by tearing our heroes away from us. Babe Ruth wasn't *always* a Yankee, he was a Red Sox first. And for every Ted Williams who played an entire career with one team (the Red Sox), or a Stan Musial with the Cardinals or a Joe DiMaggio with the Yankees, there is a Ty Cobb who started in Detroit but ended in Philadelphia.

It could be argued that way, but it is not a sound argument. The trades of Ruth and Cobb happened very early and very late in their careers. Ruth is forever identified as a Yankee, and Cobb a Tiger. Of the modern players, I defy you to identify Reggie Jackson with a particular team. And while still in his prime, do you think of Pete Rose as a Phillie or a Cincinnati Redleg?

Those heroes who do stick around almost get devoured with affection. Ted Williams is hailed like a Caesar whenever he goes back to Boston. Carl Yastrzemski will be, too. Mickey Mantle is forever a Yankee. He says he gets letters from New York fans now "that almost make you want to cry." He says he gets more mail than he ever did.

I am ambivalent on the subject, however, because (like Burman) I recognize the modern realities. The various major leagues are no more than cartels, in every sense of the word (except, of course, in their antitrust exemptions). Big league athletes, treated as chess pieces and sides of beef, have every right to pursue their own best interests. Without guilt, if possible.

But for the fan it is another matter. If he has to witness these miserable recitals over and over, and endure the threats of abandonment and the tiresome references to deferred payments and tax shelters, it is no wonder he is prone to anger, and that he has at last shown some signs of rebelling.

The assorted strikes brought out the first sublime evidences of fan resistance (heartening for me, I have to admit). The baseball strike led to the creation of a half-dozen organizations aimed at stirring fan revolt. Columnists demanded that fans write their congressmen to contest the antitrust exemptions if owners didn't (a) cut it out, and (b) cut prices. One figured that given the current inflation rate, Babe Ruth's salary would be worth $450,000 today — and Ruth would find "at least thirty-two players who couldn't lift his bat making more than that."

The football strike in 1982 resulted in seats that were showing wood for the first time in decades, in stadiums unaccustomed to such sights. In Dallas, more than 17,000 stayed away from the traditional Thanksgiving Day "sellout." In Kansas City, only 12,000 turned out in a 78,000-seat stadium for the last game of the season. In Denver, twenty-five season ticket holders burned their tickets in front of the capitol building. In 1983, attendance continued to go down.

The president of Yale himself was moved to protest the baseball strike. In vibrant prose, A. Bartlett Giamatti called it a "triumph of greed over the spirit of the garden." He called it an "act of defiance against the American people, and the only summer God made for 1981." He called it "utter foolishness."

Writing in the *New York Times,* Giamatti said there was no sympathy for either side because the "people of America care about baseball, not about your squalid little squabbles." He reminded the "princelings and sovereignlets of baseball" that they could treat the game as an industry if they liked, and play it for "whatever mercenary motives you wish, but remember that, from our point of

view, you play it so that we may all remember a past —
graceful, energetic, free in the order and law of a green
field — that never was."

Sports psychologist Thomas Tutko of San Jose State
said the football strike produced three groups of fans: fans
who got angry but would come back; fans who didn't know
any better but *to* come back; and fans who are "thinking
through their commitment." The latter, fans I have the
most hope for, "are now asking: why am I doing this? I
could be doing other things with my life."

But did all this serve to mitigate the arrogance of ownership? Not hardly. Patchwork coalitions won't change
that. Short of a wholesale fan revolt against the greed of
Big Sport, I doubt we will see improvement in this century.
If you think that is overstated, I give you the long-running
case of the well-organized, flagrantly manipulative, annual
super-scalping of Super Bowl tickets.

The actual scalping, except as a continuing noxious cus-
tom, is not the issue. As long as there are commercial
events for which the ticket demand exceeds the supply,
suckers will line up to pay opportunists more than tickets
are worth. The "American Way." Many college football
and basketball players have been financing their weekends
for years by being allowed to do much the same thing.
Scalping is scalping, and is reprehensible, but it is also
probably inevitable.

No, the shame of the fast shuffling of Super Bowl tickets
involves a greater sin: the cynical indifference the NFL
pays the people who made it the giant enterprise it is
today. The back of the hand it gives those people.

It is not the annual blackmarket trafficking of an estimated 25,000 or more tickets that is unforgivable, it is the
mercenary process that puts those tickets into the hands
of those who *would* scalp them.

It is not that some buyers pay through the nose (as much

as $500) for tickets already priced out of reach (at $40 apiece) of the ordinary fan to see Eagles play Raiders or Redskins play Dolphins, it is that the vast majority of the real fans of those teams are either priced out or shut out in the process. Fans who didn't have a friend in the NFL office, or the office of their hometown team.

For the game of their spectating lives, they either can't buy a ticket at any price, or can't afford to buy into the mysterious "package deals" that now appear regularly in newspaper advertisements across the country at Super Bowl time. "Mysterious" because the question never answered is how these packages get all those tickets.

Pay through the nose? Let us count the ways. Imagine for a moment you are a long-suffering follower of the Eagles. For twenty years, since their last NFL championship, you have endured ever-rising ticket prices (up thirty-three percent in 1980) and ever-increasing costs to park your car and purchase your hotdogs to watch a team only a Philadelphia mother could love.

What is more, you have even voted yourself the fiscal responsibility of a series of bond issues that has provided the Eagles a $51 million aviary (Veterans Stadium) to play in, a debt you will be paying off into the next century. The stadium includes a posh dinner club and plush private boxes the inside of which you will never see, but will be enjoyed to the hilt by the club owners you have helped make rich.

But it was all worth it, because your ship finally comes in. The Eagles win the 1981 NFC championship and qualify to play Oakland in the Super Bowl.

Except that the Super Bowl will not be played in Philadelphia. Nor in Oakland, for that matter. It will be played in a "neutral" city, New Orleans. Unlike any other professional league, the NFL annually sells out its title game to the tourist meccas of the nation. (Imagine the Yankees

and the Dodgers playing the World Series in Honolulu.)
This may not promote the partisan excitement that helps
make a major sporting event great, but it certainly rep-
resents a concession to commerce.

Your twenty-year dream quickly becomes a financial
nightmare. It will cost you (on the average) $800 round-
trip air fare to New Orleans for you and your mate. From
San Francisco, an Oakland couple will pay $1,300. Once
there, you will experience the tourist-mecca equivalent of
small-arms robbery whenever you venture into the estab-
lishments along the avenues, but mainly you will suffer at
the hands of the hotels. On Bourbon Street, the manager
of one admitted that he had "doubled" the prices of rooms
that already went as high as $170 a night, and was requiring
a four-day occupancy, payable in advance. He said it wasn't
unusual. Other hotel managers admitted selling large
numbers of rooms in advance to the league and to travel
agencies, who could do with them what they saw fit.

But to see the game you have to buy tickets. As a long-
suffering Eagles fan, what are your chances? None, if you
didn't have season tickets and came to Eagles games only
when you could afford it. Season ticket holders had Super
Bowl priority. But even for them the odds were not good —
about one in six.

Commissioner Rozelle's office allots each competing team
around twenty percent of the host stadium's capacity —
in New Orleans' case, 16,425 apiece to the Eagles and
Raiders. The Raiders kept 6,425 in the family (front office,
players, etc.) and offered *their* fans the chance to grub for
the other 10,000. The Eagles offered 12,000 tickets to the
holders of the 65,000 season tickets, on a first-come, first-
served basis. The great majority of those tickets were in
the end zone. Take 'em or leave 'em.

And what if you were the twelve thousand and first
Eagles fan? What if you couldn't get tickets through the

management you helped prosper? What is your alternative? Do you remember that part about paying through the nose?

The distribution of the "remaining" tickets in New Orleans went like this: the NFL office kept 10,500. The host New Orleans Saints, the worst team in the NFL, got 7,500. Every other team in the NFL got 856 apiece, or roughly 24,000. Owners of the special suites in the Superdome — one can imagine a number of long-suffering Eagles fans in that group — got 2,500.

If you correctly assume that none of the above had as much right to an Eagles–Raiders ticket as you, the long-suffering Eagles fan, and should never have gotten that chance until and unless you and your long-suffering compatriots in Oakland had first refusal, you may be on the side of the angels, but no closer to the tickets. That will take cash. And lots of it.

Here is how the final process works. The tickets go out in all those directions, to a rather indiscriminate (but not stupid) clientele. People whose life's ambition is not likely to be to see the Eagles play the Raiders. Ask yourself, if you were among the favored of, say, the Seattle Seahawks to get one of their 856 tickets, how eager would *you* be to spend all that money to see the Eagles and the Raiders?

Thus the serious scalping begins.

Allegations at the time indicated it took many entertaining forms. Oakland owner Al Davis said Rozelle himself got into the act, in a very big way. Rozelle denied it, and defended his office's rights to its 10,500-ticket allotment. Then Davis admitted that a couple years ago he sold a hundred of *his* Super tickets to a Las Vegas hotelman, at face value, of course.

Ask yourself this, then. What does a Las Vegas hotelman have that you don't have? On second thought, don't ask yourself that. You already know that. Ask, instead, what Al Davis is doing with a hundred extra tickets to a game his team isn't even involved in?

Ask, furthermore, how it was possible that a *Wall Street Journal* reporter could purchase two 50-yard-line tickets (for $325) to a previous Super Bowl in Miami from a Miami Beach bartender, and be told "there are more where that came from."

Ask, furthermore, how Larry Goss of Murray's Tickets in Los Angeles could come up with so great an inventory that he could bill the Super Bowl on his marquee? Goss claimed he bought and sold 6,000 Super Bowl tickets in 1980.

For that matter, what were the Octagon Travel Center in Kingston, New York, Alive Travel Agency in Garden City, Long Island, and Holiday Travel and Tours in East McKeesport, Pennsylvania — those hotbeds of NFL ticket buyers — doing with so many Super Bowl tickets in past years that they could promote package tours?

A friend of mine in upstate New York was thinking about going to the 1983 Super Bowl. The game matched Miami and Washington, so naturally it was played in Pasadena, California. Pasadena is about as far away from Washington and Miami as they could play and still be in the continental United States. My friend couldn't get tickets from the Dolphins, and he couldn't get them from Washington, so he called on his travel agent.

The agent showed him a circular sent from the Hermosa Beach Ticket Outlet in California, offering Super Bowl tickets at $250 apiece in the end zone, $300 for better seats, and $400 to $475 for the middle of the field. For $700, my friend could fly out, get a ticket to the game, enjoy a pre-game "mini-party," and have a van transport him to the game and back. No hotel room included. He was on his own for shelter.

My friend shopped around. He found that more than a dozen ticket agencies in Southern California had package deals, charging up to $500 apiece for Super Bowl seats. According to the *Long Beach* (California) *Press-Telegram,* several agencies could provide as many as six tickets together near the 50-yard line. The paper said the agencies "acquired the tickets from various sources, usually at inflated prices." Larry Gold, a Los Angeles broker with Ticket Time, said he had tickets from the 30- to the 50-yard lines for $300 to $350, and end zone seats for $90 to $130.

My friend called the Hermosa Beach Ticket Outlet. He talked with a gentleman named Doug. He told Doug he had "thirty guys who need tickets."

"We can take care of you," Doug said. "You want good seats or in the end zone?"

"Good seats."

"You got 'em."

My friend said, "We might need twenty more. We got a pretty big group."

"That's fine," he was told. "Send us $100 a ticket as a down payment, made payable to the First National Bank of Hermosa Beach. If you have any questions at the bank, ask for Rose. She does this for us every year."

"One of our guys is in the banking business," my friend said.

"Good. You can just transfer the funds from one bank to another."

"You sure this'll work?"

"Sir, we do this all the time."

After the ticket fiasco in New Orleans, Commissioner Rozelle was quoted as saying that Super Bowl tickets were a "mess" and gave him "a sickness in the stomach." The commissioner was right, and deserved a stomach ache. It *is* sickening. But it is also revolting. Which is exactly what the fans should be doing. If anybody has a right to scalp tickets, they do.

In the end, of course, fans are long-suffering because they are reactionary. Their attitudes and conduct are reflections of what they see and feel. And if they are violent, they are violent at least partly because of the violence they witness. The difference is that the violence they see is caused by an even greater subversion of athletics.

4.

Violence Unleashed

I DISTRUST congressional involvement in sport for practical reasons. Practically every time legislators get involved, progress begins to look a lot like desolation. I distrust it historically. Any government body that sanctions player drafts and reserve clauses deserves an active, ongoing skepticism. Such insults to the free enterprise system going unleashed for so long should tell us a lot about congressional involvement in sport.

I distrust even more the congressional subcommittee hearings that are held every now and again, not because the subjects of the hearings aren't worthwhile, but because they tend to reveal how little Congress knows about what's going on. And that, of course, is depressing.

Unfortunately, such hearings have become commonplace on Capitol Hill and they all follow the same wretched format: a bill is pushed by a certain legislator, then various aides — working for the subcommittee — range far and wide to gather witnesses. The witnesses are asked to prepare statements to be read before the hearing, presumably to help enlighten the subcommittee.

The purpose of all this paper — and foot — work is to ferret out sins and sponsor meaningful change. I imagine the system could work if the panel members did their homework and knew precisely what to ask the witnesses. But it has been my experience that they seldom do. Their questions are often repetitious and bloated with rhetoric. They have a knack for belaboring the obvious. They intimidate weak witnesses. And they frequently do not give those testifying their full attention.

At the ill-advised hearings on the NCAA, and a subsequent consideration of Representative Ron Mottl's (D-Ohio) sports violence bill by the House Judiciary Subcommittee on Criminal Justice, both of which I attended, the panel was almost always out in force for the star witnesses (i.e., those who figured to get media attention). But when it came to the lesser lights, the dais looked as though it had been hit by a killer virus. I was reminded of William Simon's exasperated reference (after several hundred appearances) to "those coconuts on the hill," and wondered why, if those coconuts could not bring themselves to listen to the constituents they had summoned, they were allowed to summon them in the first place.

The NCAA hearings were a predictable cacophony of confused testimony and did neither the Congress nor the NCAA much good. I would have gladly passed up the violence hearings but I was asked to testify, and there is something about a call from Capitol Hill that makes a fellow want to contribute what he can. Even if he knows better. (I have since testified a second time before a Senate subcommittee, so obviously I don't.)

The sports violence bill, HR 2263, in its original form, would have provided penalties — a fine of not more than $5,000, imprisonment of not more than a year, or both — for the use of "excessive physical force" in professional sports events. As it was written, the bill was ambiguous, hopelessly one-sided, and posed more questions than it answered. New efforts have since been made, but such a bill might be impossible to write because it can never get to the heart of the problem.

My own convictions on the issue as it related to football had been aired previously. Brutal tactics had led to an epidemic injury rate in football, and similar license in other sports (pro hockey, pro basketball) had been well documented. In my prepared statement I admitted to being skeptical about anything that would involve the U.S. Congress any more than it does in the procedural aspects of American sport, feeling as I did that it had not done itself any favors with such involvements in the past. I said I hoped it would let sport work out its own salvation wherever and whenever it can.

At the same time (feeling more conciliatory as my appearance neared), I said I applauded Congress's interest and conceded that any exposure to some of the mindless acts of violence that have perverted the good name of sport could only help effect a greater self-examination of the true goals and values of those responsible for it — meaning the administrators and coaches of the various teams and leagues, not the players. A key point.

I spent three evenings preparing my remarks. I hoped to alert the subcommittee to the main issues: how all of sport is injured when those at the top, who set examples, set violent ones. How win-at-any-cost ethics create a hothouse for violence that extends down to the youngest athletes. How more is at stake than just the legal (or congressional) recourse available to an injured party.

I said that some of our sports were, indeed, rough and tough and meant to be. It is part of their attraction. It would be wrong to take those elements out of a game like football, for example. If it is true that such a sport's natural roughness spawns some over-the-line bullying, we can even excuse that.

But when a barbarism becomes "accepted" and the thugs who perpetrate it glorified, and the bloody mess begins to blend into the fabric of sport, as it has, then we have a problem that certainly needs to be dealt with.

Coaches would generally deplore the vicious acts and tactics the Congress was trying to define, for a number of sensible reasons. For one, unlike most of us they live in a black-and-white world where rules violations can bring instant judgment and where there is no such thing as a change of venue or a "second set of books." Like Bear Bryant used to say, going "too far" can get your team penalized, and a penalty in a close game can get you beat. This is a practical consideration.

Moreover, brutality can break bones. Nobody that I know in the administrative end of sport wants to see his players injured. This is a humane consideration — but a practical one, too. It doesn't help the war effort to have an injured star on the bench. It's also bad for ticket sales.

But when professional sport, aided and abetted by television, took over as the role model in the 1950s and '60s, allowances for the "acceptable" conduct of our competitions began to bend. The pros succeeded beyond their wildest dreams. Few would begrudge them that. But theirs has been an irresponsible leadership, and they have made almost indistinguishable the lines of "how far" "*too* far" should be. Win at any cost. Style over substance. Accumulation of riches over achievement — those are the only values the pros brought to sport in recent years. The absolute worst examples of savage play and unsportsmanlike conduct have come from the professional level.

It does not take a stick of dynamite to get to the root of the problem. When athletes are desperate to succeed, to get to where all that money is, and stay there for a while, they do whatever they have to do. When coaches are put in a desperate win-or-else situation, they are not likely to look askance at intimidation and violence if those things can help keep them employed. This, in turn, has led to the worst part of the equation: the insane tolerance of an epidemic injury rate, and to the bloodlust that is just now being understood by sport's better thinkers as counterproductive. The bottom-line mentalities who control sport at the top have a lot to answer for in this regard.

Brutality is its own fertilizer. From "get away with what you can" it is a short hop to the deviations that poison a sport. The ugly manifestations spill into our living rooms, via television. But it is not just acts that border on the criminal that are intolerable, it is the permissive atmosphere they spring from. The "lesser" evils that are given tacit approval as "techniques" of the game, even within the rules.

There is a marked difference between what is "legal" and what is "necessary" in sport today. Often what is allowed, and gets people hurt, is simply not necessary, though it may be perfectly legal (within the rules of the game). It is this factor that needs the more careful consideration because in its growth it has distorted competition at all levels.

In distorting the competition, the games were changed. Even basketball threw in. Bill Walton, the Portland center, remembers in his early playing days that basketball was a "motion game, a movement game." He says it has become a game of "big strong guys beating up on the other team." John Wooden, the Hall of Fame ex-UCLA coach, compares pro basketball to wrestling — "no finesse, no grace, everyone holding everyone else."

Sometimes they do more than hold. Some of sport's more sensational spasms of viciousness in recent years have occurred on basketball courts, in a "non-contact" game. The blow that hospitalized Rudy Tomjanovich and led to legal action against Kermit Washington indicated that *some*body wasn't going to take it anymore, however, and it is just too bad it had to come at the expense of a cheekbone.

The fanaticism that has produced such ugliness has led to a distrust of the values of sport. I don't happen to believe that sport "builds character." I *do* believe that the lessons of sport — the willingness to sacrifice, the devotion to a mutual cause — can enhance character. But if character were that easily harvested from sport, we would have to look no farther than, say, our professional hockey teams for inspiration — and we all know what kind of examples pro hockey teams have been setting lately.

I once heard the gentleman who presides over the National Hockey League brag to a television audience, "We *are* violent. We *start off* violent." Not only does such an attitude reek of insensitivity, it devalues the very sport the man is supposed to represent. The primary attraction of sports like hockey and football is, despite such dubious advocates, still skill, not ferocity. Still technique and finesse, not intimidation. When thinking like that is allowed to fester, when it is, in fact, not discouraged, all of sport suffers.

True sportsmanship is not compatible with a win-at-any-cost philosophy. It would be hard to tell how far the influence goes, but in recent years there have been some bizarre twists. In Teton, Idaho, the principal of the local high school was angered at seeing his football coach penalized for unsportsmanlike conduct during a playoff game. The principal summoned the offending referee to the sideline — and punched him in the stomach, knocking him down. The principal was later fined $500 and banned from future contests involving his coach. He said he felt exonerated, however, when the league suspended the referee from further assignments.

In Salt Lake City, a high-school football player was

expelled from school for pummeling an official during a playoff game. The official required surgery to repair a shattered face. The player said he might have gotten his inspiration from seeing a 246-pound Brigham Young University tackle punch out an umpire during a game with Utah State.

Exposure of the problems of sport is necessary, even if legislation should be a last resort. Without such exposure too much time passes before we see how far down a wrong path we have gone. I think it is clear enough that the time is ripe in American sport to realize that a stand for sportsmanship and fair play *without* intimidation or brutality will not tilt the axis on which this planet spins. Competitive sports, in the end, must go beyond sportsmanship. They must reach all the way to "fair play."

The essential difference is that fair play involves taking a stand above the legalities of the game. A stand that places winning at a risk but at the same time preserves the dignity and value of sport. It is a moral issue, not a political one. It must be based on an inner conviction that to win by going outside the rules and the spirit of the rules is not really to win at all.

My appearance before the subcommittee was scheduled near the end of a session, so I was able to listen while others testified. It was late afternoon, and most of the subcommittee had vanished. Being one of the lesser lights, I was not surprised.

Jim Korn, a defenseman for the Detroit Red Wings, was called. The subcommittee chairman, Representative John Conyers, Jr. (D-Mich.), took the lead in examining him and was able to wring from young Mr. Korn the startling confession that pro hockey is a violent game.

When Korn further admitted that pro teams hire "enforcers" to intimidate opponents, Conyers acted as if he had found a first edition Kipling in a used book store. For what seemed like hours and hours, Conyers conjured up images of "good enforcers" and "bad enforcers," and was able to prove conclusively that a fifty-two-year-old U.S. congressman is better with words than a twenty-three-year-old hockey player.

Then Korn made a remark that the subcommittee should have leaped all over. A remark that should have been burned in the hide of every administrator of sport. Korn said he never got into fights at the amateur levels of hockey. He said he never even saw one in the Olympic Games. Why not? Because if you go outside the rules to batter another player in the amateurs, he said, you get ejected — kicked out of the game — and maybe out of future games as well.

I tried to enlarge on Korn's point when I took the chair. I was not asked to read my ten-page statement; it was "entered" into the record by Conyers, and I assumed that the subcommittee had already examined it. So I picked up where Korn had left off.

In effect, I said, the panel had just been treated to expert testimony on the cause of violence in sport, and at the same time been given the solution. While everybody was busy blaming the players, "enforcers" or otherwise, they were overlooking the fact that the brutality was orchestrated. That the violence implicated the entire structure of pro sport.

Mottl's bill would only penalize the players. Not the coaches who encouraged the borderline (and over-the-line) hits, the injurious techniques and the tactics of intimidation. Not the administrators and team owners who condoned the acts and profited from them. Not the game officials whose action, or inaction, can encourage bad behavior to escalate. All are just as culpable as the offending athlete.

And once they got into the penalizing business, would

Congress draw the line at television? Would Congress have the guts to make television responsible for its incessant catering to and capitalizing on the violence? And for immortalizing it on instant replay?

It is the *climate* of violence that must be dealt with, and sports violence bills like HR 2263 are totally inadequate for that task. But Congress need not concern itself, I said, because the exorcists were already on the job. They are called lawyers and they are swarming over our professional games like locusts, taking more and more cases of sports violence into courts of law. And, quite wisely, they are not just singling out athletes. They are representing clients who are suing coaches, suing schools, suing equipment manufacturers, suing officials, suing administrators.

(A jury in Detroit awarded former Red Wing Dennis Polonich $850,000 in damages in late 1982 in a lawsuit that charged forward Wilf Paiement of the Colorado Rockies with using excessive force in a 1978 game in which Polonich received a broken nose, a concussion and several cuts after being hit with Paiement's stick. It was the first such case in NHL history. It will not likely be the last.)

During my questioning it became obvious to me that Conyers had not read my statement. Afterward, assistant counsel Ernest McIntosh told me that though Conyers "hadn't had time" to get to it before I testified, he certainly intended to read it as soon as he could.

Representative Mottl considered my objections and asked if I would support the bill if it were rewritten. I said I didn't know, that I would have to see the revisions. But the more I thought about it, the more I realized Congress should just leave well enough alone. Sport needs less confusion, not more. It is already swamped by enough incompetence.

Nevertheless, Korn's testimony stayed with me. Such a simple evaluation, and so profound. It occurred to me that I had not seen a professional hockey game in years. That I no longer had an interest. I wondered how much it had to do with my distaste for the muddled philosophy of its leaders. And if there were many more like me out there who were being repulsed enough to stay away. Could pro hockey be turning off a vast potential audience? People who like their hockey straight and had no other way to protest the grotesque creak of brutality?

Actually, no. It was nothing as sensitive as that. For me it was no more than a matter of being bored by it. The mindless violence had become a distraction. If I wanted to pay for violence, I could get it in purer forms at the boxing arena or in the movie theaters. At least in those places it was a lot more professional.

As a young soldier stationed at West Point, I was a frequent patron of Smith Rink, both as a beginning ice skater with treacherous ankles and as a numbed spectator at the Army hockey games (numbed because the rink wasn't heated). Pete Dawkins played for the Cadets then and I thoroughly enjoyed watching him apply his football-playing skills to the ice. Cadet Dawkins was quick, tough and hard-checking, but definitely not brutal. I seldom missed a game, and I was as thrilled later on by American victories over the professional Russian teams in the Olympics, most recently at Lake Placid.

When I moved to New York from Miami, in the 1960s, I went to the Garden to watch the Rangers a few times, but after a while I lost interest. By the time pro hockey had established itself as a metaphor for hooliganism in the mid-'70s, I had forever lost the urge. My interest by then was clinical. I watched the papers only to see if anybody in an official capacity would awaken to the possibility that Rodney Dangerfield was not kidding when he said "I went to a fight last night and a hockey game broke out." And if the implications would ever be realized. And if any of the battered, stitched-up victims would ever wise up and sue, as Polonich eventually did.

With no one at the top to stop it, or even wanting to try, the virulence renewed itself annually, and grew. The 1980s came in on a wave of tacitly approved brutality. Asked about the notorious play of the Philadelphia Flyers, who had led the NHL in penalty minutes year after year, league president John Ziegler said, "If the other twenty teams were as successful, I'd be pleased, regardless of how they achieved such success." Ziegler said spontaneous fighting was a "justifiable outlet for the frustrations in hockey."

Paul Martha, chief operating officer of the Pittsburgh Civic Arena, didn't even see it as that serious. Martha said he didn't think that "fighting was necessarily violence." Martha blamed the fans and *their* bloodlust. Violence, after all, sold tickets. When Jimmy Mann of the Winnipeg team blindsided Pittsburgh's Paul Gardner and broke his jaw, a radio spot in Pittsburgh urged the fans to come out and see Mann play. There was no doubting why, or what they would see. In 109 games with Winnipeg, Mann had scored only six goals — but had amassed 400 minutes in penalties.

A game in the Boston Garden was barely seven seconds old when a fight started that led to a brawl that spilled into the dressing room runway and resulted, by game's end, in a record 406 penalty minutes and the ejection of twelve players. The colorful coach of the Minnesota team suggested that the colorful coach of the Boston team "bring a basket [to Minnesota the next week] to carry his head home in." Threats flew back and forth like poker raises. Ticket sales for the rematch were brisk.

Critics of this madness (a growing number, fortunately) finally had something to cheer by the end of 1982. The $850,000 judgment against Paiement established once and for all that the law does not stop at the ticket window. That brutality unleashed is punishable even within the boundaries of a hockey rink. Other sports had already been made to face the bench — notably, in football when Dale Hackbart of Denver sued Booby Clark of Cincinnati over a vicious foul that injured Hackbart in 1973 and shortened his NFL career, and in basketball with Tomjanovich's suit against California Sports, Inc., over the mugging he suffered from Kermit Washington in 1977.

More importantly, blame was at last seeping into the right corners. In a game against the Vancouver Canucks, a journeyman forward named Paul Mulvey of the Los Angeles Kings refused his coach's command to join in a fight on the ice. Mulvey said he would not be Don Perry's "designated assassin." In that case, Coach Perry said, Mulvey doesn't play another minute for the Kings.

Thus exposed for what was generally characterized as his sadism, Perry was suspended by the NHL for fifteen days. Dave Schultz, a former NHL player whose abilities in such matters earned him the nickname "The Hammer," but who repented and now writes moving letters to his son about the "good old days" when hockey was "fun," said he "questioned whether it will be enough." Schultz said his coach with the Philadelphia team used to send him out to fight, too, "but unlike Mulvey, I was willing." Schultz wrote a book about making a living as a "hockey enforcer" that should be required reading for Representative Conyers.

Unfortunately for Mulvey, being exonerated was not the same as being saved. He never did play another minute for the Kings, and was put on waivers.

And in the end, the real culprits were barely nicked. The real culprits being management. As an extension of management, Perry was doing no more than what has been expected — even demanded — of coaches in the National

Hockey League for years. Ordering an "enforcer" onto the ice to enforce was business as usual in the NHL. Management does not only approve, it encourages.

So how do you get to the real culprits? How do you get to those villains in the air-conditioned boxes who authorize the barbarism and profit by it without ever suffering so much as a nosebleed? You get to them indirectly, at least as a first step. *Sports Illustrated* called for an automatic five-game suspension whenever a player dropped his gloves or swung his stick, and a ten-game suspension if he did it a second time. This would discourage the player and the coach. Then, to further discourage the coach, *SI* would make the suspended player's team play shorthanded for the full term of his penalty. Coaches don't like to play shorthanded. They can lose games playing shorthanded.

In both cases, management would suffer because the penalties would affect the product. When the product suffers, gate receipts suffer. There is nothing like a blow to the gate receipts to wake up management.

The worm in the plan, and any one like it, is that management itself decides these things (suspensions, fines, etc.), and no management of *any* league has ever shown a disposition for self-castigation. Management has to agree, and management would not agree if it thought the punishment would punish *it*.

In the end, the courts may be the only hope for hockey. The courts are where the hardest blows are struck, and where the bleating is loudest when they are. When the Detroit jury found in favor of Polonich for his $850,000, an NHL general manager said he was "shocked" by the verdict. He said he was afraid it would make hockey "a very different game from now on."

According to the testimony, Paiement "planted himself and took a baseball swing" when he scrambled Polonich's face with his stick. The defense attorney whined that the jury who found for Polonich "was not familiar with hockey."

The answer is to make management squirm. Sue clubs, sue owners, sue leagues, and sue league presidents. Sue those people who profit most from the thuggery. It is not only a reasonable thing to do (getting the blame properly placed), it would be the most rewarding. Clubs can afford larger judgments than can players.

The NBA fined Kermit Washington $10,000 and suspended him sixty days for his hit on Tomjanovich. But Tomjanovich wasn't satisfied to sue Washington. He sued the Los Angeles Lakers' ownership (California Sports, Inc.), and in 1979 a jury found in his favor: $1.8 million in actual damages, $1.5 million in punitive damages. One would now doubt that California Sports will tolerate any more players who take out their "frustrations" on an opponent's face.

As for football, it has made grudging progress since being exposed to its own brute face a couple years ago. An epidemic injury rate was the chief cause of concern then. Some rules were changed at the pro level, and some were added, and some were more strictly interpreted to protect players. The net result has been to make brutality a little costlier for the brutal player, not the people who sanctioned it.

According to the National Football League, nineteen players were fined in 1981 for "flagrant personal fouls," up from seven in 1980 and fifteen in 1979. (The NFL's non-season of 1982 should not be counted in any comparison of anything.) The largest fine was $2,000, not enough to break a modern player, but a good reminder. In any case, only players were punished, not coaches or administrators.

Stan Blinka, a New York Jets linebacker, became only

the second player in the sixty-three-year history of the NFL to be suspended when his forearm blow almost decapitated Green Bay's John Jefferson. His own explanation did Blinka no good. He said he hadn't meant "to go for the head," and blamed it on Jefferson being "shorter than I thought." (Had his forearm landed a few inches lower, it might have removed Jefferson's windpipe.)

Green Bay coach Bart Starr called it the act of a "hoodlum." On a subsequent Monday night TV game, Blinka's hits on Detroit running back Billy Sims even drew Don Meredith's wrath. "I'll be doggoned, guy," sportscaster Meredith griped after another replay caught Blinka in action. "You got to knock that off. That's stupid."

NFL Commissioner Rozelle suspended Blinka for a game. One columnist suggested Blinka should spend it pushing Darryl Stingley around in his wheelchair. Stingley is the former New England player who was paralyzed for life by a similar blow from Oakland's Jack Tatum three years before.

My own interest centered more on how management would react. The president of the Jets took the practical view. He said he was "extremely disappointed" that they would have to lose Blinka for a game. He characterized the linebacker as "a fine family man and a team player."

I wondered if he would have been as generous if the entire Jets coaching staff and front office had been made to account for Blinka's actions. If *they* were suspended without pay, or if *they* were required to push Stingley around in his wheelchair or pay his weekly medical bills.

I had been in irregular contact at the time with two lawyers who had had a hand in Representative Mottl's original sports violence bill — Rick Horrow in Miami, who had drafted that bill, and Chris J. Carlsen in California. Both agreed that singling out the player alone for guilt was wrong. Carlsen objected further to the gross unevenness in the penalties meted out by the NFL justice system. Blinka, for example, got suspended, but Leonard Thompson of Detroit was only fined for his hit on punt returner Leon Bright, even though Bright missed a game with a sore neck and Jefferson missed no time at all. And, of course, no suspension was levied against Jack Tatum for his paralyzing blow to Stingley.

Carlsen's revised ideas for distributing the blame were subsequently printed in the *Southern California Law Review.* I was pleased to see they were much closer now to my own, and embarrassed to say they were better thought out. When one player hurt another maliciously, Carlsen said, the offending player should be made to pay a fine and suffer a suspension, *but:*

The offending player's *club* should be made (1) to pay the salary of the injured player during his convalescence, (2) to pay his medical expenses, (3) to pay compensatory damages if he is unable to play in the future, (4) to pay fines for failing to control its own player's actions, and (5) to pay damages or relinquish draft choices to the injured player's club for the loss of his services. To make punishment uniform, he said, a schedule of fines and penalties would have to be drawn up.

The key question remained: how do you get management to agree to such a thing? In effect, to bring judgment crashing down on its own guilty head?

Government intervention, of course. It always seems to come to that. Carlsen argued for a congressionally mandated "sports court," comprised of three appointed judges expert in athletics. The threat of such a dismal prospect (sport in the hairy grip of lawyers on a regular basis) might make the various leagues come to their senses. Horrow argued for what was essentially a rewritten sports violence bill, introduced as the Sports Violence Arbitration Act by Representative Mottl in early 1983. The Act would empower Congress to set up arbitration boards to make judgments and impose fines from league to league. And, in effect, make management share the liability for the sins of the players. And the whole process answerable to the federal government.

I shuddered at the thought. Sport, at last, taking its place alongside General Motors, the United Mine Workers and Con Edison.

But does it deserve any better? Violence is not just a physical thing. It is an influence. A process that is as damaging to the mind and spirit as it is the body — *more* damaging, actually. In sport, the influence has been as undermining as a new set of rules. But is it cause or symptom? And is it any worse than the acts that demean and intimidate in other ways?

All of sport now squirms in the grip of an incivility so vast and vulgar that a punch on the nose is almost a relief by comparison. Sportsmanship has yielded on all fronts to intimidation. Sports decorum has given way to flagrant bad manners. Offensive behavior has become the norm rather than the exception — louts having their way in every arena.

We now *expect* our sports heroes to flaunt their superiority and denigrate their opponents. We *expect* ballcarriers to spike the ball at the feet of opponents in the end zone and defensive tackles to shake their fists at downed quarterbacks in gestures of contempt. Why not? Great players in the NFL do it. We *expect* the Billy Martins and Earl Weavers of baseball to rail at umpires and kick dirt, and the Bobby Knights of basketball to scream at officials. We *expect* boxers to posture and show up their opponents. The Great Ali did it, didn't he?

And when John McEnroe or Ilie Nastase or Jimmy Connors use insulting language and crude gestures to put hapless linesmen in their place, can we honestly say it is any less violent than a kick in the shins? And can we honestly say that a rigidly decorous game like tennis, one that was once a testimony to sportsmanship, is now any less ugly than hockey?

5.

Owners and Adversaries

I HAD followed the controversy over Doug Williams's contract dispute with the Tampa Bay Buccaneers by newspaper, half interested, and then only because an old friend was involved. I had seen Williams play on television a few times and had wondered why so many people thought he had hung the moon. At quarterback he seemed to stand out primarily because of his size (large) and his color (black), and because he had an exceptionally powerful arm. At the most crucial moments of a game he seemed infinitely capable of throwing the ball thirty yards over a receiver's head.

But John McKay was the Tampa Bay coach, and McKay was a man I had great respect for, as well as warm personal feelings (if Corky McKay was not the most charming coach's wife I had ever met, she was certainly in the top three). So I knew Williams must be better than what I had seen on television. Bear Bryant once told me "nobody knows the passing game better than McKay."

I also knew McKay to be a stubborn man. It had served him well at USC, where he had won four national championships, made a dreadnought out of the I-formation, and led the free world in quick-quips. (Asked once why he let O. J. Simpson carry the ball so much, McKay replied, "Why? It's not heavy.") I wondered if he might be trying to prove a point with Williams — that, given the chance, a black quarterback could do the job as well as a white. It is hardly a subject worth debating anymore, but it raises its ugly head now and again. McKay had persevered with two black quarterbacks at USC, Jimmy Jones and Vince Evans, with mixed results.

But that wasn't the case at all, McKay said when I got him on the phone. "Dougie's for real," he said. "A wonderful athlete. Strong as a bull. When he scrambles, you can't tackle him. He got us to the playoffs three times, and he's had some great games. He's had the other kind, too, but he's still learning. He's fearless. He *wants* the ball. Some guys don't."

"Does he throw anything but sixty-yard passes?" I asked, half kidding.

"He didn't have much of a touch at first, but he worked at it and learned. The biggest thing he had to deal with was his emotions. I had to tell him, 'No matter what happens, Doug, you're the quarterback. Nobody is going to come out there and take your place when you do something wrong. So don't come off the field waving your arms and making a show.' I never pulled him from a game. I told him, 'We're building something, we're in this together.'

"Last year he said some things about what we were doing on offense that I didn't like, but within the realm of his experience, he was making what he thought was a legitimate criticism. Some people said, 'Well, he's this, therefore he's not smart,' meaning race, but it's a damn lie. There's nothing wrong with his mind. I'd love to see him reach the zenith here, not to prove *my* point, but to prove *a* point, and because he's such a nice person. But that's not why he's my quarterback. He's my quarterback because he's the best. He just hasn't played well on television."

"Why won't he sign?"

"He wants so much money we aren't even close. His agent started at five million for five years, guaranteed, and now he's 'down' to $875,000 a year for three. It's out of line, because we don't guarantee *any* contracts, and because it's just out of line. But I try to stay out of it because I've got to coach him."

He said when the impasse was reached, he asked Williams to go see Hugh Culverhouse, the team owner. "I got him to agree to sit down and talk with Mr. C. I thought it would be to Doug's advantage. Leroy Selmon got a lot of money by talking to Mr. C. But Doug changed his mind. I asked him why. He said, 'He could get me to sign anything.' It's frustrating. You can't agree if you don't talk."

"How much is Tampa offering?"

"Three years at $400,000, then $500,000 the fourth year and $600,000 the fifth. It's fair, I think. But all things are relative since the new league. Doug signed in 1978 for a $125,000 bonus and a $50,000 salary that went up over five years to $120,000, plus bonuses. We tried to renegotiate a couple times, but he said he'd rather wait. Today that contract might not sound like much, but people are getting the times confused. They see John Elway making all that money and Elway can't get the ball past the line of scrimmage. It's an accident of birth. Elway's good fortune. You can't go back."

"Will you sign him?"

"I don't know. I don't know what his thinking is, and I don't know what he's been told. He's been with me five years, we've been through a lot together. His wife died in April — twenty-seven years old. She had a brain tumor. It was a tragic thing. Cork and I went to the funeral. That had to have an effect on Dougie. But now it's this contract, and I get the impression he thinks I'm the other side now.

"The money thing is a helluva distraction in this business. Just sitting down to talk is a major undertaking. I haven't even *met* his agent, Jimmy Walsh. I got a call the other day from Eddie Robinson [Williams's coach at Grambling]. I told him what we'd offered. He said it was a terrific offer and he'd tell Doug to accept it and come in. I said I wasn't going to hold my breath."

Williams never returned to Tampa Bay, except to sell his house and pack his things. Negotiations dragged on, then came apart like a piñata. I followed the accounts. Williams's remarks and those of his agent, Jimmy Walsh, grew increasingly onerous. Racism was hinted. ("If I was white," Williams said, "it'd be different.") "Lying" was charged.

Finally, with the new season at hand, Williams signed with Tulsa of the United States Football League. I called a mutual friend, Tow McEwen of the *Tampa Tribune.* He said McKay was "brokenhearted." Tampa Bay started the season with a new quarterback, Jack Thompson, who had been acquired from Cincinnati when negotiations with Williams began to lag.

If my curiosity was morbid, it was also mobilized. In the Byzantine world of professional sport, Williams v. Tampa Bay seemed a classic case of the failing relationship between athlete and management. A spectacular breakdown in communication, loyalty and trust. Making it more intriguing was that the case involved the most crucial association I know of in team sport — that of a coach with his quarterback. And, of course, it involved McKay.

When the Buccaneers opened the 1983 season with four straight losses, I went to see him. On the morning before a trip to Green Bay for game five (and, as it turned out, the worst day of his coaching life), McKay nursed a prebreakfast cup of coffee on the sunporch of his home on Bayshore Drive and discussed the painstaking nature of such relationships, how important and pleasurable they can be, and how one coach handles them differently than another.

He said he was never one to get too close to players. We both knew others who had. To get *his* message over, Bear Bryant took long walks with his quarterbacks, and visited them in their dormitory rooms. If Bryant didn't drop by regularly to play a football board game with Babe Parilli at Kentucky, Parilli thought something was wrong. Washington Redskins coach Joe Gibbs, a former McKay assistant, called the coach-quarterback relationship a "chemistry" that becomes a "kinship," and credited a surprise nighttime visit from quarterback Joe Theisman for turning the Redskins around after a five-game losing streak in 1980.

But McKay said that wasn't his style. He had been close with some of his quarterbacks — Pat Haden had lived in the McKay house for a year in California — "but I don't put my arm around them or make a big outward display. You can show your respect in other ways."

With Williams, he said, the rapport had been solid from the start. If you could possibly characterize a short white football coach as the soulmate of a tall black quarterback half his age, then McKay and Williams were soulmates. McKay's record for indifference to color bordered on the legendary. His championship teams at USC were always well marbled, and his Tampa teams were even more so. Tampa's star players were mostly black. The 1983 official Buccaneer publicity poster looked like a flyer for the Kenyan National Guard: a montage of seven black players, including Williams.

"People said we couldn't win with a black quarterback," McKay said. "They were the same people who said we couldn't win with the I-formation, or the three-four defense. We did. Now almost everybody uses the I, and the three-four. People said there were 'rumors' about Doug's intelligence. The rumors were wrong. He's a smart young man. They used to 'rumor' about Terry Bradshaw's intelligence, too. Bradshaw took Pittsburgh to four Super Bowls. I'd love to have a quarterback dumb enough to take me to four Super Bowls."

Williams was the first black quarterback ever chosen in the first round of an NFL draft. McKay's scouts told him he was "raw talent." He was an All-American with flashy statistics, but at Grambling the opposition was suspect. (Williams once threw seven touchdown passes in a game that Grambling won 63 to 0.) A knock was that he had none of the essential "finesse" passes in his repertoire. He almost always threw what coaches call "haul-ass stuff," never to his backs.

But McKay saw films, and said Williams was "the kind of player you go with for the long pull." And he said something else, remarkable in its appositeness: "I'm fifty-five years old. If Doug Williams isn't the future, we'll have to start over, and I'm too tired to start over."

The best quarterbacks are *not* an extension of the coach on the field. They are more than that. The good coach strives not so much to dominate a quarterback's mind, but to control just enough of it so that when left to his own prerogatives the athlete's unique abilities will take over.

Just as acting is more than reading lines, so is quarterbacking more than calling plays. The play-calling itself is overrated. If the quarterback is on the same wavelength as the coach, he will usually call the same plays the coach would anyway. It is *after* the play starts, when he is on the run facing myriad alternatives (keying on cornerbacks and safetymen, reading double coverages, etc.) — it is at those most critical moments that a quarterback must shine.

"Doug had started to get that," McKay said on the

sunporch. "He was doing a tremendous job of reacting when he saw something. He was becoming — not there yet, but on the way — one of the better quarterbacks in the game. That thing about being the first great black quarterback might have been a problem, but I thought he was handling it. I kept telling him, 'No matter what happens, Doug, you're the quarterback.' "

McKay said he told that to Williams over and over again. He told him through the giddy highs, and he told him through the abysmal lows when the coach himself took so much heat he said he began to think his name was "McKay You Idiot." At times, Williams was so brilliant he took your breath away (one breathless Tampa writer described his play in a 367-yard, two-touchdown effort against Chicago in 1982 as "brilliant," "courageous," "heartwarming," "heroic," "macho," "powerful," "versatile," "compelling," and "a privilege to watch" — and that was just the first couple of paragraphs). At other times, he played as if there wasn't a single coordinating bone in his body.

In his first pre-season game, Williams's first pass went for a touchdown. In his first regular season game, his third pass was intercepted and run back for a touchdown. He *did* have trouble throwing to the outlet man or backs coming out of the backfield, but his space shots downfield won games, he played hurt (a badly swollen hand, a gimp knee), and the Buccaneers in 1979 became the youngest team ever to reach the playoffs. They went on to make them three out of four years.

But although it was a stirring improvement over what Tampa had done before, Williams was, in five years, only a .500 pitcher — won 33, lost 33. And in those crucial playoff games, he completed only thirty-two percent of his passes for only 111 yards a game, and threw nine interceptions. On national television, he had a woeful 89-

yard average. He never made the Pro Bowl; he never
ranked among the leaders in the quarterback ratings.

And sometimes he made bonehead plays, and sometimes he made bonehead remarks. Early on, after being
roundly booed, he said, "Let 'em boo, I'll still be taking
my money to the bank." A Buccaneer fan wrote the *Tribune:* "I just hope Doug's not required to throw his money
into the bank door. He'll only hit it one out of five times."
Another suggested the government should send him to
Iran because he was the only man around who could over-
throw the Ayatollah.

But through it all, McKay stuck by him. "Dougie," he
said, "is burying his critics with his achievements." Actually, it was more McKay burying Williams's critics. He
cowed writers with brusque rejoinders, an effective means
of deferring criticism. After a playoff loss in Dallas, when
Williams was 2 for 13 and 80 yards, McKay said, "I don't
think he was so ineffective." After the 1982 season, McKay
even fired his quarterback coach, Bill Nelson, when he
thought Nelson and Williams "weren't getting along."

To the end, Williams spoke derisively of "percentage"
quarterbacks — guys, he said, "who can throw three com-
pletions in a row and still not have a first down. That's
not my style." The idea of the short pass as a ball control
weapon was anathema to him. But like so many of his
contradictions, McKay believed, this was probably because Doug knew he wasn't good at it, and he worked
hard to get better. "And last year our leading receiver
caught fifty-three passes — and he was our fullback, James
Wilder. I knew then that Dougie was on his way."

What he never dreamed, McKay said, was that Dougie
would not just be on his way, but gone.

Two days later, on the most miserable afternoon of John
McKay's coaching life, with the team he had built from

scratch into a Super Bowl contender falling apart like a sand castle in Green Bay, Wisconsin, I sat with the young man he had built it around in the living room of the family's ranch-style house on the outskirts of Zachary, Louisiana. The embarrassment of his former teammates was neither lost on nor shared by Doug Williams. Their disgrace only made him laugh.

Actually, Zachary *is* outskirts, a polyp on the vine of State Road 19 that winds into Baton Rouge. And, actually, Doug Williams could not enjoy the slaughter to the utmost because the game shown on television in the area was not Tampa Bay–Green Bay, it was Minnesota–Dallas. But the network updated the score frequently (it had to to keep up) as the Packers piled it on. Sometimes the score was accompanied by scenes from the disaster area itself.

When it reached 21–0, still in the first quarter, Williams cried, "Oh, yeah!" and moved to another chair in the living room — a restless black Achilles in a blue sweat suit, unaccustomed to being so far from the front. The big color television set flickered against a backdrop of glittering metal at the end of the room: the plaques and plates and trophies Doug and his brothers had accumulated in sports over the years. Some of them were from Tampa Bay.

The house was a gift fom Doug to his family, bought with the money he had made as the Tampa Bay quarterback. It throbbed with the ebb and flow of family and friends, mostly there to see Doug. An old teammate from Grambling was there. Doug's boyhood hero, older brother Robert, now a school principal, bright and articulate, popped in and out, and there was a seemingly endless parade of pretty little girls in starched white Sunday-go-to-meeting clothes and patent leather shoes. The phone rang incessantly.

Doug's mother, Laura, monitored the calls from a kitchen already throwing off the first convivial scents of Sunday dinner. A handsome woman known, inexplicably, as "Shot," Laura Williams also cooked for the nearby grade school, a job she had held many years. One way or another, she said, her children always got plenty to eat. She and Robert senior had raised eight, of which Doug was the third youngest. Like the others — sociable, educated, athletic — she said Doug "had never caused a moment's grief, not with drugs, not even with cigarettes."

Robert senior was a former ball player and military veteran who had worked in a pipe factory until he lost a leg to arthritis. He joined the group, brought in from the back bedroom where he spent most of his time since the amputation. He sat like a soldier in a big chair next to the kitchen and made amiable small talk with visitors. Doug's infant daughter Ashley dozed in a portacrib in the middle of the room, oblivious.

The score against Tampa Bay reached 28–7, then, almost immediately, 35–7, and the phone rang again. Doug Williams giggled and cupped his hand over the receiver. "He says he hopes Green Bay gets seventy-five," Williams said of the caller.

It got to forty-two, still in the first half, and the phone kept ringing. "The Bucs will come back," Williams said. "I'm pulling for 'em." He laughed again.

A pigtailed girl in a dress swollen with crinolines and pink as cotton candy stood before him. "How come you don't play no more?"

"I play," Doug said, taking her hands in his, enveloping them.

"Number twelve?"

"Yeah."

"I don't see you on the TV no more."

"I'm in the other league. Tulsa is my team now."

"Not the Tampa Bay Buccaneers?"

"No."

"Oh."

By halftime, the Buc-kicking had reached record proportions: at 49 to 7, Tampa Bay had given up more points than any NFL team ever had for half a game. Williams said justice was being served.

Once, he said, he thought being a Tampa Bay Buccaneer "was the greatest thing in the world," but he learned "in a hurry" that pro football was strictly business. He said the business was what he got when he and the Bucs could not come to contract terms and he had had to go to the USFL for "a better deal." From now on, he said, "I play for the paycheck."

He said he'd be lying if he said he hadn't wanted to stay in Tampa, where his house was now up for sale. And, yes, he was bitter. "I bit my tongue for five years. I can't be John Boy Walton. I'm nice, but I'm not *that* nice."

He said there was no turning back, that it was "not feasible" to believe he would ever again play for Tampa Bay, even if the new league folded.

"Too much emotion involved. The fans had signs for the first game in Tampa this year: 'Doug Who?' Well, the Buccaneers will remember Doug Williams. Attendance is down. A lot of people came just to see Doug Williams play." He used the third person the way a sensitive man uses it to take the edge off self-appraisal. "Doug Williams was a novelty," he said. "In sixty-three years of NFL football, a black quarterback had never played or done as much as Doug Williams."

But he said Doug Williams was not *just* a novelty. "Doug Williams was the guy the Bucs looked to to get it done," he said. "Maybe with Doug Williams they wouldn't be zero and five. Maybe they'd be five and zero. Maybe they really *would* be going to the Super Bowl."

But by defecting to the USFL, I asked, had he not forfeited a chance to be, for want of a better term, a "trailblazer" for future black quarterbacks?

"That was never what I wanted to be," he said. "I'm a team man. That was never my problem. That was other people's problem."

He blamed the Tampa Bay "organization." He blamed the "lies" he said had been told, and the Bucs' intransigence in contract talks. He blamed Hugh Culverhouse, the owner, "a very rich man," for not making him feel "wanted." He blamed scare tactics. He blamed racism. And, finally, he blamed John McKay.

"I'll always be grateful for Coach McKay, for the opportunity he gave me. It took guts to make me his quarterback my rookie year and then stick with me through all the criticism. I always felt I could go to him. When we lost three straight at the end of the 'seventy-nine season, I went in and told him if he was going to bench me I wanted to prepare for it. He said, 'Dougie, when you get to the World Series, you don't bench your best pitcher.' I'll never forget that.

"But he's a powerful man. He shoulda done something when we couldn't reach an agreement, as much power as he has. He said, 'It's a fair offer.' If I was the owner and John McKay told me that, I'd do what Mr. C did, too."

The inmate in the portacrib had come to life and was groping for the railing, trying to raise herself. Williams bent down tenderly and lifted her up in his huge hands, turning her to reveal the lettering on her "I Love Tulsa" T-shirt.

"Janice would have wanted us to stay in Tampa," Doug Williams said. Janice was his wife. She had died less than a year after their marriage. Janice was the type of girl, he said, "who had a smile for everybody. She didn't like controversy. She would have made me stay. But it wouldn't have been right."

Before the game was over, and Tampa Bay's humiliation complete, we piled into Doug's metallic blue Dodge van for a tour of Zachary. He said Zachary was a great place for living "out of town." He said he and his daddy used to hunt the woods with his brothers. But he said he didn't like the woods. "The woods have snakes," he said. "There are only two kinds of snakes I'm afraid of. The little ones and the big ones."

He pointed out the tiny frame house he grew up in, and the places he said the Ku Klux Klan had burned crosses. At almost every turn he honked the horn and waved at people he knew. We crossed Route 19. "Nineteen will carry you all the way to Mississippi," he said.

"What carries you to Tulsa?" I asked.

"Airplanes," he said. "But it ain't easy."

I asked why he thought the negotiations had broken down.

"I wanted to be needed, to feel wanted. I didn't feel that way in Tampa anymore."

"You don't think McKay wanted you?"

"I think he coulda got me the money. I woulda played for $600,000. The $875,000 was the sticker price. They coulda given me $600,000."

"Phil Krueger said they made an offer of $600,000 just before they signed Jack Thompson."

"It was an 'if' offer. He said, 'What *if* we can get you six.' Well, what if I'd said yes and then they said, 'No, we can only pay five'? That's what they do to you. They play with your mind until you're in a weaker position."

"But you'll never know for sure."

"No. I guess not."

"Why didn't you go see Mr. Culverhouse?"

"I didn't think I was the guy to deal with him. He's a big powerful lawyer. It would be like an ant against an elephant. I had an agent for that, Jimmy Walsh."

"Did Walsh go see him?"

"No. I didn't ask him to. I wanted them to come to me."

He hit the horn again and waved.

"Next year I'll be in Oklahoma and it won't matter so much," he said, "but it would hurt me to the heart if Tampa Bay went to the Super Bowl without me. I can't be a hypocrite about it. I'll always have respect for Coach McKay, but I hope they go zero and sixteen."

He said in Tulsa he would make more in two years than he would have in three at Tampa. He said he would play maybe five more years, ten at the most, "then I'd like to coach at Grambling. Maybe even take over when Coach Robinson retires."

"Who's the coach at Tulsa?"

"They don't have one yet."

"Who are the receivers you'll be passing to?"

"I don't know yet. But I don't care right now. It's going to be the place I finish out my career."

He pressed the horn again and, from a nearby porch, two elderly women waved. Then he took a turn down a wooded road, made another turn and came up suddenly on the tidy little high school he had graduated from, in a class of twenty-five. He said there was a school play that year that featured a gypsy with a crystal ball.

"The gypsy said, 'I see Doug Williams as a big voice in a big stadium.' The gypsy's customers answered, 'Yeah, yeah? What's happening?'

" 'There's a big crowd, yelling.'

" 'Yeah? Yeah?'

" 'And Doug, he's yelling, too.'

" 'What's he yelling? What's he yelling?'

" 'He's yelling, "Peanuts, peanuts!" ' "
Doug Williams laughed.

The second half had been kinder to Tampa Bay, but only in the way that relief from the bullpen saves the battered pitcher from a prolonged embarrassment. The score, finally, was 55 to 14.

The next morning John McKay sat subdued in the back seat of a company car, shrouded in his own cigar smoke, as Buccaneers' publicist Bob Best drove him into town for the taping of his weekly television show. He had returned in a bleak mood, so down that Corky McKay had barely slept worrying about him. The half of McKay that was not depressed was incensed. After the game, he had threatened to punch the mouth of a Milwaukee columnist for asking, simply enough, why Tampa Bay had played so miserably. Past nightmares were being recalled.

In his first two years in Tampa, after a supernal college career at USC, McKay had suffered through twenty-six straight defeats without losing his wits. (Or, for that matter his wit. "What about the Bucs' execution?"he was asked then. "I'm in favor of it," McKay replied.) But in those days he was putting life into dreams, and had no illusions about what he had to work with (he had next to nothing to work with). This was different. This was dreams dying.

This, he said, "was a year I'd looked forward to so much. Now . . ."

Bob Best told McKay he had asked the producer of the television show to limit the "highlights" of the Green Bay game. McKay said there weren't any highlights. He said it was "the worst performance of any team I have ever seen, college, pro or high school. The films of that game should be burned. Maybe the coach should be burned. We play that way and we *will* go zero and sixteen, no trouble at all." He lamented the injuries the team had suffered. The offensive line had been decimated by injuries. And he lamented Doug Williams.

He said Williams's leaving "put us out of sync. You can't just go out and recruit a guy to step in, it doesn't work that way in the pros. Jack Thompson could be the answer for us, but it could take a while, too. Maybe it'll take three or four years. But if it means rebuilding, we'll rebuild. If we have to, we'll start over. I'm not going to quit."

He blew smoke.

What worried him, he said, was that the Bucs themselves seemed to believe Williams was right, that they couldn't win without him. "If you start thinking you can't make a putt, you won't make the putt. O.J. was great for us at USC, but he graduated. We continued to play. Dallas continued to play after Staubach retired. If they feel they can't play without Doug Williams, then a lot of these guys are stealing money."

He blew more smoke, and paused.

"But what really hurts is I pick up the paper in Milwaukee and Doug Williams is saying he *wants* us to lose. He's saying he's not mad at the team or the coach, but he wants the Bucs to lose. Hell, we *are* the Bucs. I'm on this team, too. Hurt? You damn right it hurts. He *had* a friend."

Where did it go wrong? How did such a fortuitous union of coach and athlete go so radically wrong so quickly? Why would these least likely of adversaries — traditionally the strongest allies of sport — become so . . . adversarial? How do these things happen (and they do, regularly, now, in sport)?

Some of his friends said Doug Williams "changed" after the death of his wife. They said he became noticeably introspective. Doug said as much: "I learned you can't

replace the things you hold most dear." Others believe
the burden of becoming the "first great black quarterback" was intolerable. That Williams sought, and found,
a way out, in a far-out league where the pressure would
be mitigated and almost any sign of life would be appreciated. In 1982 he had actually regressed. His quarterback
ratings had dropped. Improvement had been steady until
then.

It is more likely that in the confusion of the times the
questions are more complex than the answers. It is more
likely that Doug Williams — and John McKay, too, for
that matter — came to a point when he simply no longer
knew *what* to believe, or whom. Or what to believe *in*.
The hard, gray dilemma of the modern pro athlete in the
age of the Stupendous Contract and the Vendible Loyalty
is that when negotiations bewilder and break down, who
do you believe? The agent who tells you you're worth the
sun and the stars, or the people who pay you to keep your
feet on the ground?

Some answers need to be tried for nonetheless.

Was Williams being shortchanged by the Bucs? Certainly no fifty-hours-a-week construction worker would
think so, but if you compare the final offer with that of
the millions John Elway got from Denver, or to Dan Fouts's
$750,000 per year in San Diego, the answer is yes. Wil-
liams to Tampa Bay was worth more than Elway to Denver. But that is what can happen in the marketplace when
competition for talent heats up and yesterday's anomaly
becomes today's new standard. The other side of the coin
is that Joe Theisman, the Super Bowl champion quarterback, was making $262,000 at the time, Danny White
of Dallas, a Pro Bowl choice, was making $250,000, and
Terry Bradshaw, with four Super Bowl rings, was making
$300,000

Was Williams justified in believing that McKay could

have "done something" to turn Culverhouse around? Probably. Those who knew both the coach and the owner believe Culverhouse's respect for McKay was so great that he would probably have acceded to a reasonable demand. Culverhouse is a millionaire tax lawyer who, according to one rival, "doesn't just pee ice water, he pees ice cubes." He is also a man who enjoys being in sport and in the right situation (even McKay believed) was a "pushover."

I went to see Culverhouse. He is a fleshy, stockily built man in his sixties, with iron gray hair that looks pounded into his scalp and a benign, soft-eyed expression that would make him seem vulnerable to almost any entreaty. His record speaks otherwise, of course. A lawyer friend told me, "Hugh Culverhouse *always* knows the bottom line." But if you were a Girl Scout selling cookies and could gain admittance, you would probably make his plush Tampa offices a first stop.

Culverhouse said he was not all that pleased when Williams and his agent called the first Tampa Bay offers "embarrassing" and "an insult" in the press. He said as far as the money went, the lines had hardened when, with Williams unsigned and McKay on pins and needles, he had to shell out $200,000 and a first-round draft choice for Jack Thompson. Thompson at the time was an insurance policy they didn't want to have to buy. It was then he figured $400,000 was enough, although he "never talked it over personally" with Williams or his agent, Jimmy Walsh.

Walsh had complained that in five years Culverhouse "never had dinner with Doug Williams." As stumbling blocks go, that would seem a minor one (dining with the boss has obvious pitfalls) but I asked Culverhouse if he liked being involved with his players. He said he did. That he had helped Leroy Selmon make a profitable business connection with the First National Bank of Tampa, and had secured a thirty-car limousine order for Jimmy Giles for the 1984 Super Bowl (Giles was making a second career in the car rental business). Culverhouse said he "tried to help the players" whenever he could.

He then produced a copy of a registered letter he had sent to Williams on June 7, 1983. The letter outlined an offer he had made weeks earlier to cut Williams in on a $200 million real estate development called TampaSphere, a Culverhouse project. According to the letter, there were no strings attached, and no initial cash outlay was required. Williams had declined. Walsh later said he thought the offer's timing was "suspect," coming as it had during negotiations.

Culverhouse said the deal would have made Williams a lot of money. He was "saddened," he said, by the "lack of trust" shown. He said the one thing that bothered him about owning a pro football team was that it was "awful the way we don't trust each other."

Was Williams lied to? His complaint there was that when he signed his original contract for "so little," Phil Krueger, the Bucs' contract negotiator, told him he "wouldn't start for two or three years." In retrospect, it was not the truth — Williams *did* start his first year. But most rookies don't, no matter how good they are. Krueger would probably have been lying if he had said otherwise. McKay said it was not in his plans to start Williams. "The pressure is too great. Look at what happened to Elway."

Were the differences racially motivated? Well, what isn't these days? Certainly Williams had heard his fill about race. But given the racial epithets black athletes often endure (they are, of course, heard everywhere, not just in Florida), and the early heat Williams got (McKay himself went into the stands after one heckler), it is still true that Williams enjoyed exceptionally good treatment in Tampa. A Doug Williams fan club sprang up his first year, and the Tampa press gushed his praises. (McKay was not so lucky. He is not as popular now as he was in California.)

If anything, the Tampa press bent double on the race issue. Williams's infamous quote in the Milwaukee paper ("I hope they be 0 and 5") was corrected in the *Tampa Tribune* to read, "I hope they'll be 0 and 5." One Tampa columnist openly suggested that Culverhouse "go find Doug Williams and pay him what he wants." And, of course, McKay pushed hard for Williams's acceptance.

What saddened McKay in the end was that Williams himself seemed so obsessed with race. In their first meeting, when Williams came to his home after the decisions were made, he told McKay how "proud" it made him that McKay played so many blacks. He said whenever he stood for the National Anthem he "always counted the black players and coaches on the other team." (Williams later told me he had been "doing that since high school.")

Far from being flattered, McKay was appalled. Imagine, he said if it were a white quarterback with that kind of thinking.

Could a contract compromise have been worked out? Not when you negotiate this way. Initial offers and counteroffers aside, it came down to one fateful day in June.

McKay was "getting antsy." There had been no communication in three weeks. He had not drafted a quarterback; he was counting on Williams. Camp was about to open. To "do *some*thing," the Bucs shopped around and found Jack Thompson, a second-stringer in Cincinnati with a $200,000 salary, available for a first-round draft choice.

On June 2, with McKay and personnel director Kenny Herrock sitting in his office, Krueger called Walsh. Their versions differ on the conversation, but they both agree it was brief.

Krueger said he told Walsh that they had figured it up

and if they added the $200,000 they would have to give Thompson to the $400,000 they were offering Williams, it would come to $600,000, and they could save the draft choice. " 'I can't say Mr. C will go for it,' " Krueger said he told Walsh, " 'but *if* we could get Doug the $600,000, would you go for it?' Jimmy said no, that his bid of $875,000 was final. I said, 'Then it would be good business on our part to make the trade?' He said, 'Yes.' I think he thought we were bluffing."

I went to see Walsh in his Manhattan apartment-office on 51st Street, near Third Avenue. He is a short, thick-set young man with an appealing Irish mug and a bubble of sandy hair. His conversational style runs the gamut from emphatic to bombastic and, although a nonathlete, when he talks football he speaks in absolutes.

Walsh had made his splash in the agentry business by getting the Cleveland Browns to pay $700,000 for a line-backer named Tom Cousineau a couple years before, but he actually got his start, he said, by securing a shaving cream commercial for Joe Namath. In the commercial Namath shaved off his mustache right on the air, live.

A picture of Namath, resplendent in a three-piece suit, perched atop the television set in Walsh's cluttered outer office. Walsh said he and Joe had been college buddies at Alabama. He said he had had nothing to do with Joe's original contract with the New York Jets, the $400,000 deal Sonny Werblin orchestrated that started the money hype in the 1960s, but that he handled Joe now. He said besides Namath, Williams, and Cousineau, he had no other athlete-clients.

I asked what he thought had gone wrong in Tampa Bay.

"They gambled with Doug and lost," he said. "They knew his value, his ability. He's the greatest quarterback in the history of the game. But they figured he'd never leave. As the months went by, he got more and more

frustrated. Then he *wanted* to go. It's as simple as that.
The Bucs lost their leader, and a chance to go to the Super
Bowl.

"The question you have to ask is, 'Why did they let it
happen?' I told Phil Krueger, 'Give this man a terrific
deal. Make him feel wanted. If you don't, you might de-
moralize him.' The signing of Jack Thompson was a slap
in Doug's face. I told Doug it was a negotiating ploy. If
he'd held out, he'da got a million dollars from Tampa
Bay. The reason Doug Williams is going to the USFL isn't
because Jimmy Walsh got him a better deal, it's because
Doug Williams got fed up."

I said it was a shame, breaking up the Williams–McKay
combination. That they seemed to have a lot going for
them.

"That's a fiction. The coach in Tampa is as much a
reason for Doug leaving as anything. Culverhouse wouldn't
have let it happen if McKay hadn't told him something.
McKay could have gotten Doug the money."

"Did you talk to McKay?"

"I never met the man, I never had a conversation with
him. I ask you, 'Why?' I met Carroll Rosenbloom. I met
Weeb Ewbank, Joe Namath's coach. A *great* coach."

"McKay's a great coach."

"He was a great *college* coach. What's his function now
at Tampa Bay?"

"To coach."

"You gotta be kidding. When he decides to quit coaching, he's going to be the *president of the club*. He has a
financial stake in this thing. Did it ever occur to you that
they were trying to make an example out of Doug Williams? Make the quarterback play for less and you don't
have to worry about the others."

"You think it was racially motivated?"

He lapsed into a Southern drawl, mimicking an imaginary meeting with Hugh Culverhouse in which Culverhouse would say, "C'mon in heah, boy, and you 'n me'll do some business." "Let's face it," Walsh said, abandoning the accent. "We're talking about Tampa, Florida, not New Brunswick, New Jersey."

I asked if he remembered the particulars of Krueger's pivotal compromise offer of $600,000 on June 2.

"The $600,000 was never mentioned, not until later and it was all over. We had asked for a lot more than that."

"Doug says the $600,000 *was* mentioned. He says you told him about it and he turned it down because it wasn't definite."

"Well, maybe it was mentioned, but I swear to you I don't remember it. All I remember is that the conversation was brief and to the point. He said, 'Are you holding firm at 875?' I said yes, and that was it. We had had no conversation from May nineteenth to June second. No meetings, no calls."

"Why not? Weren't you concerned about him getting signed and ready before camp opened?"

"There was plenty of time. I knew signing Thompson was a ploy to get Doug to panic. I told Doug he didn't really need to report until the second or third exhibition game, anyway."

"If other players thought that way, a coach would never get a team ready," I said.

"Ask Joe Namath," Walsh said. "Hell, he told me if it came down to it Doug wouldn't have to report until the first or second regular season game."

"You can't be serious."

"I sure am. I knew if we held out long enough, we'd get a million a year. Doug Williams was the franchise at Tampa Bay. It's that simple."

The contract with Tulsa, signed August 28, 1983, would not make Williams a million a year, Walsh said, "but he'll be well paid, and he'll be appreciated." He said, however, that if he had his druthers, "Doug would still be in Tampa Bay. But I'm not the one to blame. I'd like to be, but I'm not. I was merely a conduit, a front man. The principals were Culverhouse, McKay, and Doug Williams. The question they have to ask is, 'Why did we let it happen?' "

He said it was a moot point and that time would exonerate Williams. "Doug Williams was a far better quarterback than he was ever allowed to prove in Tampa Bay. He'll prove it now. Doug Williams will break every passing record in the history of pro football."

"In Tulsa?"

"Yes."

"I remember something Don Shula said when Larry Csonka, Jim Kiick and Paul Warfield jumped to the old World Football League. He said he couldn't begrudge Csonka the money he would get, but he thought it was a shame that when honors were passed out on some future date Csonka would not be there for the recognition he deserved."

"That won't happen to Doug," the agent said. "He'll go down in history as the greatest of all time."

The breathtaking salary spiral in professional sport, leading to the stupid, counterproductive adversarial position good athletes like Doug Williams find themselves in with good coaches like John McKay, is a boomerang management threw out some time ago and is now getting back. In force. With a vengeance. Or, to confuse the metaphor, a mechanism the owners and administrators of sport painstakingly put together in order to shoot themselves in the foot.

The mechanism includes the player drafts and reserve clauses and "arbitration agreements" and all other restrictive covenants that bind players and lead to their rebellion. The rebellion is not over. Neither is the money spiral (where it stops, nobody knows).

But the most damage it has done from the standpoint of fallout is that it transformed the relationship between player and management from familial, or even paternal, to adversarial (management meaning coaches and administrators, as well as owners). That's the worst thing.

My tendency is to blame owners — a blanket indictment. I have trouble with that, however, because many of the men who have made the greatest contributions to sport "owned." The Art Rooneys and the Tom Yawkeys and the George Halases and the Lamar Hunts. But, on the whole, the owners of sport *have* been the architects of this lunacy, especially since the owning business passed over from expensive hobby to highly profitable enterprise and the patrons opened their ranks to those for whom "owning" was perceived as a license to steal.

Almost all post-1960s stories about owners read like variations of the hillbilly banging his hoe on a rock and oil gushing out of the ground. Writing about such opportunists is no picnic, I can tell you that. I live most of the time in Miami, where Joe Robbie owns the Dolphins, which is to say he got rich quick. Robbie is a one-time prairie lawyer from South Dakota who, according to *Sports Illustrated,* never paid taxes on more than $27,000 in any one year before he became an owner.

Robbie invested less than $100,000 of his own capital to buy the Dolphins in 1966. Former partners in the venture say his cash ante was more like $15,000, but no matter. He now controls millions. He is a great success story, and can afford to tell the city of Miami to chew coconut when it tries to get him to pay the back rent on the Orange Bowl, or to threaten the entire area with moving the club if he doesn't get his way (i.e., a new stadium by sundown, with sky boxes, or else).

In one story about his rehiring of the late Joe Thomas as an "assistant to the president," I told a number of bald-faced truths about the canny way Robbie ran the Dolphins, and he responded by trying to get me with a press release. In the release he disowned me as his "friend." I was surprised to know he thought of me that way. I certainly didn't go around saying that about him.

My favorite owner is Peter O'Malley of the Los Angeles Dodgers, whom I wouldn't know from a resin bag. I love the way O'Malley owned the Dodgers to the pennant in 1981. He did a terrific job of owning. A *tour de force*. For me he was the single most refreshing sports figure of that year and any year since.

O'Malley owned an entire season and never made a headline. He was colorless, nondescript and noncontroversial — as big league owners go, a plate of boiled cabbage. He *never* had his name in the paper. When the Dodgers won the 1981 Series, he wasn't quoted. In fewer words, he was a man to be exalted, if not remembered, which is exactly what owners should be.

This is not to say that I don't think George Steinbrenner is a great act. I do. George is also a man's man. If he said he beat up those two guys on the elevator, I believe him. If he said he beat Rosie Ruiz in the New York Marathon *after* beating up those two guys in the elevator, I'd believe that, too. I think he's entertaining and makes a very good beer commercial.

And it's not that I don't think Georgia Rosenbloom Frontiere is a man's woman and also a great act. I do. As an ex-nightclub dancer who qualified for ownership of the Los Angeles Rams by being the widow of Carroll Rosenbloom, Georgia has broken new ground in the business. At her late husband's memorial service, in the backyard of a Bel-Air mansion, she had a fifteen-piece orchestra, two open bars, and many Hollywood personalities on hand.

The master of ceremonies, Jonathan Winters, delivered what was described as "an hilarious monologue" instead of a eulogy.

In the Rams' press book, owner Georgia Rosenbloom Frontiere (those are not her only names; she has been married other times) gave her age as forty-two. Later she was reported to have a younger brother who was forty-seven. Georgia Rosenbloom Frontiere also inherited from the late Mr. Rosenbloom a head coach named Ray Malavasi. Malavasi took the Rams to the Super Bowl in Ms. Frontiere's first season. The next year, he made the play-offs. The next year, Georgia Rosenbloom Frontiere fired him.

It is not that I don't think George and Georgia are fascinating people. They are. It is their kind of "owning" as a force in sport I don't like, and for another reason besides their exquisite bad taste.

Modern-day "owning" has changed our conception of big league sport. It has exposed many owners as greedy and vulgar and overbearing and disgusting, and sometimes even boring, but nevertheless bad for sport. The tactics of the Finleys and the Robbies and the Steinbrenners and the Georgia Rosenbloom Frontieres have advanced the arts of bullying and self-aggrandizement and wiped out every illusion of belonging that sports fans must have.

People forget those illusions ever existed. The illusions of allegiance. Of loyalty to team and place. Owners used to be people who willed sport to the people, like philanthropists. They didn't do it for the money; they usually had enough of that already. They did it for the joy of sport. The involvement. To be loved in their hometown, or in towns they made their homes.

They were the players' patrons and friends, not their adversaries. They were more buddies than bosses. The Wrigleys and the Rooneys would have been in it even if they couldn't make a dime. Before television a dime is about all they *could* make. Sometimes they lost their shirts. But they weren't entrepreneurs, they were "sportsmen."

And the fans, as direct beneficiaries, were encouraged to believe that the team they rooted for and bought tickets to see play really was *their* team. Boston's team. Chicago's team. It was important.

But now the illusion is gone. The losing team in the 1981 World Series clearly wasn't the New York Yankees, it was the George Steinbrenner Yankees. Don Shula coaches the Joe Robbie Dolphins, not the Miami Dolphins. As long as Charlie Finley owned the Athletics, they were the Finley A's. Owners nowadays own like Barnum and Bailey — cross 'em and they pack the circus out of town. Refuse to build them a new stadium or give them a fat share of the concessions, and they threaten to go to Memphis.

The players have known for a long time that they were being alienated. They knew the owners weren't their patrons anymore as soon as all that big money started rolling in, with a hint of bigger money to follow. They knew the owners weren't going to divvy up voluntarily.

When the lying reached epidemic proportions, the players started organizing unions and hiring lawyers to nose around in the fine print and say inflammatory things on their behalf. The basketball players got the ball rolling with Larry Fleischer as their legal representative in 1962. Marvin Miller became a household word in baseball, as popular with the owners as a month of rainouts, and football introduced Ed Garvey, and the free world was treated to an orgy of labor relations, including seven strikes in the last fifteen years.

The American Way? If it is, Americans don't want it. Fans of sport would prefer to be comfortable with their teams. They want to feel the benign human vibrations, not the throb of machinery as Chevrolets roll off the production line. They don't want to hear about tax dodges, and deferred payments, and compensation for free agents, and a lifetime .270 hitter like Jason Thompson getting a million bucks a year to play baseball. They wouldn't mind seeing some evidence that Thompson is *worth* a million a year, but that's not going to happen because nobody is.

The players, of course, are merely picking up the cards management dealt them. Dubi Silverstein, the economist, is a baseball fan, but he told it straight: "Baseball is a game; major league baseball is an industry." And a monopolistic one at that. Steinbrenner himself told us what saps we were to think otherwise. On *60 Minutes* he said, "Baseball is show biz, it's no longer just a sport." It has been decades since it was.

And yet, despite such confessions, Big Sport continues to get away with fiscal murder. The greatest insults to the free enterprise system in America today are the various pro player drafts. From a constitutional standpoint, they are indefensible. From the standpoint of labor, they are unconscionable. Say, as an analogy, you are an M.I.T. graduate with an engineering degree. How would you like to be told you have been "drafted" by Dow Chemical and are being sent to Dow's "farm" in Blister Rock, Utah? Player drafts are excused and allowed as a necessary evil, held in place to protect the "competitive balance" of pro leagues. Actually, they are there to protect the club owners from each other. The owners would *really* be at it if they had to bid for players on the open market, as they find themselves doing every now and then when a new league springs up and starts raiding for players. Owners simply do not want to have to compete for players, and the government, alas, goes along.

It is anachronistic to argue that abolishing the player drafts would make the rich richer and the poor poorer.

Since Big TV, *every*body is richer, and every new-breed
"sportsman" in North America drools over the chance to
get in on the action. A baseball owner with a team that
has never seen the bright lights of the first division puts
his club up for sale and finds himself the center of a bidding
war for the franchise. With the various writeoffs and de-
preciations available, potential owners flock. The line forms
to the right. The NBA cries every year that five or ten
owners are on financial thin ice, but how many throw in?
None.

Owners, of course, make terrific extortionists. They bully
entire communities into believing the sun will not rise over
their fair cities if the pro team is not kept happy. NFL
owners are especially adept at it. They soak season ticket
holders up front with far-in-advance purchasing, and let
the money grow in interest-bearing accounts for months
before the season starts. It is a license to steal, and since
they have granted themselves that license they were un-
derstandably piqued when they had to make refunds in
1982 after the player strike killed half the season. The
owner of the Rams said she just *couldn't* give it back. "I
already spent it," she said.

Joe Robbie drags his feet when it comes time to pay
the rent at the Orange Bowl and badgers Miami all the
time about a new stadium, but in 1981 his Dolphins grossed
almost $16 million. I had 1982 Dolphin tickets. I had to
submit a formal request, with the unused tickets, for a
refund for games that were canceled in September and
October. I got my refund in January. Right after that came
word that the Dolphins were raising their ticket prices in
1983. So did other NFL clubs. The strike "cost" them,
but *they* weren't going to pay, the *fans* were going to pay.

Owners moan and groan about the high salaries, but
they are the ones who leak the figures, a publicity ploy
carried over from the 1960s when Sonny Werblin got all

that ink signing Joe Namath for $400,000. And they are the ones who decided to pay the salaries — *if* they pay them. The terms of more than one player's contract have borne the telltale marks of creative accounting — or at the very least been the subject of gross exaggeration. Herschel Walker was supposed to have gotten $16 million to sign with the U.S. Football League. He got one-fourth that.

Meanwhile, what are the players supposed to do? Tell the owners to please quit paying them so much? Hardly, knowing as they do that management will dump on them in a minute if they falter, or embarrass them in the press the way Steinbrenner does, or blast them by phone from the press box the way Robert Irsay of the Colts has done. Charlie Finley made a career of embarrassing Alvin Dark in public when Dark managed the Oakland Athletics.

It's an ugly new world, this world of owners versus athletes. We have seen the last of the Ted Williamses asking the Tom Yawkeys for a pay cut. We have seen the last of the Bob Mastersons. Who is Bob Masterson? An All-Pro end for the Washington Redskins. He played sixty minutes in the NFL championship games of 1940 and 1942, and received $606 for the first, $965 for the second. He was reminded of those windfalls when the Redskins received $36,000 apiece for beating the Dolphins in the 1982 Super Bowl. He said, "The Redskins still hold a special place in my heart."

A modern Redskin does not talk about special places in his heart. He talks about taking the $36,000 and running somewhere else to play if the offer is right. *No* place is special. In the baseball strike of 1981, owners tried to get back some of the freedom they relinquished to the players through free agency. The owners realized they had maneuvered their forces into a box canyon. They were hurling money at mediocre athletes with both hands. They said they needed some "relief" from the extravagance.

The players said fine, show us the books. In collective bargaining, if management claims financial stress it has to open up the books to prove it. You never heard such hemming and hawing. The owners backpedaled so fast you would have thought they had touched an open flame, which, of course, they had. They lost their case.

The NFL owners have the best system, lopsided in their favor. If a player plays out his option and signs with a new club, the old club gets "compensated." They have a formula, with draft choices used as collateral. If my club loses a player who is making more than $200,000 a year, I get a first-round draft choice as compensation. It works because it is designed to scare off buyers. The last I heard, during a period from 1977, baseball had 176 players change uniforms while the NFL had one — Norm Thompson, a cornerback who went from the Cardinals to the Colts. No club wanted to risk losing a high draft choice to sign the "free" player. Which means the player isn't free at all. I think it is better all around for players to stay with one team, but only if it is *their* idea.

But how about competitive balance? Would an open market destroy it as owners say? Well, the colleges don't have player drafts and they don't have a problem with balance. In the last four years, the national championship in football was won by teams that had never won it before — Clemson, Georgia, Penn State and Miami. Miami also won the college baseball championship for the first time. North Carolina State, and not UCLA, won the basketball championship. If anybody needs competitive balance, it is the colleges, as farflung and dissimilar as they are, but the uproar would be deafening if coaches in the NCAA asked for player drafts.

Player drafts, moreover, do not raise a ship that has gone to the bottom. Intelligent, incisive leadership does that. No matter how low in the draft he picks, no matter how depleted his resources, Don Shula gets the Dolphins back in contention every year. When were the Browns in contention last? George Steinbrenner spends all that money, and gets all that talent, and look what a mess the Yankees made of the '82 and '83 seasons.

Make no mistake; the club owners are still *the* force in pro sports, and if you needed a clinching argument you could have gotten it from the NFL players' strike: twenty-eight greedy owners against fourteen hundred greedy players, and the owners won in a rout and made Ed Garvey look like a rube. The players got no real concessions. They folded because winter was coming on and they couldn't take the losses the owners could, averaging only $100,000 a year, and because they really didn't like having their greed exposed. The owners were used to that. The whole thing was a big waste of time.

It was argued during the strike that the players' demand of fifty-five percent of the television money was excessive. Was it? They are one hundred percent of the show. Fifty-five percent was no less than they deserved. Owners of professional teams do not produce anything. They do not build anything, except stadiums with taxpayers' money. They erect no monuments to commerce, or to architecture, or even to industry. The game *is* the players. Period. It is their talent, their sweat, their blood. Of course, coaches contribute, too, except for the blood. But fifty-five percent was a pittance.

And who are these owners? By most indicia, a bunch of skinflints. The NFL Charities made a thing about the $4 million it gave away from 1974 through 1982. The figure was impressive until you realized it represented less than one percent of the NFL's gross revenues. The Boosters Clubs of America tried to solicit support for the high schools from all the big pro sports leagues, and got virtually no response. Pro franchises seldom respond, except when doing so will get them a lot of publicity, or help them get rid of a lot of lousy seats at discount prices.

Situation ethics prevail among the managements of pro sports. I have to laugh whenever anybody from the NFL makes a snide reference to the U.S. Football League playing in the "off" season, hurting other sports. What does the NFL care about "other" sports, with *its* ever-expanding season, and ever-expanding television schedule? But the canniest thing owners in all Big Sports do is make fortunes in new stadiums and arenas while misguided taxpayers get saddled with expanding debts on the financing.

Pro owners are masters at this kind of exploitation. They get concessions of all kinds, they get sky boxes, they get sweetheart gate percentage deals, they get outrageous rental agreements. Three years ago the Mariners paid a measly $1,395 per game to rent the Seattle Kingdome for one year. New York taxpayers awoke one season to find that the Yankees paid only $170,681 in rent on a $13.4 million gross.

Judge Roy Hofheinz made over a million one year just exercising his right to charge visitors a buck apiece to come in and gawk at the Astrodome. Meanwhile, the stadium kept costing Houston taxpayers more and more. Local governments have shelled out more than $750 million in the last thirty years to build or refurbish stadiums for big league football and baseball teams. The debt to taxpayers will reach $6 billion by the turn of the century.

None of the big new stadiums generates enough income to pay off the interest charges, except the ones that hold rock concerts. The Super Dome in New Orleans will never get out from under. Originally it was approved at a $35 million construction cost. It wound up costing $300 million. The Busches helped get the stadium in St. Louis financed with private capital, but they are an old baseball family and that kind of commitment is considered naïve by today's entrepreneurs.

Peter O'Malley would seem to be the exception, on all counts. O'Malley doesn't fire managers every other weekend. O'Malley does not pay his players three times what they are worth, then storm into the clubhouse and blast them for not playing a "kids' game" well enough to earn what *he* paid them in the first place. Steinbrenner did that. And O'Malley doesn't say he's in it for the ego, the way Steinbrenner does. The Dodger players are sixteenth among the twenty-eight big league clubs in player salaries. They have only one "millionaire," Valenzuela. Their announcer, Vin Scully, makes that much.

And still they win, and average 45,000 in a 56,000-seat stadium for all eighty-one home games. And for the first twenty years they were in Los Angeles they did not raise ticket prices one time. Even now, you can get into Dodger Stadium for as little as a buck-fifty — seventy-five cents if you're a kid.

A logical first step to striking an armistice with owners is to grant pro athletes a revenue-sharing plan, one that opens up the books so that they will know they are getting exactly what they deserve, and no more than the club can afford. The club's profits would then be their profits. My own preference — being convinced as I am that owners will never change — is for a more drastic measure.

I think municipalities should own professional sports franchises, the way Green Bay does.

The cities that bear their names and put up with their flops and foibles should not only run these professional teams but benefit from them, fiscally as well as socially and emotionally. The time is right, with all that television money floating around. The fans of pro sports deserve a

return on their investment, which is considerable when
they have to tax themselves heavily for stadium and highway construction just to have a pro team.

How would the cities ever gain such control, presuming
they would want it? Nationalization is probably out. Legal
confiscation, for a fair-market price, would be a way. But
a negotiated sale would be more agreeable. Then let the
municipalities appoint boards of directors to run the teams,
with the general managers who run them now making
deals, hiring and firing, trading, and so forth.

In the end, the Yankees would truly belong to New
York, not George Steinbrenner. And they would be assured of staying there.

For ten years, major league baseball — and only baseball of all pro sports — has employed a labor-management
expedient known as "arbitration" to settle salary disputes
between players and owners. Arbitration calls for an in-
dependent party (a qualified arbitrator) to decide a player's monetary worth, at least until the player gets the itch
to challenge his contract terms again. If you believe that
what's good for the United Auto Workers is good for the
Baltimore Orioles, you would have to think arbitration is
good for professional sports. If, on the other hand, you
believe as I do that it is just one more step down the road
to the devaluation of sport, you might not be so sure.

Players and players' agents who invoke the process *love*
arbitration. They love it almost as much as they love free
agency (the right of a player to declare himself "free" to
entertain other offers after his contract expires). They love
it because it is the key to the vault — down there where
the *big* money is. Since arbitration became a way of life
in baseball in 1973, the average major leaguer's salary has
soared from $35,000, to more than $240,000.

Naturally, owners hate arbitration. They hate it almost

as much as they hate free agency — or anything else that makes players realize how much money owners control and how much they are willing to pay to exploit the players' skills. The owners reluctantly agreed to the practice in the first place because (1) they knew the reserve clause which bound a player to a club like a serf was not going to escape judicial reckoning forever, and (2) they hoped to stave off free agency as the first alternative to the reserve clause. They have rued the day, and, in 1975, got free agency anyway. So much for the prescience of baseball owners.

But like striking oil when they meant only to dig a sewage ditch, the owners early on discovered that in their willingness to leak player salaries as a promotional gimmick they had exposed the greediness of athletes. The players' public quibbling and whining over money matters assured the populace that they were much more concerned with how much they were making than with how well they were playing. As often as not, the athlete was typified by the petulant pro basketball player who tore up his airplane ticket when he learned the club wasn't flying him first class.

In this propaganda windfall, owners doubtlessly expected sympathy for the millions they had to shell out. When pitcher Ron Davis, the three-game winner, got a $175,000 raise to $475,000 from the Minnesota Twins through arbitration, owner Calvin Griffith's outcries not only made sense, they made headlines. Additional arbitration led to additional extravagances.

Fernando Valenzuela, the Los Angeles Dodgers left-hander who sneaks a conspicuous glance skyward just before he delivers a pitch, had his salary balloon from $350,000 in 1982 to $1 million in 1983 through the process. (Now we know why Fernando has been glancing skyward. He has been thanking Heaven for arbitration.) A Cubs relief pitcher named Bruce Sutter was awarded $700,000 in

1980 — twice as much as the Cubs had offered him. Using Sutter's salary as a standard, an arbitrator awarded relief pitcher Tom Hume of Cinicinnati $595,000 in 1982. The Reds had offered Hume $350,000. As other players joined in the prospecting, the money under contract dispute reached $4 million in 1983. More than one hundred players had filed for arbitration.

We must remember, however, never to feel sorry for owners, at least not until they start showing *us* the books, until they start revealing how much *they* take. In the same newspaper that carried the lament of the Cincinnati assistant general manager who called the arbitration process "disastrous to management" and a portent of doomsday, an adjacent column had a story announcing the sale of forty-nine percent of the Kansas City Royals to a successful real estate developer named Fogelman. I am sure if we asked ourselves why a successful businessman would be willing to shell out $10 million to invest in a "disaster," we wouldn't take long coming up with an answer. Mr. Fogelman knew exactly what he was doing.

But at the same time, we can, and should, feel sorry for the game the process debauches. The growing alienation between players and management not only makes the bargaining process odious but it is blatantly counterproductive. When management disprizes the contributions of a player in order to keep his salary down, how can it possibly keep the player happy in his work? Conversely, how can management successfully promote something that it publicly devalues? It is not only bad business, it is dumb.

It is dumb because it cannot help but incur the disfavor of all those $20,000-a-year biology teachers and plumber's helpers who pay the freight in sport. Spectator sport cannot afford their estrangement. But it is just as bad for what it does to the "family" of sport. The gulf it helps widen between the athlete and his bosses.

When the Don Reese story came out revealing the drug horrors in the National Football League, I went on the *Today* show for NBC with two ex-NFL players, Carl Eller and Dave Meggysey. Eller, a former user, represented the league, Meggysey the players' association. Bryant Gumbel moderated. When I got my turn, I said that in all of Reese's testimony there was one sad recurring theme: that he "didn't give a damn" about the Miami Dolphins, or any other team he had played for because he didn't think they gave a damn about him, at least not personally. (Actually, what Reese said was, "Screw the Dolphins.")

I said that an "adversarial relationship" existed between the players and the management of sport, and that it was getting worse every day.

Meggysey interrupted to say that he "didn't think so," that he didn't think management and labor were adversaries. Then he launched into a controlled and impressively articulate tirade against the league and the owners. He talked of dirty tricks and bad-faith bargaining. He suggested the whole drug issue was a plot to discredit the players and their union in the current contract negotiations.

After the show I reminded Meggysey of his inconsistency, and the fact that his own book, *Out of Their League,* told of the alienation he had suffered as a player. But Dave was in a crusading mode at the time and seemed more interested in moving on to the next battleground. We parted, agreeing, at least, that the game was the big loser because of the conflict.

A short time after that I was in long-distance telephone conversation with Alvin Dark, the former big league manager (Giants, A's, Indians, Padres), and was reminded of what Dark himself recalled as the saddest case in his managing career. He was at Cleveland at the time, handling the dual role of manager and general manager, "something you should never do," he said, "because it requires you to play both ends against the middle."

Tony Horton, one of Dark's standout young players, was angling for a raise. He deserved one — a slugging first baseman, he had made the All-Star team that year. Dark, the manager, had praised his performance and told him what a bright future he had.

But Dark, the general manager, had to tell the young man no, he wasn't worth what he was asking — a hike from $30,000 to $100,000.

Negotiations dragged on. An impasse was reached. Proposals and counterproposals went back and forth, and in and out of print, and Horton slowly but reluctantly retreated from his original position. A step at a time he retreated, like a boxer under siege. He grew sullen and suspicious. His confidence waned. His play suffered.

One afternoon during a game, Dark said, the boy seemed to lose touch competely. "He looked like he was dream walking. When the game was over and everybody else headed into the clubhouse, he went back out onto the field and took his position. I went and got him and told him everything was going to be all right, but I knew better."

Tony Horton had suffered a nervous breakdown. He was institutionalized for a while after that. He wasn't allowed to go to a ball game or watch it on TV, or even listen to one on the radio. He never played again.

6.

The Amateurs

THIS was a long time ago, in Mexico City. The athlete's name was Ron Clark. I wonder if the name means anything anymore. It did then.

For all but a very few Olympians, the star burns out quickly. One could argue that this is as it should be. For the true amateur, sport is a love, not a life. For such an athlete the Games would be a highly personal quest and the achievement something to treasure, like a consecration or a battlefield heroic, not to flash around in hope of landing a color job with NBC. To put it another way: a quest not to *be* a star, but to reach one. The difference isn't really so subtle.

Whatever the case, I am always amazed how few names have stayed with me from the Olympics I have worked. And how the ones that have — Willye White, Billy Mills, Al Oerter, et al. — stayed not because of the events they won (those statistics have left me entirely, although Oerter was a discus thrower who never lost, so I have a pretty good idea about his), but because I thought they were special people. Ron Clark was one.

In Australia, Clark was a national hero. A tall, handsome, dark-eyed young man with an endearing stutter that surfaced ever so slightly when he got excited and a slash of gray in his close-cropped black hair that looked as if it had been added with a pallet knife. Although thick-legged for a distance runner, he was the best in the world at the time. He had won everything there was to win at a variety of distances, and had set world records (don't ask me which), albeit without having achieved an Olympic gold. As I recall, he competed in three Olympiads.

We had first met in Tokyo. Those of us in the *Sports Illustrated* contingent were charmed by his intelligence and candor, and because unlike so many other prominent athletes he seemed genuinely appreciative — not to say surprised — by the perks that came his way. (I remember once when we had bought him dinner at the New Japan Hotel, and the waiter came around to ask about dessert. Clark whispered cautiously, "Would it be all right if I had the peach melba?")

By the time we got to Mexico City he was a little more practiced in accepting a meal, and I was buying him a late breakfast when the subject came up. Actually, it had come up the night before, at a party we had thrown at the villa *SI* had rented for the Games on the outskirts of town. There had been rumors about payoffs to athletes by equipment manufacturers, and, as always, talk about the "chemicals" (steroids, or their forerunners) Russian women athletes reportedly took to increase their strength (and thicken their mustaches).

We were in a group standing by a grotto where the villa owner kept a menagerie. Somebody said it was apropos because the conversation had gotten quite animated, even though it was "mostly conjecture." The wife of an English sporting goods rep, herself an athlete but well out of training at that moment, said it "certainly was *not* conjecture," and started a new round of wild guesses.

Clark, nursing a pineapple juice, had listened for a while, and then, as if in passing, and with a certain resignation, had said, "It's all related." And more or less dropped it.

As I remember, he was into his second orange juice

and I my third cup of black coffee when he picked it up again.

"They do it, all right," he said, meaning the drug-taking. "I've been all over Eastern Europe, and I know they do it. They do a lot of things in Eastern Europe."

"It doesn't seem to bother you."

"It doesn't really affect me. Distance runners don't use them. If I was a hammer thrower, I'd probably be mad as hell."

"What do you think about them?"

"Well, it's not like taking heroin. They're doing it to get bigger and stronger, not go off into space. If they want to do it, I suppose it's bloody well their business. What bothers me is that it's not fair to the other athletes. If they're going to do it, they should declare themselves."

"It still wouldn't make it fair."

"No."

"It'd still be cheating."

"Yes."

We stayed on the subject for a while, deciding, as I remember, that the only thing to do was to divide the future competitions between the freaks and the nonfreaks. Have a special Olympics for those willing to go beyond reasonable "training" procedures, even to pumping their bodies full of poison in order to excel.

(I remembered this when the steroid issue came up at the 1983 Pan American games and, after sophisticated testing, a number of athletes were banned and stripped of their medals. The irony of that particular scandal was that after it broke, athletic clubs around the country had a run on people who *wanted* to use steroids. Women as well as men willing to risk dangerous side effects to accelerate their training regimen. One weight trainer in Miami put on forty pounds in two weeks.)

The winning edge is many things in sport. You have

one if you are naturally gifted. Nothing beats that. God is on your side. But you may cut the difference, even go ahead, if you practice harder, run longer, gulp thousands of vitamins, lift tons of metal, eat truckloads of healthful, fibrous, unappetizing foods, etc., etc. You can even luck into it by having better coaching or by having access to better facilities.

But fair competition requires that you draw the line somewhere. And I think what Ron Clark was saying is that when you have drawn the line, it is not just dangerous to go over it, it is unfair. It is cheating. It is unsportsmanlike. It is, if you will, un-Olympian.

Then, stuttering slightly, Clark began to talk about other corruptive influences of what he said was the "amateur" in only the loosest sense. He said the size and scope of these competitions leading to so great a prize as the Olympic Games made it almost "imperative" that the better athlete "take things" (meaning "unwarranted expenses," the euphemism for payoffs) to get by, to be "at his best" when he was required to be, and that he was guilty himself.

"We're talking about reality," he said, "not idealism. The Games and all the major amateur competitions are big money-makers. Everybody knows it. The sponsors make a bloody fortune, and the associations who run them go first class. The athletes squeeze in three across in the back."

Clark said he was weary of the duplicity. To fly to the corners of the world to compete (for him it meant all the way from Melbourne), and to compensate for time away from gainful employment, the best "amateurs" *had* to have help. "Unless we're bloody heirs, we can't make it because the expenses we're allowed aren't realistic. So we take, and the bad thing is we have to take under the table. Dirty money. Usually from people who stand to gain a whole lot more by paying it out."

"The manufacturers?"

"The shoe companies are the worst here."

That had been the rumor, all right. That Adidas and Puma were the biggest spenders. It didn't take long to prove it out. Anita Verschoth, an *SI* colleague, made a number of discreet inquiries among athletes she knew, and I did the same (a pole vaulter admitted that by competing in the shoes of one manufacturer he now put his foot to the pedal of a new convertible), and when the Games were over she and I went to Germany to confront the brothers who ran those rival companies.

Adidas was founded by Adi Dassler (hence, "Adidas"). His younger brother Rudolph had started Puma after a falling out. They didn't speak, and Rudolph didn't speak to us. (Through an intermediary, he responded to the charges in the customary manner of the culpable. He threatened to sue.) The Adidas family, after some shadowboxing, told all.

Adi's son, Horst Dassler, outlined the payoff procedures, and the extent of the bidding. *Sports Illustrated* ran the story with a cover picture showing silver coins spilling from an Adidas and a Puma track shoe. To be on the safe side, we kept the estimates well within the thousands of dollars of bribe figures we could prove.

And, of course, nothing else happened. No athletes were called in or censured. No meet or competition sponsor was condemned. No action of any kind was taken. U.S. Olympic officials said they heard about the "illegal payments," too, but when they checked it out they found the reports "exaggerated." Years later, in the Orient, I talked with an athlete who had competed then and was, as she put it, "on her last legs" as a runner. She said nothing had changed. The manufacturers were still shelling out, and the athletes were still taking.

And why not? The inequities are lost only on the deaf,

dumb, and blind, and I wouldn't be too sure about them. In big "amateur" sport, only the athletes are asked to be amateurs.

What is the answer? *An* answer is to quit the sham and leave the athlete to his own devices. Let him scrounge for his expenses any way he can, from any source save the government. Let him be his own keeper, and not a sponsored member of the Bolshoi Ballet. Require only that the ceiling he reaches not exceed a *reasonable* expense allotment, and if it does, or if he demurs, declare him a "professional."

That won't happen, of course, first because we have made our major amateur competitions into orgies of nationalism, and with that kind of false pride on the line, we cannot keep governments out. (The solution therefore becomes the opposite one: subsidize our teams entirely and send them into battle with the best of preparation, like an army with banners.)

But mainly it won't happen because we have invested too much passion, too much "interest" in our amateur sports. From the cradle to the draft we inculcate the thinking of an outstanding athlete with dreams of glory, and gilt trips. From those "gentlest of beginnings," we lift their noses from the grindstone and point them to the sky. Where the pie is.

Coach "Jack" is a friend of mine, too good a friend to stretch his soul across these pages without benefit of some concealment. I have known (liked, respected) Jack for twenty years, from his coaching days in college to his eventual disenchantment in the pros. Our times together were irregular over that period, however, so to my eyes his deterioration was dramatic as the pressures on him increased. His complexion sallowed. His eyeballs retreated in their sockets, and toward the end he looked like the poster for a national campaign against tar and nicotine. His jackets hung on him as if the hangers were still in them. He developed tics. His nerves jangled almost audibly, and he did not answer questions so much as he jumped at them, like a man startled in the dark.

Jack is out of coaching now. He says he misses it. But he doesn't miss it enough to go back. For one thing, he says he found to his delight that he could make more money in "civilian life,"and that he actually could sleep past five A.M. One day recently, we sat in his basement den where the walls are festooned with plaques and there is a gallery of pictures showing Jack with famous people. Almost every successful coach has such a room somewhere in his house. Some include a large color portrait of the occasion himself, done to look like George Patton or Leonidas at Thermopylae. I suspect it helps confirm their position in life and assure them that they really did make it.

I especially like Jack's picture wall, however, because I'm on it, in a relaxed moment with Jack at a 1970s cocktail party. Jack said it was put there because he needed an eight-by-ten to balance the alignment on the right side and I shouldn't take it too seriously. He laughed, in the easy, robust way he used to laugh. I noticed, with some relief, that he had developed a small potbelly.

"I wanted to coach from the time I was a kid athlete in Ohio," he said. "Coaches were more important to me than parents. I thought they were gods. They were wise in all the ways of life, and they knew the game so well. And, of course, I loved the game.

"I can still smell the grass where we played growing up. You know how you smell it when you're playing. You get your nose pushed in it, or you sit around during a break chewing on it, and it's something you smell forever. You can't say why. It's like when you make a big tackle and you feel it through your entire body, and maybe you get a shot in the mouth and it stings, and maybe even bleeds, but at the same time it feels good because *you've made the tackle.* It's something you can't explain to anyone who hasn't played. And it has nothing to do with winning or losing."

He got up and stood in front of the pictures on the wall, surveying the field. He reminisced over the pedigrees there, and the players who had kept in touch over the years and came to call when they were in town, and the ones who had made it big in the pros.

"I think I loved high-school coaching more than college, because I got so close to the boys. Some of them still call me. But I think I got a bigger charge out of college because there was so much more at stake, and I got so much attention. I used to think the pressure was the price you had to pay for all the attention — the friends you made, the deals you got. Free membership at the country club. A new car to use every year. I never bought a sportcoat for full price."

I told him the sky blues and bright oranges he chose never sold for full price anyway, and he laughed.

"The pressure got to me, I admit it," he said, sitting back down. "The cheating got to me. I hated that. You can rationalize so much of it, but we had one school in the conference that didn't know how to do it any other way. They'da paid players and phonied up transcripts even if they didn't need to. It was a way of life."

"Bear Bryant used to say that about ———," I said. "He said, 'They might as well put a sign up out front: "We Cheat." ' He said they couldn't help it. I asked him why he didn't turn 'em in and he said somebody already had, but it wouldn't matter anyway. 'They'll go right back and do it again. It's in their blood.' "

"We cheated, too, in our own way," Jack said. "Our

guys sold their tickets for a profit. That's a rule we broke.
I had an alumnus who owned a lot of horses and helped
some kids with some jobs and things, and I knew it wasn't
right, but I figured if he didn't somebody else would, and
I could manage him if it got out of hand. He was a big
contributor to the university as a whole, and he just liked
to help out. Some of those things the NCAA should allow
anyway. Not pay the athletes, but give 'em some realistic
spending money when they're going through two-a-days,
and then through the season, and all they know is practice
and study, and a lot of them, the blacks especially, don't
have nothing to live on.

"I know some of those guys didn't belong in school.
That bothered me more than anything, bringing in the
academic cripples, because it was such a struggle for them.
I know we got guys admitted who shouldn't have been,
but I knew of others who were worse students who wound
up at —— and ——, and came back and beat hell out
of us, and I knew if I was going to survive I had to do it
too, to a point."

"Either way it's cheating," I said. "If you cheat off the
field to win *on* the field, it's the same as breaking the rules
of the game and getting away with it. If you thought you
could play thirteen men and get away with it, would you
do it? Of course not. You want to win by the rules. When
I play tennis, no matter how good the other guy is, I don't
want to play the doubles court while he plays the singles.
I want to play by the rules. The sporting way.

"What's so sporting if you play a bunch of guys who
are getting paid, or aren't going to class, and I play a
bunch of guys who are clean and are really students? It's
not fair. It's cheating. It's the same."

"That's very noble sounding," Jack said, "but you have
to see the world coaches see before you condemn them.
Not every coach has the budget or the backing Bear Bryant

had, or Joe Paterno has. The administration *told* me I had
to *make* money to break even. The whole athletic department hung on our making money. That's pressure,
brother. I never stopped worrying about budgets. I never
stopped worrying about getting television dates, or a bowl
bid.

"I worked my tail off to make it a first-class operation,
we even had a new stadium planned, and I knew we were
going great because the faculty started complaining about
the football tail wagging the university dog."

Jack chuckled. "I had a professor who was on me all
the time. He wrote letters to the school paper blasting the
program. Not me personally, but the concept of big-time
college sport. That meant football. He was persistent as
hell, and I liked the old rascal. So I disarmed him."

"You *disarmed* him?"

"Yeah. I invited him to come on a road trip with us.
Be an assistant coach and see how much work our guys
do, and how tough it is for the players. He loved it."

Bryant used to do that, I said. "A great public relations
ploy."

"Where do you think I got it?" Jack said, grinning.

But in the end, he said, he got his fill of the deceits and
the pressures. The desperation he always lived with.

"Desperate? You bet your fanny I was desperate. We
planned for every game like it was the last roundup. When
we had to get a kid that could make the program, we *got*
the kid, even if it took ten visits, even if it took a ton of
white lies, and a half-dozen black ones. Half the time I
couldn't believe the things I was saying myself, so how
could I expect them to?

"That's the thing about the rationalizing. What it does
to the athlete. Most of 'em are good kids. Inherently good.
And athletics only made them better. But how can they

pass through the system and not feel used? Or become users themselves? They can't.

"When I got to the pros, I thought that would be behind me, but it was worse because then you just weren't dealing with a boy's athletic career, you were dealing with a man's life. I hated having to cut a guy, and you have to cut a lot more than you keep. But my whole perception of sport soured in the pros. I think I enjoyed it as much as anybody, because it can be fun and it can be rewarding. But there was a coldness to it, and a meanness, that I never got used to. Even the crowds are meaner — probably because they bet so much. And you *never* get close to your athletes in the pros.

"I think now that the best time for me by far was coaching in high school. The involvement was complete there. You treat kids there like they're your own. Amateur sport at its best.

"But I've seen my kids go through the process since then. I've seen the pressures on them, even as little sawed-off runny-nose kids trying out for the little league team. I thought I was hard on my players. I've seen coaches yell and scream at ten-year-olds like I *never* did. It would have been funny if it wasn't so sad."

Jack paused, and then laughed — a big, startling laugh.

"Do you think anyplace is safe?" he said. "It's four o'clock in the afternoon. Do you know where your little leaguer is and what he's up to?"

The lowest form of "spectator sport" is little league sport. It is, of course, exactly (and lamentably) that — spectator sport. It is an involvement that goes so far beyond the mere participation of an aspiring athlete that it boggles the mind. Not to say ruins the experience. Those "gentle beginnings" are not gentle at all.

I am against little league sport. Not *some* little league sport. *All* little league sport. In principle, in fact, in perpetuity.

I will go to my grave believing little league sport is bad for the youth of America, because I don't see the swamp being cleared in my lifetime. Just the opposite. The swamp gets bigger every day.

I have in front of me a picture that depicts little league sport in all its glory. The picture got wide currency. As a brute-face example of human behavior, it probably could have been worse, but it involved women and that made it *seem* worse.

In the picture, one woman, identified as a mother from Burlington, Ontario, is wearing brief shorts and a tank top and high-heeled wedgies. She is shown lashing out with her wedged foot at another mother from East Brunswick, New Jersey. Mother number two is in a stance reminiscent of the basic feminine approach to schoolyard aggression: she has her hands up tentatively and her mouth thrust forward. Her tongue appears to be out. A third woman, looking harried and small, is in the middle, arms spread like a referee's, trying — well, manfully — to keep the combatants apart.

The altercation occurred not outside a bowling alley or a PTA meeting or some other likely arena, but on a children's soccer field after a game between two teams of ten-year-olds. According to accounts in the Toronto *Globe and Mail,* the game had been marred by unsightly incidents. Players on both sides were flagged for rough play; their fathers argued on the sidelines.

As the sportsmanship and language on and off the field deteriorated, at least one adult male was seen making vulgar gestures. The two mothers happened onto the field and into the fray immediately after the game. They were suddenly the center of it. East Brunswick Mom said she was kicked and scratched, and had her watch knocked off. Burlington Mom said she had only retaliated because her son had been "whacked on the face" by representatives of the other side. She said her kick missed the target, and she was sorry it had.

According to the *New York Times,* which hopped on the picture for its social implications, the embroglio served as still another reminder of "what can happen when adults become involved in the play of their children." The *Times,* quite accurately, saw it as an indication that the recent growth of kids' soccer had finally brought the game down to par with other organized kids sports (Pop Warner and various brands of football, Little League baseball, etc.) in their ability to distort youthful competition.

The scenario contained all the familiar elements.

Involved soccer parents building fields, making schedules, holding player drafts, conducting car pools, all-star games and tournaments, peddling Cokes and candy bars, and generally butting in on every phase of the operation.

Soccer moms and pops crowding the sidelines of every game to encourage their pint-size warriors, their teeth clenched and the veins standing out on their necks.

Full-grown officials towering over the action like Gulliver over the Lilliputians, their whistles blaring authoritatively.

Coaches yelling and screaming at the players, and sometimes at the officials. And vice-versa.

Right on their heels were the sports psychologists, professional and otherwise, always out in force nowadays to measure the fallout from such activities. They got it from every corner. Parents complained about unfit coaches (pictured as frustrated ex-jocks and fantasizers, pressuring children into the hard lessons of "win-at-any-cost" sports ethics). Kids complained about both, albeit with less volume. (What, after all, did they know? Participants in youth sports are not obliged a say in when they play, or how much they play, or what position they play. Just be on time, Sonny, and make sure your jersey is laundered.)

In other words, soccer had arrived. Business as usual in the little leagues. And except for the photographic evidence (Burlington Mom versus East Brunswick Mom), even the violence was not new. Stark examples of how really obsessed adults can get over the games of their children have, in fact, been frequent newsmakers.

Cheating in every form, intimidations, threats, fistfights, riots, bribes, lawsuits — youth sport has been treated to all of it. A few years ago in a small Florida town named Kissimmee (imagine that) a mob of adults acknowledged the efforts of the four coaches of a winning team of twelve-year-old football players by attacking them with clubs and pipes. One coach wound up in the hospital. A cry from the crowd ("He's dead!") apparently sated the mob and it withdrew just before the constables arrived.

The more organized they are and the broader their physical and fiscal demands on the community, the closer youth sports come to being one long, jangling repository of criticism.

From the watchdogs of our collective psyches, they now draw an almost unanimous condemnation.

"Abolish the little leagues," says philosopher Paul Weiss.

"They're destructive; they delude us with their chummy qualities and we fail to see the disabling psychological effects," says Dr. Rollo May, the psychoanalyst.

"Forbid 'em," says Harvard's David Riesman (*The Lonely Crowd*). Riesman says the cradle is robbed for girls by preteen pregnancies, and for boys by "this kind of athletic flirtation."

Whom to blame? More appropriately, whom to blame first?

Although it would not be inaccurate to say Mom and

Pop and all those facsimile Knute Rocknes who clutter the sidelines of play every weekend, it would be better to examine first what atmospheric change occurred to create such boors. The first, the most prominent one, is the indirect influence: the unfortunate emergence (thanks to television) of an imperfect role model. The professionals.

The change from the adulation of the fictional athletic hero who played for fun (or whatever Frank Merriwell and Chip Hilton played for) to the real ones who play for pay has had a grotesque ripple effect throughout sport, even to levels where fame and fortune are only the stuff of adolescent dreams and wishes. Even for those who want nothing more than the healthy diversion sport should provide.

The model is irresistible, because it is brightly packaged and ubiquitous. A pervasive influence. "Big league" is easily perceived as "the only way to do" sport. If you can't *be* big league, you can *act* big league and *look* big league, and never mind that you are only nine years old. Those responsible for the conduct of kids' sports, themselves willing foils, pass this on, even to those who have absolutely no idea of the fallout — the parents.

To visit on such small heads the pressure to win, the pressure to be "just like Reggie J or Dr. J," is indecent. To dress them up to look like professionals, in costumes ten times more costly than they need for play at such experimental levels, is ridiculous. With such overkill, we take away the very qualities that competitive sports are designed to give the growing-up process.

I discussed this by long distance one afternoon with Dr. Benjamin Spock, the baby doctor–activist. Not surprisingly, he agreed. As an ex-Olympian who appreciated the need to start early in sport, Spock was nevertheless appalled while living in Cleveland to find parents bringing bleary-eyed pre-teenage figure skaters to the ice rink at five A.M. to practice. "That's not fun," he said, "that's a family conspiracy."

The one clearcut incentive for sport, at least at these formative stages, is to have fun. Period. When you take the fun out, it is not sport but exploitation. One could argue correctly that there is no hope for this at the professional level, where the stakes are so high and the ideals so confused, but at least those athletes are rewarded for their toil.

The ultimate exploitation is the little leagues. There, adult domination deprives children of the chance to grow naturally in sport, the chance to learn about competition's ups and downs without parental approval (or worse, disapproval), and without the weight of "big league" settings and imitations. To learn, through trial and error, entrepreneurial gifts as well as athletic skills. Organizing games. Playing them. Being their own umpires.

A game should never be more important than the child who plays it. The outcome of an athletic contest should never be as significant as the pleasure and education the participant might derive.

Such an activity totally loses its meaning when sport is transformed into a plaything for a segment of society *other* than the kids. A segment that very well might be making sport a refuge for its own hangups — a place to go not to appreciate the intrinsic values of pure sport (the joy of competing just for the hell of it), but to get away from the inflation, the bomb, the refugee influx or the impending visit of the divorce lawyer.

Too many parents confer on sport their worst anxieties, bequeathing to children the same dogged intensities that make them the cocktail party bores they are. Or, for that matter, the deadbeats they are. There have been many sick-sad examples. Recently a Dallas father who had coached his four children in little league football, baseball, and basketball, was found to have "borrowed" $10,000 from a kids' league treasury. He said he needed it to cover his losses in the automobile business.

For many parents, involvement is a form of "buying in," much the same way they buy in to a pro team — wearing silly T-shirts, unfurling banners, screaming obscenities. Some psychologists say it is a sign of their own failures to achieve, of trying to identify with the success of their progeny. In this setting success is measured totally by win or lose, and when their children lose, it is as if they have lost themselves. And that they *really* can't take.

Sports psychologist Bruce Ogilvie told me he once took a tape recorder to a little league football game and set it up near the stands. "You've never heard such vile, vicious language," he said. "With clenched fists and livid faces those parents goaded their children with nasty needling [and] yelled at the referee as if he were a criminal."

And what happens to the children through all this? To begin with, says Ogilvie, "they are mostly lost in the maze of extrinsic things going on around them. The activity no longer has any sustenance for them. They are merely the vehicles from which the adults derive their kicks." Watch for yourself, he says, when a team of eight-year-olds is on the field — staring at the sky, twirling their gloves (or helmets) in the air, turning to watch the planes go over. Detached, uncommitted, turned off.

I filled in one afternoon — with more than some reservations — as the substitute coach of my son's team of eight- and nine-year-olds. The regular coach, an Earl Weaver impersonator, had to get a tooth extracted and told me "somebody had to be there for this crucial game." Crucial or not, I made up my mind I would not interfere. I screwed myself to the bench and, except for helping the boys make out the lineup card and yelling out an occasional "thattababy," clammed up.

From there I watched as (1) the other team's coach baited the teenage umpire into an ugly argument, (2) a third team's coach "scouted" both teams with elaborate charts and colored pencils, (3) a gung-ho mother of one of our star players gently prodded me for "not caring," and (4) our team won or lost the crucial game. I'm not sure which.

As we were driving home, I asked my son if he liked baseball. He seemed to think the question called for honesty, and although he knew I loved the game and welcomed any opportunity for a little catch, must have sensed my impartiality. "Not really," he said. I was disappointed but not surprised.

Being turned off is the one extreme. At the other is the totally addicted child who finds in sport (or has been made to find) an opportunity for status and expression, maybe even with an eye out for the money when time and his own well-charted development take him to the stars.

Parents of such children literally get inside their progeny's bloodstream. They become obsessed with the heady notion that they have sired the next Tracy Austin, the next Kurt Thomas, the next Steve Carlton. Forcing (or at least encouraging) their children to give up social lives, and other sports, and maybe even academics, to gain — what?

More often than not, to wake up on the far side of the experience to discover that there were thousands of other eight-year-olds doing exactly the same thing. Believing implicitly that dogged determination and countless repetitions would get them to the top — or to whatever they perceive the top to be. Only to find it doesn't happen that way at all, except for a select handful.

Parents who fall into this trap, says New Yorker Emily Greenspan, a former "obsessed ice skater," see the "spark of athletic precocity in their children and [being eager] to produce a winner, change fun to fear." For parents who become immersed in their child's athletic career, says Ms. Greenspan, it soon becomes *their* career, and the confusion does not reveal itself as "bad" until it is too late.

The John McEnroes and Dorothy Hamills who succeed would tell us it was "worth it."

But would we get the same response from the thousands who are shoved into this time warp and do *not* make it? Even to a local championship? These veterans of domestic sports wars who were never told by a caring, qualified person that they were just not good enough to aspire so high? Who woke up at thirty without medals or, worse, without the sport that had kept them sociologically afloat all those years? Who found too late that the odds were frightfully against them from the start?

The return to earth can be traumatic. Psychologist Terry Orlick of Ottawa, himself an ex-jock, handled the case of a girl who, due to injury, had to give up competitive swimming. Her life had been rigidly programmed in what Orlick calls this "industrialized" kind of specialization, where the high expectation of the individual in one field makes it difficult for him to enter others, and, not wanting to risk failure, he avoids or withdraws from anything else.

The girl reentered society with some shocking realities. She had "terrible identity problems. She was totally withdrawn. It was a painful process. She did not even know how to buy a regular brassiere for herself."

And what of the coaches? Not just the coaches of these special kids — for most of them are, at least, qualified — but the vast number who stumble and bumble into youth sports. Well-intentioned fathers who offer their time, but also their twisted notions of what coaching children in competition is all about (what it is *not* all about is their trying to imitate Earl Weaver). Turning kids off or burning them out with their own bizarre applications of win-at-any-cost.

Larry Csonka, the former all-NFL fullback, followed the progress of a kids' football team near his home in Fort Lauderdale. Csonka is not a man who recoils from spilled blood — his or anybody else's. But he was horrified by little league football. "The coaches didn't know much about what they were doing," he said. "They just yelled a lot. They acted like they imagined Lombardi or Shula would act. Why, they had those eight-year-olds running *gassers* [post-practice wind sprints], for crying out loud." Csonka would not let his kids play little league football.

Influenced by the wrong examples, plagued with slogans about the "need" to win and the "fanatical drive" to win, such men make the score its own biggest reward, and dilute for their own children the pleasure of the competitive experience. The worst thing to be said about them, however, is that they are not qualified. An unqualified coach is a dangerous person.

Thousands of youngsters are injured every year because they have been taught improper techniques for their size and skill level. Damaged elbows are common among young baseball pitchers (so common that "Little League elbow" is a recognized name for a specific ailment); freestyle swimmers suffer a specific kind of shoulder injury; football players get hurt in many ways, even at a level where the danger of injury is minimized because they just don't deliver that many foot-pounds at impact.

Whether the potential for damage is physical or psychological, the threat is always there, and even coaches at the more advanced levels do some astonishingly stupid things when the well-being of their athletes·interferes with their drive to win. A high-school football coach in the Midwest lost a star player to appendicitis before a key

game. The game was lost. The next day the coach had the
team physician check those players whose appendixes were
intact, and tried to get him to have the appendixes removed. The doctor refused. He said the coach had no
right to make such a demand.

But youth league coaches *do* have the right to say who
gets to play and how much they play, and it is here that
organized youth sports do their dirtiest work. Bruce Ogilvie laments the "sickening arrogance" of little league
coaches forcing eight-, ten-, and twelve-year-olds to sit on
the bench while others participate, learning nothing beyond the elitism of sport. To practice and not to play, or
to play "a little," is a downer for a youngster who is getting
his feet wet in sport. There is nothing right or good to say
about it. Token appearances — an inning or two, a couple
minutes in the fourth quarter — are no less demoralizing.
They may, in fact, do the greater harm.

There is a growing concern among the custodians of
youth sports that many kids who are so stigmatized (you
can bet *they* know what sitting on a bench means) are not
coming back for more. The dropout rate is epidemic, especially in football. Instead of being a place where the
love for competition is inspired, the games become a place
where interest dies, especially among white middle-class
kids who have so many alternatives to flee to.

My own son never returned to baseball. I was saddened — not for myself, because I had no illusions about
what it could lead to — but for him. He was turned off
to a great game.

A couple of years ago, the Concord, New Hampshire,
Pop Warner team won the state championship with a
9–1 record that included seven shutouts. The next year,
when the coach called his first practice, instead of a hundred
or so, only twenty-two players reported — and two of
them were over the weight limit. The coach said he "couldn't

understand it." Alarmingly, the discouragement apparently filters *up*ward. High schools across the country are suffering drastic turnout and attendance declines in football, and many schools have dropped the sport.

The negatives in the experience are compounded when the child not only suffers the premature rejection that bench-riding imposes, but is channeled into positions in team sports that deprive him of the joys that make the game fun in the first place. Eventually, physical development and skill limitations will make those positions acceptable as the best way to stay in.

But you do not protect a youthful baseball player from his inadequacies in the field by making him a "designated hitter." And a right guard on a little league football team, tasting football for the first time, will *never* know the pleasure of running the ball, passing it or catching it. The fun things of football. Worse, he will probably get bored right out of the game. Maybe all games. When you take the fun out, you risk turning a kid away from competitive sports, never to return. Afraid. Turned off. Tuned out.

All in all, the process adds up to what one former high-school and grade-school coach calls "no more than a sophisticated form of child abuse." Brother R. E. Piqott, C.F.C., says that many kids who play at eight or ten stop playing in high school because they get fed up with "the excessive competition, the screaming adults and the absence of fun."

Adults calling ten-year-old basketball players "chokers" and berating little guys who are afraid to take a bat off their shoulder as having "no guts," is pressure of the worst kind. To think that kids learn in this crucible of scrutiny is not rational. It not only takes the fun out, it could very well kill their chances to progress. A double whammy.

*   *   *

What, then, do we do about it?

It would be simple enough to say that the first thing to do is dissolve the partnership. Turn in the fancy uniforms and tear up the schedules. Sweep the sidelines clean of screaming parents and ersatz coaches. Go back to the sandlots. Certainly no other country organizes children for play the way we do, and there is evidence enough that when he or she is *too* organized, *too* structured, the young athlete winds up dispirited.

An ironic object lesson in this kind of bungling was provided in *Sports Illustrated.* A Canadian coach lamented that the Soviet Union's hockey program had benefited from an *un*regimented approach to the sport, an ideological contradiction he could not believe. The Russians had routed coach Scotty Bowman's Team Canada in the Canada Cup tournament, and Bowman said he thought he knew why.

On a visit to Moscow he had been struck by the contrast between the approach to the game there and in U.S. and Canadian cities. In Russia, he said, the neighborhoods were alive with kids skating on their own; "they did not even start organizing until age twelve or so." Bowman said it would be better to let youngsters learn skating skills that way, and was joined in his belief by the National Hockey League's Bobby Orr: "Parents," said all-timer Orr, "are ruining hockey by organizing kids too early."

As a child growing up in South Florida, I divided many of my summers between Miami and Key West, playing the days away at the nearby parks and playgrounds. Without coaxing, without instruction, we moved from game to game and sport to sport with effortless enthusiasm. We made contests of little "practice games," not just to improve techniques but to get more out of the fun parts of the game — hitting "pepper" in baseball, playing one-on-

one basketball. We concocted new methods to score so that we could play no matter how many we were or how limited the field. Stickball, of course, was a must.

Ed Kranepool, who played for the New York Mets from age seventeen to his retirement at thirty-four, fondly recalls growing up in the baseball sandlots of the Bronx, choosing up sides, setting the rules, playing two or three free-form games a day. "Adults had nothing to do with our games," he says. "We weren't an organized entity. The games were, in fact, disorganized fun. That's what sports for little kids should be. My initial frustration in sports began when I joined the local little league as a ten-year-old."

But nostalgia is one thing, hard realities are another. It is too late to go back. Times *have* changed. Youth sport would be better served if we thought more in terms of accommodating the need for fun with the facts of community life as they now exist. By its very definition competitive amateur sport implies "love" (from the Latin *amator,* "lover"); an amateur competes out of love.

But the vacant lot other generations played on as kids, for the love of it, is not likely to be there now. . . .

And the fields our tax monies have provided for "organized" play are. . . .

And adjusting to the change might be imperative because, alas, kids no longer just naturally gravitate to the athletic fields on Saturday morning. Affluence has had an anesthetizing effect. Kids sleep in on Saturday. Kids watch cartoons and play electronic games, and complain about the heat if they are asked to leave their air-conditioned caves.

In this respect, the little league Moms and Pops are doing their children a great service by getting them involved. Waking them up, getting them out.

It is also true that the world these kids now face *is* more structured. Being more crowded, it needs to be. The trick, then, is to modify the programs so that the children will be the first, not the last, to benefit. In a sense, therefore, part of the problem — organization — is also part of the solution.

By all means organize, or help the kids do it. Schedule games and fill the fields with players. Outfit them (reasonably, inexpensively), car-pool them, encourage them. Get them to the field on time.

But then step back and let them play.

Let *all* of them play.

Step *way* back so that even if you are seen you will not be heard. Resist the urge to monitor and regulate, and to choose their teams for them.

And, most of all, resist the urge to coach them.

The need for coaching is understood in sport. Being a coach for youth is a high calling, but it would be far better for children if we separated the coaches of little leagues from those who would be coach but have no business at it.

The time has come to understood the need for a basic separation of interest and support: that it is one thing to encourage your child, and play catch with him, and hit balls to him, but it is quite another to take on the mantle of coach for him and his peers.

Qualified coaching is essential to the learning process, but kids at that formative stage should not be over-coached, and not be coached at all by well-intentioned part-timers. Kids just starting in sport need an adjustment period, a time to "fail" in private. They need *ample* time to experiment, to try things, to test the limits of their own bodies without close scrutiny.

When the time is ripe, one professional coach for two

or three or even four teams at the park should be adequate. One qualified person to provide the needed guidance and instruction.

The money parents spend "getting involved" could well go toward paying the salary of such a coach, and supplying *his* needs, since they will directly benefit the children. To such a coach (a physical education major, preferably; one who has participated in the games at a skilled level) the youngsters can come to learn techniques, or to satisfy a rules question, or to referee an argument.

A coach who would be there but only to instruct, not to involve himself in the winning and losing of what, after all, are inconsequential contests.

A coach, in short, who would stand above "win-at-any-cost."

Child's play is not trivial. It is important stuff. But first it must be fun. Win-at-any-cost *dulls* sport. The games themselves are robbed of the qualities that make them exciting for us (a reason we invent them in the first place) when a coach's frantic need to win translates into dogged efforts *not to lose.* Play, then, instead of freewheeling and uplifting, becomes conservative, cautious and calculated — the opposite of uplifting. The skills of players are "sat upon" while the coach protects his lead.

Such distortions of sport happen all the time at the professional and major college levels. They should *never* happen at the little league level. But, of course, they do.

The influence of the role model filters down rapidly and helps create men and boys so paralyzed by exaggerated importance of "the score" that they think it's okay to make bench-riders out of ten-year-olds. That it's okay to shut lesser players off from the learning process while their more adept peers get the job done. The job being to win.

What makes this profoundly sad in little league play is that it is sanctioned by the very people who should be most opposed to it — the parents. Eventually they even become accomplices in the crime.

There is nothing wrong with Mom helping arrange for bats and balls and caps, and maybe solving a transportation problem or two. And there is nothing wrong with Dad hitting fungoes to the guys or filling in when an adult is needed for counsel. But it *is* wrong for them to contribute in any way to a distortion of the purpose of playing games. And it *is* wrong for someone who only *thinks* he knows the game to coach young people in the development of their skills.

A little leaguer is in far greater danger of being over-coached than he is being poorly coached. Of being numbed by drills and practices rather than discouraged by his own lack of skills. Every study I have seen on youth sport has come up with the same conclusion: kids would rather play than practice. They are not interested in "refinements" and "techniques" when they are just starting out; they are only interested in playing.

Terry Orlick surveyed the motivational instincts of one thousand children involved in youth sport; of those, ninety-five percent chose "fun" as their reason for playing sports. *Ninety* percent said they'd rather play for a "loser" than sit on a "winner's" bench.

Because most parents instinctively sense this, much deceit is practiced by little league administrators to keep parents from revolting. Many leagues brag of rules that say "everybody plays." More often than not what that means is a token involvement for the lesser kids, while the best play every down or every inning.

The ill effects of such deceit should be obvious enough. If all an unskilled youngster does is make brief appearances (at positions where he can do the least harm), he will not improve. And he will in all likelihood have his confidence shaken as well. He may, in fact, wind up knowing sport only as what writer Robert Lipsyte calls the "chain-gang joylessness of drills and practices." *Not* fun, but a dead end of pseudo-participation.

The solution here is so simple. But to reach it we must accept all around that *to play* is the object. The only reason to have a league.

And in youth sport, *every*body plays.

Every game.

The whole game.

If the league is so loaded with players that the benches are crowded on Saturday afternoon, divide the teams again. Create more teams. Let them play on another field, or at another time. But let them play without concern for "starting lineups" and star-status.

Those discriminations will come naturally later, in high school, say, when skills are clearly defined and a level of team excellence is worth striving for. Eight-year-old kids don't have to know how good or bad they are; they don't need to be reminded by adults, or discouraged from the outset by elitism. They will gravitate naturally to the players whose skills they are more comfortable with — school friends, neighborhood buddies.

In this light, it would be infinitely better to let them choose their own teams. Player drafts of pre-adolescents are the height of absurdity. Let the coach at the park set the game times and structure the leagues, but let the kids pick their own teams, away from the pressure (and needs) of their parents.

And then let them forgo ninety percent of the practicing they do to play. Play *instead* of practice. Kids are great imitators. Most of the things coaches and quasi-coaches try to teach at that level they will pick up themselves anyway. They will learn faster by playing. A baseball or basketball game a day if they want. Maybe two if there is time.

Kids ten to twelve years old could play a football game every day. Not eleven-man-to-a-side, blood-and-guts football, but six- or eight-man football, where they can all get a chance to pass and catch and run with the ball, and to sharpen their skills without drudgery, and to quit if they get tired. Or if they get bored.

Let the kids decide because they know more than you how much they want to play, and at what position, and how much the game means to them. Take those decisions away from the coach and that legion of parent-coaches who get in the way.

(Make no mistake. The kids expect more maturity and good sense from their coaches than they are getting. A questionnaire was sent to parents and players in a Southwest youth football league a few years ago. Forty-one percent of the kids complained that the coaches yelled too much; thirty-six percent said the coaches were poor losers and poor examples.)

Furthermore, youth sport should throw off the trappings of the "big time" — the expensive costumes, the extravagant awards and trophies, the banquets, the all-star games.

"Look at some of the trophies kids are awarded," says Kranepool. "Where's the incentive to carry on after getting that kind of hardware?" Kids, he argues correctly, will develop in sport without bribery. "Don't worry, the good players will stay with the game, and plenty of kids written off as failures will blossom into fine players. I've seen a lot of premature stars in the little league. I played against them. They aren't playing now."

As for the conduct of the games themselves, two changes should be made across the board. The parameters of play should always reflect the size and abilities of the players (e.g., the fields they play on should be tailored — cut to fit). Kids do that naturally in the sandlots. And then, most importantly, let them learn the rules and be made to go by them without having policemen blowing whistles in their faces. Let them take on for themselves the burden of sportsmanship by umpiring their own games.

Children should learn for themselves that rules are made for a reason, and the reason translates into the betterment of the sport. To deprive them of the chance to develop a respect for playing *within* the rules is wrong. When they learn this sensitivity, sport will be made more meaningful because they will know that it is not only unfair to win by cheating, it is not sporting. That to win outside the rules, or by bending the rules, is not to win at all.

Ideals are set in childhood and tend to erode and be corrupted with age. But we should at least *start* with high ideals. A principle of sport (beyond fun) is that it teaches us to sublimate aggression and violence and cheating, not encourage those things. When this is not done, it is appallingly clear that sport suffers. When you push a kid away from the good lessons of sport, toward "anything it takes to win," he suffers.

We have a lot to work on — and to work against. Youth sport is serious stuff because it may well be the youngster's most powerful influence. Its course *can* be redirected. Throwing out the little league babies with the dirty little league bath water is not necessary. The mechanics of youth sport are not unalterably bad. Life at the park is possible without the bloodcurdling yells and bloodthirsty parents, and without fanatical coaches living out their fantasies. We have gone out of control, but we can get back *in* control.

Beyond the above, what it will take is not more criticism, but more caring. Dad has to know that he may have "gone too far" by professionalizing Tommy at eight or ten; that organization is not all bad, that some specializing is necessary at times to refine the skills of a gifted youngster, but we have "gone too far" when we make his specialty a tryanny instead of a simple quest for excellence. That we have gone "out of control."

Dad has to know that a *laissez-faire* attitude will not close the playgrounds or stunt his child's development in sport; that pressuring the child, and burdening him with winning, is counterproductive. And Mom has to be made to know that her screeching when Tommy drops the ball *is* bad — bad for her, and bad for Tommy. Most Moms want Tommy to have a good experience; they just don't understand how counterproductive their conduct is. They have to be made aware that they are "out of control."

Almost any great athlete who has reached star status will tell you how excellence in sports has had a lifelong benefit, knocking down personal and social barriers, learning how to interact with people, overcoming prejudice. Ronald Reagan once described in glowing terms the "inner confidence" he learned from playing sports. *How* he learned is every bit as important as the fact that he learned. That is where the reform in youth sport is needed. Says Jeanne Austin, mother of Tracy and four other tennis-playing Austins: "The child has to want it, not you. Don't emphasize trophies or being first. *Do* talk about the fun, and the friends you can make, and the benefits of exercise."

Be assured. The most important thing about playing sports is to *play*. To take part, with all the good that implies. It is okay to try to win, and there is an undeniable joy in winning. But it is enough to take part. Because from *that* pleasure springs all the benefits that sport can provide. To insist on it for our children is the least we can do.

7.

The Dishonored Campuses

GIVEN the extent and persistence of its failings, I tend to regard any sign of improvement in intercollegiate sport with a dubious confidence — the kind one might feel, say, toward a sleeping grizzly.

Those of us who look to college sport for the best of sport should, I suppose, be more tolerant. Or at least be willing to concede that in an imperfect world there has been precious little else to encourage us lately. The professionals set such breathtakingly dismal standards that we tend to overlook anything else, which is, of course, what the professionals prefer.

Furthermore, it is possible to find good reasons to believe that the colleges aren't completely beyond hope. Ralph Sampson is a reason.

I know Ralph Sampson only as a man I would not stand next to in a buffet line — he is a dwarfing seven-four — but I think I would like to know him better.

Ralph Sampson could have gotten the $1 million a year he now gets playing pro basketball in the National Basketball Association instead of the tuition, board, books and peanuts he received playing college basketball at the University of Virginia for four years if he had taken the money and run instead of passing it up and staying put the way he did.

When he played his last home game in March of 1983,

Sampson was brought back to the floor by ringing applause and thanked the school he "loved" for the education it had given him. Every year Sampson had said "no" to the NBA hardship draft, made All-America, and advanced with his class toward a degree he thought might be important in the long run. Asked why he clung to such a radical course, Sampson said, "Money isn't everything." I knew some people thought that way, but I didn't think big-time athletes did. Not anymore.

The Reverend John LoSchiavo, president of the University of San Francisco, is a reason. I don't know Father LoSchiavo, either, but I feel a kinship and will send him a get-well card if he ever gets conked by a San Francisco basketball fan.

LoSchiavo didn't think it was all that wonderful to field a big-time college basketball team if the way you did it made ugly headlines every time the wind changed. Facing a third NCAA probation in four years, LoSchiavo did a remarkable thing. He neither fired the cheating coach, disciplined the unruly players, nor implicated the underhanded boosters club. He canceled basketball. Pulled down the shades, doused the lights and closed the store. He said the university could "no longer afford to pay the price [in integrity and reputation] that the basketball program is imposing on it."

He said (and it should be on the wall of every college president in America):

"All of us involved in these problems have to face a fundamental question. How can we contribute to the building of a decent, law-abiding society . . . if educational institutions are willing to suffer their principles to be prostituted and involve young people in that prostitution for any purpose, and much less for the purpose of winning some games and developing an ill-gotten recognition and income?"

With that, he arbitrarily, unequivocably, dumped bas-ketball. Now neither the coaches, the players, nor the alumni boosters can embarrass Father LoSchiavo's school anymore.

David Rimington is a reason. After four distinguished years of football for the University of Nebraska, Riming-ton had won the Lombardi Trophy and twice made All-America. The last two years he was awarded the Outland Trophy as the outstanding college lineman in America. Nobody had ever done that before. Certainly not anybody with a 3.21 grade point average in business administration. In 1983 he was named to the Academic All-America team. The NCAA should have Dave Rimington bronzed.

Joe Paterno is a reason. I especially like this reason because Paterno I do know, and if ever a blow was struck for goodness it was the one that won his Penn State foot-ball team its first national championship New Year's night, 1983, in New Orleans.

Bill Lenkaitis, a former Penn State player, said the "greatest testimonial to the Penn State football program is its list of graduates." Penn State's players have gradu-ated at a rate close to ninety percent in the sixteen years Paterno has coached them. Three on his 1982 team made the Academic All-America team, including the quarter-back, Todd Blackledge.

Paterno espouses sanity and reason in college sport. He thinks of himself as an educator first, a coach second. Some newspapermen say he bores people with his harping on the subject. He doesn't bore me. Sometimes we harp together.

The twenty-two college and university presidents who made up the American Council on Education's ad hoc committee demanding tougher new academic standards for student-athletes are reasons. This distinguished posse — Father Ted Hesburgh of Notre Dame, Derek Bok of Harvard, Charles Young of UCLA, et al. — took their cry for relief to the NCAA in January of 1983, and it had the unmistakable ring of a fed-up group that wasn't going to take it anymore.

They proposed — and got, tentatively — higher eligibility requirements for scholarship athletes (not just a 2.0 grade-point average coming out of high school, but an average gained through a core curriculum of eleven academic courses, as well as a 700 combined score on SATs) and stricter normal progress rules (with the proviso that a minimum number of credit hours be completed toward a specific degree in the year preceding competition).

The former would, perforce, put a greater burden on high schools to educate their athletes *before* they graduate them, and would thus help relieve the colleges of what one president aptly called the "academic salvage operations" they have been attempting (unsuccessfully) the last decade or so. The latter would make it tougher for coaches to shelter their players from a meaningful education while they used up their eligibility. The whole system would benefit, most especially the athletes.

To be sure, these are but shining fragments of encouragement, and (alert as always to the sleeping grizzlies) I am only cautiously optimistic as to what they signal. There are many other pieces of evidence still too fresh to ignore that do not shine. College sport has suffered a Niagara of abuses for so long that it is often hard to distinguish the ill from the hearty. Too often they occupy the same ward.

The twenty-two college presidents might have won a battle on the NCAA convention floor, but the war was far from won. The new rules for tougher standards could scarcely be called a mandate for sweeping change — they were not *that* tough. Too, they do not go into effect until 1986, and even before they were passed the shrill cry of the offended could be heard throughout the land. As we shall also see, college administrators are less than unified in the methods needed to clean out the cesspool. Some of them can't even see the cesspool.

Herschel Walker was an exemplary Heisman Trophy winner, but the one before him, George Rogers, admitted to a $10,000-a-year cocaine habit when he got to the pros. And a Heisman winner before that was so questionable a scholar that he raised eyebrows every time he opened his mouth in public.

Penn State might be an unsullied champion, but Clemson won it the year before and by the time the crown changed heads Clemson was languishing in the NCAA doghouse on a two-year probation for violating more than 150 rules. One would have to have a passion for self-delusion to think that the violations did not help win the championship.

(Bobby Layne, the ex-pro quarterback, joked about the method he would use to win if he got the head job at Texas Tech. He said he would recruit with $100 bills. "If they'd named me the coach, we'd win, and then we'd be on probation, and then we'd win, then we'd be on probation again." Come to think of it, maybe Bobby wasn't joking.)

At last count eighteen schools were under some form of NCAA penalty. Another twenty-five or more were being investigated by an NCAA enforcement wing that has grown to frightening size. Frightening because it is not progress when more (and more and more) investigators have to be added to the NCAA's far-ranging investigative staff. To the contrary. That college sport needs a police force at all is vulgar and depressing.

And the outlaws did not all have outlaw names. Some of them had John Wayne names. UCLA was on probation for recruiting violations in basketball. Wisconsin, SMU, Arizona State, and Colorado were on probation for recruiting violations in football. When Clemson got thrown in, the prosecution charged sixty-nine violations related to recruiting and "benefits." The *New York Times* said that probation had become "almost fashionable," an indication to alumni and boosters that a college is at least "trying" to win. How sad.

Recruiting, of course, is the pounding heart of the problem. Under NCAA aegis, it is a mishmash of abused and abusive regulations — more than three hundred pages in an NCAA manual — that no one seems to understand but almost everyone runs afoul of sooner or later (two hundred fifty NCAA members have been penalized since 1951). Recruiting is the bane of college sport. It is an obscene, indecent, immoral, and disgusting process that demeans coaches and humiliates schools. It is a ritual of bribery, and distorts honest competition. Outside of that, I can't think of anything bad to say about recruiting.

I have been on recruiting trips with three coaches, each of whom was at the top of his sport at the time, and none of whom did himself any favors by having me along. (I either told them at the time or wrote later that what I had witnessed was beneath them.) Bear Bryant of Alabama and Johnny Majors of Tennessee were selling their programs to beardless eighteen-year-old football players; Bones McKinney of Wake Forest was making his pitch to a seventeen-year-old basketball player. Watching them in action, I thought how ridiculous it seemed, these men of stature, reduced to vacuum cleaner salesmen.

Majors had been coach of the year at Pittsburgh the season before. In a bleak Kentucky farmhouse, I sat in abject discomfort as he tried to impress a hulking defensive tackle with the noble credits of the University of Tennessee. The tackle was obviously used to having big-time coaches drop in. He paid Majors the utmost indifference and never removed his cap. As Majors talked, the boy watched a Jerry Lewis movie flickering from the television set behind Majors's left shoulder. The only responses I remember the boy making were occasional snickers at the jokes. Lewis's, not Majors's.

It would be interesting to know how many great college coaches got out (or were forced out) in their prime not because of the rigors of coaching itself, but because they got a bellyful of buttering up teenagers and lying to Mom about how good the pumpkin pie was. Darrell Royal came to hate recruiting at Texas, he said, because he "deplored" having to go back again and again to win a prospect. Having to make sure what he said in his last visit had not been overpowered by the subsequent sales pitch of a rival.

Recruiting, of course, is where the cheating begins, and where the athlete learns to accept cheating as a fact of life. Where he learns how much honor there really is in college sport. A Notre Dame defensive end named Scott Zettek told one writer that it was his experience that the "majority" of coaches were "dishonest" in recruiting, and that "for a while, I confused honesty with lack of interest." Finally, he said, he decided that if a school would cheat in recruiting, it would cheat in other ways, maybe to revoking his scholarship, so he went to Notre Dame, which he said didn't cheat.

Recruiting, too, is where people get involved in athletic programs who have no business being involved. Alumni and "boosters" with warped ideas of what "helping" a program means, and with too much freedom to horn in. People who themselves have such a base sense of what winning is all about that they are as paranoid as coaches about the success of rivals (if the other team beats us to a hot prospect, it must be cheating, so let's get hopping and cheat better). They compound the problem by cheating on their own, or by doing it by fiat as the coaches' undercover emissaries. Booster clubs have a lot to answer for in the corruption of college athletics, but they would not be in the position to corrupt if the schools did not sanction them and coaches did not encourage them.

When UCLA went under, a man held partly responsible for its sins was a sixty-nine-year-old nongraduate named Sam Gilbert. A multimillionaire contractor, Gilbert was "a friend" of UCLA basketball for fifteen years. Everybody loved him. He arranged for players and their families to receive goods at discount houses. He helped players get cars, stereos, clothes, airlines passes, and scalper prices for tickets. All of which, of course, is illegal under NCAA law. The one thing he denied was the charge that he helped basketball players arrange for abortions for their girlfriends.

When braced about his actions, Gilbert made a cogent rebuttal. He said that many of the things he did — feeding kids, sending them home for family funerals — were "morally right" even if technically wrong. And he was absolutely correct.

NCAA rules on recruiting and aid to athletes are archaic, a curious, cumbersome patchwork of the serious and the silly. One college president said they "offend every concept of good manners," and by doing so "increase the likelihood they will be violated." He said in the end they undermine respect for the more significant regulations. In particular, the president was talking about an NCAA rule that allows a school to buy a prospect dinner on campus, but if his mother comes along she has to pay for her own.

When John McKay was still at USC, we talked frequently about the laughable inequities of the system — laughable if you weren't an athlete.

"The thing that kills me about the NCAA," McKay said, "is that every piece of legislation that came along the past few years wound up being against the athlete. 'We're going to save money,' they said. 'No more fifteen-

dollar-a-month laundry money. No more money for sup-
plies,' which is a big item in engineering and architecture.

"Now they've taken away some of the tickets the player
gets, and they want his letter jacket, too. They had us cut
scholarships, then told us we couldn't dress over a certain
number for a home game, even just to sit on the bench.
If we went on the road, we could only take forty-eight
players. We took forty-eight to Notre Dame — and a 250-
piece marching band. Tell me how that saved money?"

(More than one coach will admit privately that he frequently breaks the rules for "humanitarian reasons." A
basketball coach at a Division II school in New York said
he often lent players money. He said he wondered if the
NCAA was concerned "with the reality of the situation.
Where a guy doesn't have money to eat . . .")

All things considered, why, then, do we act surprised
when a boy accepts a bogus credit or a cashmere coat,
knowing as he does that there are rules and there are
rules? If he hasn't seen that the recruiting process debases
the educational process, he has certainly seen how the
former works.

The solutions are so simple that it boggles the mind —
and therefore will be considered too difficult to try. Recruiting should be seriously curtailed. The time permitted
to recruit and the distances allowed to travel for the talent
should be drastically reduced. Contact between coach and
athlete should be limited to one visit in the home, one at
the school. Coaches should be made to stay home, or at
least not be allowed to travel back and forth across the
country wining and dining athletes and their parents.

A sphere of influence, based on the number of high-
school athletes available, should be established around the
geographical centers of the schools, and coaches should
be kept within that circle. No personal recruiting trips
should be allowed outside it. If a remote prospect wants

in, or vice-versa, the coach and the athlete can exchange letters, or even phone calls. It would be cheaper, and safer, and saner. A lot of money would be saved — money that could go toward loosening up those restrictions that only encourage the participants to cheat, and insult good manners to boot.

Make no mistake. Every day, in every area, the unholy depreciation of intercollegiate athletics goes on. Some months before he died, Bear Bryant told me it was "going on all over the damn country, and don't ever kid yourself that it's not."

Bryant named a team in his own conference. "I wish they'd just take the rules off ————," he said. "Let 'em do whatever they want. Just put a sign up out front: 'We don't have to go by the rules.' They're not going to anyway. It's in their blood.

"The last time they got caught buying two kids, the principal of the high school had to turn 'em in. What did the NCAA do? They told 'em they weren't going off probation for a while. Forty-eight counts against 'em in football, thirty-six in basketball. Probation doesn't scare 'em a damn bit."

Bryant himself had been caught for illegal recruiting when he was at Texas A&M. He said at the time he considered it "meeting the competition," but it was "the best thing that ever happened to me." I asked what he would do to stop it now.

"You only have to do one thing," he said, "and then you'd only have to do it once. Rule the player ineligible for life, and fire the coach. Make it a policy. Do it one time, at any school, and that would end it everywhere else. Everybody would be scared to death. They're not scared now."

What makes the cheating so ironic, as well as ineffably sad, is that it flies in the face of everything that sport stands for — in a word, sportsmanship. Most coaches I have known would be outraged if an opponent cheated on the field, or if you suggested they do it. As much as anyone's, their professional lives are ordered by the ethics of hard work and the careful preparation of developed skills, and a strict commitment to winning by the rules. The scoreboard is inviolable.

How, then, does it square when they cheat *off* the field in order to gain a competitive edge? Bringing in academically deficient athletes, manipulating their qualifications, paying them (one way or another) illegally? It doesn't square, of course. It is as unacceptable as cheating on the field. To win in such a manner is not to win at all. There is no glory in it. People think so in the present context, but they are sadly mistaken.

Cheating is anathema to sport. If you pay your quarterback under the table and I don't, you have created an unfair advantage. It is cheating. When you shuffle your star forward through a meaningless high-school curriculum while the other guy's star forward is taking all the required courses and staying up nights to pass; when you bend the entrance requirements to get him into college, and then keep him eligible through phony accreditations while the other guy is going by the book, you distort competition. You are a cheat. It is as damaging to the spirit of competition as tactics that physically abuse an opponent.

The one place we should, without question, be able to expect honest competition is on the playing fields of our college campuses. Institutions that deal with the life-making processes of our youth should be so sensitive to rules-bending, so repulsed by cheaters, so on guard against the athlete who "hears the cries of the crowd but never the rustling of a page," that cheating at that level would be a rare and exceptional thing. If we can't count on that, they are an insult to education and anathema to sport. They should close the store, as San Francisco did.

Be assured that if more college presidents had the guts of Father LoSchiavo, there would be a greater sympathy for this position. Unfortunatly few seem to grasp it, and some never do. Wichita State has been caught cheating and put on probation seven times.

Why, then, do coaches cheat? Mainly for the same reason they always have. There is no mystery to it. Because we make desperate men out of them. Desperate to win, to fill the stadium and get the television money and pay the growing bills.

We give them inflated salaries and massive responsibility, and no security, and insult their intelligence by suggesting they are just one of the professors. They are highly motivated, highly competitive people, but we tell them we don't think they'll stay that way if we make them safe from the unemployment line. Instead of tenure after a reasonable period of proving themselves — five years is a figure Father Hesburgh uses at Notre Dame, and I'd think that fair — the only assurance we give them is that if they don't win they'll be on the street.

We have told them at every level that it does not matter how clean they keep their program. It does not matter what percentage of their athletes graduate, or take their place in society as assets. It does not even matter how well they teach the skills of their competition. All that matters is the flashing scoreboard lights.

Coaches become so inured to this madness that they think nothing of jumping a contract, or packing up at the first tremor of discontent. They know where the priorities are, too. When the president of Bethune-Cookman told football coach Bobby Frazier his four-year record of 23–18–1 was "not good enough to get them into the [television] money," Frazier took it for exactly what it meant and resigned.

Most of the bottom-line mentalities who run big-time pro and college sport have an infinite understanding of profit and loss, and no appreciation at all for the perplexities of coaching. To the inescapable ordinance of games that says for every winner there has to be at least one loser, they give a grudging observance that borders on the obtuse. Don't make it complicated. When in doubt, fire the coach.

After eighteen years as head football coach at LSU, and despite a fine record, Charlie McLendon's contract was not renewed. McLendon's bittersweet valedictory included a remarkable concession to the times: "The pressures to win are unreal," McLendon said. "Football and basketball are the income producers and if you don't sell tickets, you're out of a job. So a coach who needs a player real bad will bend the rules a little to keep him eligible. Once you bend the rules a little, you bend them a little more."

Most coaches would agree with McLendon that what they are doing is what educators have forced them to do. Like boxers, coaches stand alone. If they lose, they can't call a meeting and throw off on a sales manager or a minor executive. The head of the English department simply fails an unqualified student. Good coaches don't do that. They are not only obliged to get that student in school under the rock-bottom standards now allowed, but they must nurse him along, finding ways to keep him eligible so that the team will hold up and they will win and stay employed. I have heard more than one coach put the system in this perspective: "They'll fire you for losing before they'll fire you for cheating."

The paradox is that coaches, perhaps more than any profession, live daily with the hard realities of rules.

Their competitions call for immediate punishment of rule-breakers; there are no stays of execution, no appeals to a higher authority.

But off the fields and courts, coaches see the other hard reality: that apart from the competition, but directly influencing it, are a lot of people who cheat and nothing happens to them. Nothing except that they go to bowl games and are heroes in their home states — in some quarters even bigger heroes for having beaten the system. Why should it surprise us, then, when coaches say they would rather get caught cheating then lose?

How desperate is desperate? Ted Owens was fired as basketball coach at the University of Kansas, despite an outstanding 348–182 record. Owens's teams had won six Big Eight titles, and had gone to postseason tournaments nine times. But his 1982 team had done poorly, and the athletic director, Monte Johnson, citing the "tremendous amount of pressure" to win at that level, terminated his contract with time remaining. In a statement that did not hide his bitterness, Owens said Johnson's decision "not to honor the university's contractual obligation to me" deprived him of a chance to lead Kansas to better days. He had been on the job nineteen years. He was fifty-three years old.

At Arizona State, football coach Frank Kush was sued by a player who accused Kush of punching him in the face on the sideline during a game in 1978. Kush had a reputation for being abusive and physical with his players. Never implicated in court was the intensity of the environment that made Kush prone to that kind of behavior. The player sued for $2.2 million, but lost in superior court. Nevertheless, Kush was fired. A rival coach said afterward, "It's hard to see the outcome as a victory for anyone."

In January of 1982, the former tennis coach at Arizona

State and the head coach of track and field at Arizona shot and killed themselves, ten days apart. Both were forty-one years old. Friends and family of the two men blamed coaching pressures. A girlfriend of Marty Pincus, the tennis coach, said he had been "frustrated and depressed" over the loss of his job two and a half years before. He had been fired despite a good record (164 victories in 195 matches and three Western Athletic Conference championships). The friend said they had talked about it until the early morning hours the night before he killed himself; she said Pincus "never accepted the idea that they should have fired him."

The wife of Willie Williams, the Arizona track coach, said the fun for him had "vanished" under the pressures of winning. He had turned, she said, from a "calm, caring man" to someone who was always "uptight." When his program was investigated by the university on budgetary matters, he apparently had had enough. Besides his wife, Williams left four children.

Good coaches are special. Their influence on young people is massive, and they are not blind to it. Most of them handle this trust tenderly, even to the point of taking on educational responsibilities that should never have been theirs in the first place. Most of them now spend considerable time and energy supervising tutoring and counseling programs, and have cultivated an appreciation for a student's classroom status that makes the concern of academic deans puny by comparison.

When coaches wind up on the seedy side of recruiting — promising money, promising grades — or are revealed teaching techniques that might get somebody hurt, it is usually their fellow coaches who come down hardest on them.

But neither do coaches miss the essential flaw in the process: that desperate ethics and a dubious job security are the byproducts of money, and the need to generate it. There are no desperate water polo coaches. Wrestling and soccer coaches stay on the post forever, "fixtures" in nonrevenue sports. It is on the coaches who can fill the stadiums with paying customers that we confer large salaries and celebrity status, and the oppressive weight of win-at-any-cost.

John Robinson is now out of college coaching. At USC, he won conference and national championships, and saw his football program racked by academic scandal. I have always thought of Robinson as unusually sensitive for a football coach, but I admit that neither he nor the coaching profession would consider that a compliment. Near midnight some months before he quit, we sat in an almost cleaned-out Italian restaurant in Santa Monica. Oiled just enough on vodka and white clam sauce (served separately but in that order), he talked about what life as a big-time college coach had become.

"Every year that I've been here I've had death threats," he said. "I have to have police escorts out of the stadium. You say, 'Hey, wait a minute. It's only a game.' Only a game? You gotta be kidding. But at the same time, *I'm* responsible, and *I'm* criticized if my players don't go to class. Well, I could live with that. But some changes will have to be made.

"If coaches are teachers, they should be given faculty status. I should be paid what a faculty dean is paid. No more, no less. I should be given tenure. I get a hundred speeches offered me a year, for extra money. If I'm going to function as a teacher, I can't accept a hundred speeches a year. I've got to say no. I'm not going to New York for a clinic. I'm not going to Hawaii. I'm going to stay home and behave like a schoolteacher.

"But then my organization of coaches is going to have

to say, 'We're going to cut recruiting back so you can be on the campus twice as much.'

"My school is going to have to assure me it will be my teaching ability and not my won–lost record that will give me longevity. The president of my university cannot say, 'If you don't win, you're gone.'

"The media is going to have to look at John Robinson and say, 'This man has done a great job over a period of years,' and when things don't go quite the way they like, when we tie a game, they'll not take advantage of me to get a better story."

The business of firing coaches and managers is mostly a bizarre practice that has been advanced to a science by the George Steinbrenners of the professional leagues. It goes on all the time, so there is nothing really new to report, but as a reference: Of the twenty-six managers in big league baseball in 1983, sixteen were either in their first or second year with the club, and only two had managed the same club for as long as seven years.

I was especially amused (as much as one can be at the misfortune of another human being) by the canning of Ray Malavasi by the owner of the Los Angeles Rams. Ms. Frontiere said of the dismissal that Malavasi was a "fine and loyal person." She said she had "strong personal feelings of friendship" for him. She fired him by telephone. Naturally, when she hired the new man — my old friend John Robinson, I am sorry to say, because he is too good for the pros — she did it in person, and in front of cameras.

So coaches know where the bodies are buried, and in increasing number so do the athletes, and this is the most portentous factor of all. Lo, they can see, and the consequences have made for intriguing twists, not to say stunning turnabouts. Some of them in courts of law. One in particular caught my eye. When a basketball player named

Mark Hall was ruled academically ineligible by the University of Minnesota, he hired a lawyer to challenge the ruling. And a district court judge made a shocking decision. Judge Niles Lord ordered that Hall be reinstated on the grounds that he was brought to that school not as a scholar "but as a basketball player."

Within the context of Judge Lord's ruling was the nut of the issue. I hope somebody was listening. Said the judge, "It well may be true that a good academic program for the athlete is made virtually impossible by the demands of their sport at the college level. If the situation causes harm to the university, it is because (college administrators) have fostered it, and the institution rather than the individual should suffer the consequences."

What Judge Lord meant, in effect, I believe, is that our coaches are at least paid to enter the maelstrom, and they go in with their eyes open. If we persist in suffocating our athletes with cost-of-winning pressures, too, we may bargain for more than we can afford.

Long ago we opted to make them athlete-students, as opposed to student-athletes. We did this via recruiting and its obscene abuses, and by requiring, as Judge Lord suggests, the lion's share of their time and energies while they are in school. It is an admission we should at long last fess up to, (1) because it is true, and (2) because they perform a great service in that posture.

Varsity athletics are considerably more than games for the scholarship athlete. Practice is long and hard. There are films to watch, wounds to heal, training table and meetings to attend. The player leads two lives: a tough one as a student, a tougher one as an athlete. His academic schedule is interrupted by travel and absences. He is chronically tired, often injured. He is really asked to lead a "semidisturbed life," says psychologist Thomas Tutko.

When center Steve Tobin admitted he had dropped all

but four credits during his last football season at Minnesota, he blamed a football commitment that kept him busy "from one in the afternoon to seven-thirty almost every night." The average student does not have to commit himself like that, he said. "People don't seem to understand what we go through. I'm a lineman and I have to sit and rest at least an hour when I get home from practice every day until my headache goes away. There's no way I can open a book. When we travel, we leave Friday morning and usually don't get back until sometime late Saturday night. I'm not saying I would study the whole time, but if I wanted to, I can't. The weekend's shot."

Only the most sanctimonious of college coaches (who would have wanted his scholarship in a minute if he broke a leg) or the most cynical of National Football League officials (who would have grabbed him in a minute if they weren't fearful of tilting the balance with the colleges, the one that preserves the latter as their farm system) could possibly have blamed Herschel Walker for taking the U.S. Football League's money and running. Under the circumstances, and considering the above, there was nothing else for him to do.

Pass up millions of dollars to play another year at Georgia? How naïve, and how inconsiderate. A poor black boy from Wrightsville, Georgia; his father a nightshift worker at a chalk mine; his mother a day worker in a garment factory; six brothers and a sister — and a chance to escape a grinding poverty and take the whole family with him on winged feet. Would the University of Georgia have provided such deliverance if he had crushed a knee playing that last year?

It could be that Walker will go back to get his degree, being only a year away. Most who quit don't go back; Steve Bartkowski tried, and found it too awkward ("it was like I had been away forever; I was so much older than everybody . . . I'll never do it. I know I won't."). But Walker is "different" so maybe he will, even if it doesn't matter a whole lot. And despite the braying of college coaches, the one defection will not ruin their game.

I would be concerned for others who believe that they also have great talent and quit their chance for an education to chase the dream. Team sports are beguiling that way. There is no unyielding par, no impassive stopwatch to tell a youngster how good or bad he is. A halfback breaks a fifty-yarder and thinks he's Jim Brown. It's the nature of the beast. There are, alas, already far too many young men who think they are on their way to prosperity, and will forgo their education for it.

But the larger sin lies in not dealing up front with the true definition of the college athlete in today's market. By vigorously upholding the comic pretense that he is a student-athlete, and not the opposite of that, we have mandated the perversions of the academic process that have caused so many spectacular failures, no longer possible to disguise.

I will never understand why we are surprised when our athletes resist the classroom. Why we are shocked when they accept bogus grades (or sports cars, or whatever the recruitment currency of the day might be). Or act like cons and thugs. They see excess all around them; they are weaned on it.

How many times do they have to have their education stilted by the exigencies of the budget before it sinks in?

How many times do they have to see their athletic department in its hunger for funds change dates, rearrange schedules, accept matches in the middle of exam week (or halfway across the globe) to gain a monetary concession from the insatiable television networks? At the expense of their valuable study time.

The player around whom much of the controversy at

San Francisco swirled, and who now plays in the NBA, was convicted in 1982 of assaulting a coed while in school. He said what happened was "part of life."

It is a money ethic that now dominates college sport. It has been pointed out (I'm not sure by whom; probably Sonny Werblin) that NBC paid more for the rights to telecast the Rose Bowl than Thomas Jefferson paid for the Louisiana Purchase. When USC was put on probation for multiple violations of NCAA rules in its football program, its president threatened to sue mainly because it was going to cost the school "millions" in TV revenue.

Do the colleges throw in the towel? President Howard Swearer of Brown has suggested that colleges end the hypocrisy, drop pretenses entirely and pay scholarship athletes as if they were pros. Work out a salary schedule, require no class attendance and generally treat the athletic department as if it were a Burger King franchise. If I were a college president hearing that melody I would give it the ear Dr. Swearer's stature deserves, and resist to the death.

Aside from proving beyond a doubt that college athletics are no more than a business, such a move would do the business in. The rich would get richer, the poor would go bankrupt, and it would do nothing to help get anyone educated. It would be economic suicide (even USC could not have afforded O. J. Simpson; Georgia, with all its bowl and television money, could not have afforded Herschel Walker under any circumstances).

But worst of all, it would strip away the final illusion. What illusion? That the athlete is in the school he plays for because he *wants* to be there.

And why is that important? Because the fan of sport in America is increasingly alienated from the practitioners of sport, the players at the top levels, and increasingly hostile toward them. Turn the college jock into a hired gun, allow him to be perceived as a nonstudent who is no longer "one of us," and he will be expected to perform "just like the pros."

His final devaluation will have taken place. When he fails, as he surely will sooner or later, he will be treated just as shabbily and in the same derisive manner as the pro athlete. The alienation will be complete. College sport does not need that. It needs the reverse of that.

But most of all it needs to erase once and for all the image of exploitation that has plagued it ever since it got into the Big Sports business, and allowed that business to pollute the academic mission. The recent spectacle (by wire service photo) of a lanky young black man looking miserably out of place in a Chicago elementary school classroom told it plain enough.

He was not the freak result of a physiological quirk; he was an adult basketball player named Kevin Ross, twenty-five years old and trying to correct the legacy of sixteen years of a misspent education. The last four years were misspent at Creighton Unviersity. He could read at no better than a fourth-grade level.

8.

The Academic Sham

His name was Billy Harris. "Billy the Kid," he called himself. The name, he said, had meant something before the dream died.

We met in Chicago, in the sparse inner-city offices of Athletes for Better Education. He sat drinking orange juice from a plastic cup — a stringy, handsome, goateed black man pushing thirty. Tight coils of hair covered his head. His dress was relaxed and airy — white sweater, blue cotton shirt, white cotton pants, sandals with socks. His manner was neither. A mouse in a cat's cage would have been more relaxed.

We talked for more than two hours. It was not so much a conversation as it was an address. His words — sharp, glib, challenging — came in drumming bursts, like hail on a flat roof.

He said he had "been lucky." He said he had "had some things."

He was raised on the South Side, in a four-room apartment in a ghetto called Robert Taylor Homes. "The Project." There were four brothers and a sister. He was the second son. His father was gone. His mother was on welfare. She was "very religious," he said, and "unique." She emphasized the "solid things."

"I grew up on Thirty-ninth and Federal, you understand? There's graffiti on the walls that we made, gang-

banging [street fights, not sex]. Gang-banging is peer pressure. It wasn't like you had a choice. I never grabbed
pistols and stuff to go out and shoot people, but there was
times when I had to bug a little bit to make it, you know
what I mean? That's not something I'm proud of, that's
just survival. You can't survive being neutral.

"I played organized basketball as early as grammar school.
I could dunk when I was twelve years old. We had a little
crip line going, the other young dudes my age, and I came
in, man, and I went up on it, you know, and *boom,* I
threw one down, you dig? These dudes at the other end
of the court are high-school All-*Americans,* and they stopped
and came down there and said, 'Hey, Blood,' you know?
'Let's see you do that *again,* Jack.' I was five-foot-*nine.*

"So I came down, and *boom,* threw another one down.
They said. 'Hey, come down to this end.' It didn't dawn
on me then what was happening. In less than two months
my game went from, you know, being a beginner-type
dude that could jump and play to being a *force* in the
game. They wanted *me* to shoot jumpers, you understand
what I'm saying? I knew right then there was something
different about my game.

"In the seventh, eighth grades at Crispus Attucks, I'd
hit as much as sixty, seventy points a game. I didn't measure myself on if we won the game, you know what I mean?
I measured myself if when the game was over I had my
thirty or thirty-five. If I got twenty-six, I didn't feel good.
If I got twenty-nine, I didn't feel good. I had to do that
because I knew I could.

"I was recruited from one high school to another. I was
at Lindbloom Technical. A coach from Dunbar saw me.
He said, 'Hey, you don't need to be there. You need to
be *here.*' I never had a problem with books. I was lucky.
I'm above average with that student-type thing. But you
cannot be a superstar athlete and not be affected.

"I went to this school where they graded you every ten weeks. At the end of ten weeks I had a B in this English class, but the teacher died. For the next ten weeks they gave us a series of substitutes. I decided not to go. At the midterm in order to be eligible I had to be passing all my subjects. The last substitute had only been in the class a couple of weeks, but he wanted to fail me, because I hadn't been there. Half the teachers in the school went around to explain to him that he couldn't do that. I got my grade and everything was cool.

"Somebody says, 'Hey, man, that was bad for them to do,' and in a way it was. But this is the start of that shit. Some type persons woulda relied on that all the way, but I say, 'Hey, you were lucky that time,' you know? If this teacher had a little more guts he wouldn't have passed me, and that would have been better in the long run. But it's hard to make a guy ineligible if he's packing your gym.

"The teachers see this. A guy looks at an athlete and says, 'Well, he's an athlete, he's not going to be into books.' The stigma starts there. He can read every play in the playbook, but he can't read his books, you dig? It's like they're imbedding the seeds. You don't have to 'ask' for anything. You get it. Only time you see a counselor is if you're in trouble. Your counselor is the coach, understand what I'm saying? You're not a part of the regular school. This is what people refuse to deal with. An athlete is not a part of the student population.

"I graduated in the top third of my class. I had the second highest SAT score at Dunbar, and was number one in the ACT, you understand what I'm saying? But I knew where the future was. I was 'Billy the Kid.' I wore the special uniform number of the star. My brother had the number when he started. Before him, Kendall Mayfield, drafted by the Knicks. Marvin Stuart, drafted by the 76'ers.

"I'm gonna tell you the prime thing, what this is all about. I came from a very humble background. I had friends thirteen, fourteen years old involved in strong-arm robberies. I couldn't do that. I knew the difference between right and wrong. I thought about the afterwards — about getting caught, about going to jail.

"But basketball let me know I could get anything I wanted, as long as the eligibility held out. Hey, man, I got *paid*. In *high* school. I got free lunches, clothes. I went to the prom in a limo. I had *money*. I was able to give my mother money. We did all the things that were supposed to be illegal. We practiced every day of the year, which was against the rules. When you practice that much, it makes whatever you're practicing the most important thing in your life. How can a guy tell you it's not if you're out there practicing on Thanksgiving Day? We *did* crap like that, man. Then when you get to college, you don't go home for Christmas. You're at school practicing on *Christmas Day*. You're not a regular student, you're not a regular person.

"When the college scouts started coming around, my mother had so many steaks she didn't wanta see another steak. We were going out to dinner every day. I had people come to me with the *cash,* you understand? Imagine being seventeen years old and living on the basic necessities and people showing you seven thousand dollars.

"In high school I had thought of being an engineer. Scored off the board on the tests. But when you become a *talent*, the last thing the coach wants to hear is, 'Hey, coach, I can't make it to practice today because I gotta go to the library and catch up on my engineering.' Or, 'I gotta do some research,' or 'make a book report.'

"They don't wanta hear that shit. Coaches steer you away from stuff that will tax your mind. They don't give a damn if you're brilliant as hell, they want you in P.E., or anything they have some control or input. When you're dealing with an engineering prof he don't give a damn what the coach is trying to do. You talk about putting a ball in a basket, that shit is meaningless to him.

"I came out of high school, man, I was seventeen years old, you dig? From being a high school student to having to deal with this business aspect. That's what college sports is and nobody should think otherwise. I was recruited by every major university. I had guys come to my mother's house and put five, six, seven thousand dollars on the table and say, 'Here, all you gotta do is sign this piece of paper.' I'm not going to hurt anybody by telling who, that's not my thing.

"But, hey, I wound up going to a school like Northern Illinois, in *DeKalb*. All right, hey, 1969, I was Public League scoring champion, and I went to Northern Illinois, a school that nobody heard of in any sport. The next year James Bradley, recruited by everybody, including UCLA, *he* came to Northern. And Cleveland Ivey was there, from Carver. He'd been Public League scoring champion, too.

"You understand what I'm telling you? Northern Illinois, the little school out in the corn. We were ranked twentieth and got featured in *Sports Illustrated*. We woulda had a championship team but the NCAA came out and started looking. Don't think that Northern got there by saying, 'All right, we're going to give you guys four years of *education*. In order to take me they had to take other people. There are people walking around right now that's got a college education because I went there, understand what I'm saying? It's a cold world, man. Everybody wants the dollars. Everywhere it's the same. Nobody discussed academics with me. That wasn't important to them.

"When I left college I took a pay cut. People wanta think guys don't get paid for playing basketball in college, that's their business. We're psyched into thinking that it's

good, healthy, All-American fun. That's the thing that
hurts the most. All the shit they shoot in your mind. But
I was treated super at Northern Illinois. I drove a Mercedes
back and forth to the city. It was mine to come and go.

"But if you get ineligible, or decide you wanta be in
business school, which is what I wanted to do, they're
going to come snatch that scholarship from under your
ass. I coulda got my degree at Northern. I coulda graduated the time I was supposed to. I had a 3.2 average. I
always carried a full load — *over* a full load. But I was
going for a B.S. in phys. ed. and I took a lot of history
courses — Roman history, all of 'em. Hey, it ain't so tough
to get good grades. There's always a way to get around
anything. I'm very intelligent, but I'm not above taking a
break.

"But I went from being almost like a god to no one
really caring. You don't see that until you're twenty or
twenty-one, when your four years of eligibility are up. I
need six hours to get my degree. They can *give* you that
piece of paper. Some of them do. Some of them guarantee
you will graduate.

"When I was drafted I just had a week of classes left.
I had to report to the pro camp. This dude that was teaching me had been instrumental in recruiting me. I said,
'Hey, let me take the test a week early.' 'No.' 'Is there
any way I can go and come back for the final when you
give it?' 'No. You must put in the time.' He didn't care
anymore.

"I was drafted by the Bulls in the seventh round in 1973.
It was a big letdown, you understand what I'm saying? I
went from seeing headlines, 'Harris Near Silver Lining,'
'Million Dollar Decision,' to being drafted in the seventh.
Hey, *that* will make you deal with reality.

"The Bulls gave me a two-thousand-dollar bonus, and
I wound up getting cut. They called it an 'attitude prob-

lem.' They had to say something. I was in good shape, I was a good draw. Big crowds both times Northern played in Chicago, against South Carolina, against Oral Roberts. Everybody's in there cheering Billy the Kid.

"I've been kept in limbo since I left college. I played in the Eastern League, I played overseas — in the Philippines, in Europe, you understand what I'm saying? I could still be a force in the league. But I get by. I can get up in the morning and put on Pierre Cardin slacks. I've got two Cadillacs to drive. A lot of guys work all their lives and never get to drive a 'hog.' Women like athletes. I've been taken care of, you dig?

"I got a chance to be a counselor for a job-placement agency. I interviewed kids at a halfway house. I was into it, trying to show 'em what's in my life, you understand what I'm saying? I want to be a positive influence. I tell young dudes, 'Hey, get you some money, get it now. But if you come out of college without a degree, you're still short.'

"It's wrong for the guy who gets to taste the pie and then doesn't get it anymore. The experience was more disappointing than if I'd never been in the NBA. Like going to the desert and getting one sip of water.

"I can't say in truth that basketball and athletics were worth it. But I'm lucky. I'm not on the streets doing dope. To be twenty-seven and be able to turn things around and make something of your life is a good thing.

"I ride through the old neighborhood. I see the graffiti. I think about the things we did. After all the shit, a lot of the time I think, 'Maybe I'd be a lawyer now, or even a doctor,' you understand what I'm saying? I had potential."

For as long as intercollegiate and interscholastic sports have been taken seriously in this country, the image of the "dumb jock" has endured. In caricature, he is not an altogether unappealing figure: the fullback whose neck is a size larger than any score he ever made in math class; the kid with the rampant pituitary gland who dribbles behind his back and slam-dunks but breaks into a cold sweat at the prospect of diagramming a simple sentence.

This was always an exaggerated image. The good of a system that encouraged the less-studious to develop his physical skills to the point where they might carry him to academic opportunity had overshadowed the specter of the few morons who got "helped along" via a phony academic certification. Despite occasional scandals, the image was more playfully than seriously advanced.

No more.

The "dumb jock" has come to full flower in the American educational system. He is a national catastrophe, and a national disgrace. About the only good thing that I can say about him is that his blossoming inadvertently exposed the larger failures of the educational process.

What happened? Why is it different after all these years?

First, it is different because the educational system itself is in chaos, its spirit inert and preoccupied, its standards blunted to a point where almost anything that passes for curricula is permissible.

In a nation that once prided itself in being the most advanced, twenty-three million American adults are functionally illiterate, unable to fathom a restaurant menu. College freshmen read at a level ninth-graders read at fifty years ago. A University of Miami geography professor found in a survey that forty-two percent of his incoming students in 1982 could not locate London on a world map.

High schools — many of them — do not educate, they merely graduate. Junior colleges — many of them — have such meager academic requirements that they are fertile ground for any angling coach who feels the need to do some academic cheating to keep his players eligible. The sins of the high schools and junior colleges are visited on the major colleges, where the buck stops. Colleges with any academic fidelity at all may not be squeamish about consuming an athlete's eligibility (his playing time), but they usually draw the line at granting him a degree he has not earned.

Second, it is different because declining enrollments and inflated costs made the fear that the bucks will stop a real one for many colleges. They became vulnerable to the rationale that a little academic malfeasance might not be so terrible if it kept them off the fiscal rocks. They saw the excesses and maneuverings of other coaches, other administrators, other booster clubs leading to big money — directly via TV windfalls, or indirectly by making the school more visible to potential students. Only lately, when the corner-cutting almost brought the house down, did they realize the error of their ways.

Third, it is different because academic standards have eroded and been undermined to the point where more unqualified "student-athletes" than ever have been getting into college. Not just underprivileged young men who need a chance, but uneducated young men who have no chance, not in the classroom. Through their playing days at college they are kept "eligible" via an eventless and immaterial habitation of the classroom. They wind up down the road with neither of the things they need most: (1) an education, and (2) a degree.

Fourth, it is different because the administrators and academicians who have traditionally tried to keep "Big Sport" in its place have themselves been the architects of all this chaos, and have created the ultimate irony: they have subverted their own system. Caught up in the money-madness, they have made a legion of scavengers of their coaches — coaches desperate to win, desperate to get and keep in school those players who can help them win, and thus keep business booming. The failures of administrators are as joined to the sins of coaches as a man's leg is to his hip.

Fifth, it is different because under the guise of "affirmative action" and other civil rights programs, athletic administrations have only made athletes more exploitable — and exploitive — than ever. Short of successful prayer, "eligibility majors" will go through the process doomed to failure and a future of disillusionment. To do this to black youth, in this society, at this time, is unconscionable.

Sixth, it is different because in the last twenty-five years the colleges have allowed their "money" sports, football and basketball, to become farm systems for the professional leagues, and in so doing permitted their athletes to embrace the terrible myth: that the "logical ascension" to the pros is compatible with the academic environment, *even at the expense of scholarship.*

Scholastic cripples are thus invited into college to pursue an impossible dream: to become one of the infinitely small number (less than two percent) who make it in the NFL and NBA. It is the hoax that sucked in Billy Harris and thousands of blacks like him, and enrages such black activists as Harry Edwards, the Berkeley sociologist. Says Edwards, quite accurately, "They have a better chance of becoming surgeons."

Finally, it is different because the coaches themselves — traditionally the heavies in this long-running melodrama — see it better than anyone else. They are at once culprits and victims, and many of them have had enough of being both. "Our administrators tend not to deal with the problem at all, but to gloss over it with a lot of fancy dialogue," said Bill Walsh after he quit as head football coach at Stanford to go with the San Francisco 49ers.

"When you enroll a kid who has no chance to cut it academically, you're guilty of manipulating that kid. When you protect him from an education instead of educating him, you're guilty again."

When I first examined the scene of the crash for *Sports Illustrated* two years ago, there were so many scandals in the news that it took two pages of solid type just to provide a summary of the current offenses. High-school and junior-college transcripts had been falsified. Grades had been given college athletes for courses never taken, or courses that did not exist. Bogus credits had been granted athletes who weren't even in the same state at the time their classes were held. Extension courses given at lesser institutions were being exploited by so many major colleges in so many ways that within a week after the *SI* story broke the NCAA ordered a clampdown on the guidelines governing their use.

Among the defrocked were such prominent athletic houses as USC, UCLA, Arizona State, New Mexico, San Jose State, Purdue, and Utah. Bodies flew in all directions. New Mexico's basketball coach was indicted by a federal grand jury on multiple counts of fraud. The school fired him and his assistant. USC fired its academic counselor and a speech instructor. Oregon fined its football coach, four of his assistants, and the swimming coach.

It was especially troubling to me that so much dirt had been uncovered at USC, long a favorite of mine because of the outstanding coaches and administrators I had gotten to know there. For a school with such a rich academic tradition and enviable athletic record, including more NCAA team titles (sixty-three and counting) than anybody, it seemed way out of whack. It was as if a collection of panhandlers had popped up behind the counters at Tiffany's to run the business.

The dirt did not sweep, either; it got deeper. An in-house investigation revealed that 330 "marginal" students had been admitted under USC standards in order to play on varsity teams in recent seasons. It was an admission of turpitude that could not have been more disappointing.

(I felt no better a year later when USC was brought to the dock again, this time for generating cash payments to its football players through a ticket-scalping scheme. The scheme was handled by an old friend of mine, Marv Goux, who had been an assistant coach there for twenty-five years. The NCAA banned USC from bowl games through 1983, and television appearances through 1984. The new USC president, James Zumberge, whom I did not know, threatened to sue the NCAA. The ban, after all, would cost USC "millions" in revenues. Never mind the cheating. Never mind the tarnished image. Protect that TV money! I decided I did not *want* to know President Zumberge.)

In the aftermath of all the revelations, a tidal wave of indignation, righteous and otherwise, rolled over college sport. Old enemies resurfaced en masse. Educators who traditionally are blind to the good of mixing sport with scholarship found their platform crowded with breast-beaters. Crackdowns were declared in almost every quarter. Hardly an issue of the *NCAA News* went by that a guest editorialist did not rail against the system.

Then, finally, inevitably, gratefully, came the twenty-two college presidents with their recommendations to the NCAA to upgrade the standards for admission and normal progress. The vital, overdue changes were voted in at the NCAA convention in San Diego in January of 1983, to go into effect in 1986.

I knew exactly what was going to happen next. I hoped it wouldn't, but it did. Even before the convention was over.

Black college leaders almost unanimously condemned

the proposed changes. The changes were called "racist" (among other things) by the presidents of Grambling and Southern universities. The requirement of a 700 score on the Standard Aptitude Test was singled out as particularly "unfair" because blacks taking the test averaged less than that nationwide. The SATs themselves were called "racially biased," although they had been modified to meet that charge years before. Most absurd was the rating of the Grambling president, who called the reforms a conspiracy by white administrators to rid intercollegiate rosters of black athletes.

The response was shortsighted and overwrought, not to say self-defeating, but it was not inconsistent. (*Lowered* standards were partly to blame for the black athlete's shameful exploitation in the first place.) For me it was a tap on the shoulder. A reminder of things that had bothered me about my report in *SI* two years before. The nagging belief that I had been too broad with my criticism, or, rather, not quite precise enough in certain areas. Specifically:

— That the pro influence on the academic life of the young athlete, black or white, was more pernicious than I had stated. That until the high schools and colleges realized that the pros were coyotes in the henhouse, they would be forever at their mercy. (The pros had to do very little to effect this, of course. Just be there when the system spewed out the willing athletes.)

— That high schools — and, down the line, even grade schools because it starts there — needed the strongest possible signal from above to jerk them into accepting their own irresponsibility. That they needed to be blamed outright for pushing academic oafs up the ladder to failure at the college level. To be told that *they* were accountable, too, when the uneducated star athlete was left in the lurch after his eligibility ran out.

But where I had missed the mark entirely, or had been unwilling to say it forthrightly because it is "not for the white man to say," was that the real issue was wrapped up in the continuing dilemma of the black athlete. That the underlying problem was a black problem.

That the sin was not just exploitation, but exploitation working hand in glove with the unwillingness of black leaders to see the terrible mistake of compromising standards. To realize the calamity they permitted in allowing the academic process to be subverted, even if it got black kids into college. And until they did there would be no understanding and no healing.

The system had failed the black athlete, but with the exception of enlightened critics like Harry Edwards, a prime factor was that too many black educators had sold him out. They had unwittingly encouraged him to be entrapped by the pro myth. Indeed, had helped him nurture it through the hapless academic regimens their own demands for lower (and lower and lower) standards had created. When he failed, the only reason they could come up with was the catch-all "racism."

It did not take a detective to see it. The testimony spoke for itself, loud and clear. With sickening regularity, the voices that cried out for justice within the system were black voices, and they were saying, "Give us a break."

I reviewed my notes on Billy Harris, and listened to the tape I had made. I remembered what a waste I thought he was — a bright, sensitive, worthwhile young man who had conned and been conned right out of a future.

The file included a heartfelt letter to me from a "sophemore" in high school who said I had "maid" him think about giving up football. His "coathes," he said, had "teached" bad examples.

It also included copies of memoranda signed by college athletes in NCAA infractions cases: "I thank [think] the offer was made at home . . . I think he [the coach] did visied me a school one [once]. . . . Since I have been at ——, Coach —— have not give me any money, period. But he have lend me five to tin dollars but I have paid it back to."

Another: "Mr. —— has give me . . . up to 10 dollars went I needed to go home. To see my mother who is sick I have paid him back sent then."

There were other voices, in other testimony.

To help qualify him for a basketball scholarship to Indiana State University, a special verbal examination was given a black athlete at Englewood High in Chicago. He was asked to name the twelve months of the year. He passed the test by naming ten. A halfback in Kankakee, Illinois, qualified for a scholarship in the Big Ten Conference when a substitute teacher who took over the course in the final three weeks of the term "gave" him the C he needed to pass the English course he had been flunking. The C raised his grade point average to the minimum 2.0.

After sixteen years of primary, secondary and college education, Fred Buttler was a C-plus student, at least according to grades given him by his teachers. At Cal State in Los Angeles, he was a star defensive back, but flunked out after his last season of eligibility. His life's dream to be drafted by the pros into big money did not materialize.

For the next two years, Buttler's unsuccessful attempts to find work created a growing tension with his father, an auto mechanic separated from his wife. In the heat of an argument, the father threatened the son with a shotgun. The young man picked up a pistol and in the confusion shot and killed his father. The son was arrested and charged with murder, but eight days later was freed when a judge ruled it an accidental homicide.

Still grieving for his father, Fred Buttler then tried to drive to the nearby cemetery where the body was buried.

It took him more than an hour to get there. He kept stopping along the way to ask directions. Once in the cemetery he still could not find the gravesite, and finally gave up and returned home. He could not read the road signs.

The possibility that some young men, black or white, athletes or not, simply aren't college material and will never be does not deter the efforts to exploit them.

The pro myth is fed by an irresistible hype. There is a pot of gold at the end of the rainbow and its names are "National Basketball Association" and "National Football League," and a number of lesser aliases. The sports pages crow with the figures to be made. Agents swarm into the ghettos like bull ants to tell how those figures are enhanced by "clauses," and how financial coups are available for superstars. Hardly a day seems to go by that another talented nongraduate does not sign another multi-million-dollar contract.

The colleges sucker in. They have to; they are part of the machinery. Since television got its thumb on the windpipe, there is so much money to be made in big-time sports that everybody cooperates. (When asked once why the pros did not have farm systems, general manager Red Auerbach of the Boston Celtics replied incredulously: "What for? We have the greatest farm system in the world — the colleges.")

College recruiters know they cannot justify the sell-out on scholastic terms, so they try to justify it with dream talk. They brag about their ability to place players in pro ball. They pitch the pro myth to eighteen-year-olds, and get O. J. Simpson and Tony Dorsett to make a call.

Their publicists send out press releases ("The Big Eight Conference has more players — 135, count 'em, 135 — in the NFL than anybody") and decorate the pages of their athletic brochures with those who have "graduated" to the pros. One school in the South shamelessly produced a four-color recruiting poster that included pictures of those who "made it," under the caption: "*A Pipeline to the Pros.*"

It is a pipeline to disillusionment and heartbreak. Never mind that four out of five NBA players have not graduated from college. Never mind that almost two-thirds of all NFL players do not have diplomas. Never mind that. They're the ones who "made it." The great multitude of hooked youngsters who are throwing away their education a little bit every day to follow the pro dream is the real tragedy. There are no publishers of puff sheets for them.

According to the National Federation of State High School Athletic Associations, 700,000 boys play high school basketball and one million play high school football every year. At the NCAA level, the numbers reduce to 15,000 in basketball and 41,000 in football. About 4,000 players complete their college basketball careers each year; some 200 get drafted by the NBA, around 50 actually make NBA teams. The average player's career lasts 3.4 seasons. In the NFL, about 320 college draft picks go to camp each year; roughly 150 make it. Those who succeed play pro ball for an average of 4.2 seasons.

If the odds were displayed on an infield toteboard, only a fool would take them. Thousands and thousands to one against making the pros: 6,000 to 1 for a boy playing high school football; about 15,000 to 1 for a boy playing high school basketball. It *is* easier to become a surgeon. "The myth of sports as a way of upward mobility" for young black men like Billy Harris reaches its "true definition in the pros," says Harry Edwards.

Edwards has his own figures. "There are fewer than a thousand blacks making a living playing professional sports," he says, "while every black kid is busting his ass so he can make it, too." Spurred on by misguided notions of athletic black supremacy and served a diet of pro athletes as role models, "perhaps three million youths between thirteen and twenty-two are out there dreaming of careers as pro athletes. The odds against them are better than twenty thousand to one."

Ron Johnson, several times All-Pro runningback with the Browns and Giants, calls it "the rude awakening. All those skinny little guys with glasses? Always studying? Well, by the time they're thirty, they're doctors or lawyers or successful businessmen, and just beginning to cash in on those years of struggling. But the [uneducated] football player is almost always through by that age, and then he goes from earning maybe $100,000 a year or more, to maybe nothing."

Maybe to worse than that. Johnny Sample, the former Jet All-Pro, tried to make a living as a ticket broker. He got into legal trouble and spent a year in jail. Bob Hayes, the erstwhile "fastest human" and former Dallas Cowboy, received a five-year prison term for selling drugs. Mercury Morris, the ex-Miami Dolphin, is serving fifteen years for dealing cocaine.

The bottom line is crowded with tragedy. The late Bob Presley's failures at the college level (he did not come close to a degree at Cal, says Edwards) were exacerbated when he got a tryout with the Bullets as a six-foot-ten center and was cut. "He couldn't make it," Edwards told me, "and he couldn't take it. At first there were incidents where his wife had to call the police on him. He was writing bad checks. Somehow he was able to get probation.

"Then he got a job working for the phone company repairing telephone lines. He was out in public and people were always asking him if he played basketball. Some guys develop a sense of humor about it, but Presley never did. Things went from bad to worse. One day he showed up

at the Seattle Supersonics locker room. He started screaming at Tom Burleson's shoes and shooting basketballs into
a trash can and begging for a tryout. By then he was long
gone. A few months later, he jumped off a bridge."

Walter (Flea) Roberts, a former roommate of Edwards's at San Jose State, made it to the Cleveland Browns
as a 152-pound kick returner, but did not get his degree.
But Roberts was one of the lucky ones. He did well as a
San Francisco sales executive and is not a bitter man. He
has a Kierkegaardian approach to life — you are, he says,
"the prime reason for what happens to you." If you allow
yourself to fall into a pattern of relying on someone else
to hold your hand, as so many black athletes do, he says,
you'll surely wind up "a goner."

The worst of all, says Roberts, is the after-shock. "If
you don't get that diploma, there's no way you're going
to be better off going back to Bedford-Stuyvesant, or Watts,
or the Hough area in Cleveland. There's nothing there.
I've been to those places, and there's nothing there that
I care to be around.

"If you expose a guy to hope, if you show him a light
at the end of the tunnel, then put him back on the streets
with limited skills — I mean, what can happen to the guy?
Get a job for five dollars an hour? What's that mean with
inflation? It won't buy anything. To have a little sampling
and then be detoured away is a depressing situation."

The dilemma of black athletes in American education
took on a new dimension in the years after Jack Olsen
examined their exploitation fifteen years ago in *Sports
Illustrated*. For one thing, the sheer weight of their presence, both on athletic teams and in the student bodies as
a whole, all but obliterated the "tokenism" of the '60s.

Schools that were once bastions of segregation now applaud, from well-mixed grandstands, basketball and foot-

ball teams that are richly integrated. The University of Arkansas, for example, had one black athlete in 1978, or less than one percent of its athlete-students. By 1982 the figure was up to forty percent. Last fall, when coach Lou Holtz suited up seventy-four football players for Arkansas's opening game with Oklahoma State, more than half were black.

But only a fool would argue that being black is no longer a liability in America, and where the dilemma has not changed, except to get worse, is in the fact that "getting in" a university and "getting out" with the paper to prove it are two different things. More black athletes graduate from colleges every year — but the ratio of those who do to those who don't has declined. Every study made, officially or otherwise in the last fifteen years, suggests that fewer than half, and maybe as little as twenty percent, of the black athletes on scholarship wind up with degrees.

An official from one school in the Deep South admitted to me that in the first twelve years of integrated classrooms, it had not graduated one black athlete. Another school had ninety-one blacks on its varsity teams over a ten-year period and only ten had graduated. It is still true, as a study by George Hanford of the American Council on Education showed eight years ago, that "twice as many white athletes graduate as blacks."

Many factors are blamed for the grim statistics, and most of them are not new: the socioeconomic handicaps; the failures of education at the lower levels; the declining standards that allow the "pampered" athlete to be carried piggyback through the system while his potential slowly petrifies, only to find, in college, that there are no baccalaureates for illiterates.

Black academicians in the NCAA consistently led the movement for lower admission standards, getting them as low as possible and keeping them there. They did this on the reasonable grounds that opening classroom doors as wide as possible would create an atmosphere of acceptance that would lead to greater achievement.

But permissiveness is not policy, and the results have not been gratifying. To the contrary. Allowing athletes, black or white, to go unchallenged scholastically is a permission slip to heartbreak. Educators have a term for it: the "Hawthorne Effect" — students performing up to or down to the levels expected of them. More often than not, black athletes were the ones getting the slip.

It was not just an educational mistake, or a social mistake, it was a moral mistake. And as Edward B. Nyquist, former head of the College Boards, has said, "What is morally wrong can never be educationally right."

The lowered standards created an atmosphere, all right. An atmosphere of license made to order for abuse. And when you let the monster out of the closet, you risk not being able to get it back in. In such an atmosphere, lazy parents do not have to encourage their star halfback to read. Lazy teachers do not have to make him toe the line in class. Their only aim is to trundle him through the system as painlessly as possible. The high school diploma may be little more than a certificate of attendance, but it will get him into a college of his choice.

Flaws in the American school system (overcrowded, underfinanced, classrooms in turmoil) are well documented and need not be reviewed here. It is enough to recall that not many years ago a student needed a reading knowledge of Latin to get into many colleges. Now teenagers advance into upper academia barely equipped to handle instruction booklets and train schedules. A Long Island boy sued New York State for $5 million because he had been allowed to graduate and could not even read a restaurant menu.

From this national pattern of neglect emerged an expediency known as "grade inflation." The "B" of today, like the five-dollar bill, is simply not as valuable as it was fifteen years ago. Teachers succumb to expedient grading practices because beleaguered school boards can't afford to have bottlenecks of failing students. What can happen to the pampered young athlete in such a lax environment is predictable.

Chick Sherrer, the ex-Princeton basketball player who is president of Athletes for Better Education, deals with "grade inflation" every day. Sherrer's Chicago-based firm has centers in New York and Los Angeles and for six years has been trying to find ways to acquaint underdeveloped minds with the need for scholarship. He has on file the case of a Chicago boy who in his junior and senior years took College English, U.S. history, geometry, French, trigonometry, and biology. He finished high school with a 3.2 average and ranked forty-fifth in a class of four hundred.

"On those figures alone," Sherrer told me, "he was a prime college prospect. But then he took the college entrance exams. In his SAT [Scholastic Aptitude Test], he scored 208 of a possible 800. In his ACT [American College Testing], he scored a 9 of a possible 36. A very well-trained monkey could get a 9."

"Colleges," Sherrer said, "simply don't know what they're getting. The 'Great Society' has spent fifty billion dollars on public education since 1964, and all it has to show for it is more illiterates."

By Sherrer's accounts, the Chicago school system graduates a number of outstanding basketball players every year who cannot read above the sixth-grade level. One who wound up in a four-year California school was reading at a fourth-grade level through the eleventh grade. Sherrer's group, AFBE, monitors the progress of area high-schoolers and channels them into camps and reading programs, then tries to help place them in an appropriate college. It alerts college recruiters to potential problems through an annual report that details the athletes' academic progress.

For example, this evaluation of one boy who read almost to grade level but had consistently made poor marks: "D——— is anything but dumb, but the message has not come across that you cannot hustle or con your way into academic success. If he doesn't shape up his act, he may never see the inside of a four-year school."

When a high-school transcript makes better fiction than *The Grapes of Wrath,* it is a good bet that the school has compensated for the miserable job it has done by "helping the kid out." College recruiters complain of an all-too-familiar pattern. The requirement for a football or basketball scholarship is a C average through high school. A school finds out a college coach is interested in one of its boys. The boy reads at the fifth-grade level. The boy suddenly becomes an A student. The NCAA has a case on file of a New York athlete who showed colleges three different transcripts — three different sets of grades.

You cannot cure cancer with powder and paint. When kids pass who don't deserve to, teachers know it, administrators know it, and other students know it. It erodes the whole network of discipline and respect that makes the educational process viable. When beleaguered colleges accept more and more inferior merchandise, no matter how unused it is to the smell of an open textbook, they risk something else. Decorum.

De facto appeasement of what amounts to educational fraud is not only self-serving, it is self-destructive. Giving an athlete a "break" to get him into college only makes for a continuum of cheating and failure and increases his distrust for the system. There are no noble monuments to cheaters. Worse, the cheating could very well serve to make the athlete antisocial — and even a dangerous character.

The practice of allowing — on any pretense — misanthropes and potential sociopaths into an environment that will demand more of them than they can handle has created a climate for mischief that has shamed one institution after another (Kentucky, Arkansas, Florida State, et al.), and threatens to disgrace others. The system is almost guaranteed to make brooding misfits out of poor students. If the misfits are freighted in from a completely alien socioacademic background that is halfway across the continent, they may also develop confused loyalties and identities. Sports psychologists have had a field day diagnosing the felonies that pass for the behavior of some "student-athletes."

It was into this breach that the NCAA finally moved in January of 1983 with its proposed upgrading of admission standards — Proposal No. 48 on the convention agenda, pushed by the select ad hoc committee of twenty-two college presidents.

Beginning in 1986, incoming freshmen, to be eligible for varsity competition, would have to score at least 700 of a possible 1600 on the SAT (or 15 of a possible 36 on the ACT), and have accumulated a minimum 2.0 grade point average in a specific number of college preparatory courses. As improvements go, they didn't exactly tear the house down to start over, but it was better than changing the wallpaper. The Football Coaches Association had proposed far tougher standards three years before — a "triple option" of either a 2.5 average, or 800 on the college boards (SAT) or 18 on the ACT.

But it was a first step, and would certainly serve as a signal to the high schools and junior highs that the colleges weren't going to settle anymore. That primary and secondary educators had until 1986 — plenty of time, but not forever — to prepare their athletes for the reading and writing they would have to do once they matriculated.

Proposal 48 was voted in overwhelmingly — and, just as overwhelmingly, was hotly contested by the presidents of historically black colleges within the NCAA. The black leaders thought the new standards too high, and prejudiced to boot. They pointed out that black students on the average scored slightly below those standards nationwide.

Well, of course they scored below those averages. At least partly because they had never been challenged to do otherwise.

In their ire the blacks even criticized Joe Paterno, the Penn State coach who has an almost spotless record for sending his athletes — black and white — down the aisle on graduation day. Paterno had had the guts to say that it was time the colleges stopped "raping" black kids who "bounce basketballs and run around tracks and score touchdowns" but aren't prepared for the demands of academic life. Dr. Joseph B. Johnson, the president of Grambling, said he was "offended" by Paterno, who, he said, "doesn't know anything about blacks."

A few days later Harry Edwards called his colleagues' objections "misguided." He said black educators were "underestimating the intellectual capabilities of black athletes. . . . Dumb jocks are not born, they're systematically created."

Johnson said white administrators were sending out a message that "there are too many black athletes on NCAA teams," and that it was time to cull the crop.

Well, he was right. Partly, There *are* too many *unqualified* black athletes on NCAA teams. And too many unqualified white athletes, too. If they are not students, they do not belong in college. If they are there just to fill up space before shipping off to the pros, they do not belong. They are an insult to the system and unfair to the coaches whose teams are made up of athletes who go to class, with the time and effort that demands.

The sooner they are brought up to qualification, or relegated to an industrial league or to whatever provision the pro teams make to prepare them for athletic employment (at the *pros'* expense for a change), the quicker the college rosters will be truly representative of colleges. Until then, they are fraudulent.

But *do* we sell our black athletes short? And is there really a way out of what Dr. Roscoe Brown calls the "jock trap"? What if blacks *can't* cut it? What then? Would that not be the final disillusionment? It is one thing to be told you have failed because of extenuating circumstances, it is quite another to find out you can't cut it.

There is a least one place in America where they are told they can, and where they do. Where it *is* cool for black athletes to carry books. And make good grades. And aspire to something more than athletic aggrandizement. If there ever was a time to look to such a place, it is now.

Father Thomas B. James is not a radical. He believes in athletics, and the possibilities they generate for young men. He also believes blacks should quit blaming the system and start looking to themselves for deliverance.

Father James is a Catholic priest with a master's degree in English from Loyola University in Los Angeles. He is athletic, urbane, tough, outspoken, just past forty years old — and black. He is the principal and former academic counselor at Verbun Dei High School in inner-city Los Angeles, near Watts. Verbun Dei has an all-male enrollment of 306 — mostly black, a few Chicanos.

For much of its twenty years, Verbun Dei has been well known for the crack basketball teams it produces. Its football teams in 1981 and 1982 won twenty-five straight games and two district championships. In recent years, it has made other significant contributions. Eighty percent of Verbun Dei's seniors go to college. Sixty percent get college degrees. One Verbun Dei graduate was a Rhodes Scholar.

"When I came here twelve years ago, I wanted to teach Shakespeare," says Father James. "The kids laughed at me. I teach Shakespeare now. And every kid in school has to take *two* English courses."

Father James is sitting on the floor of his room at the parish on Crenshaw Street, wearing bermuda shorts and lounging at an angle to catch the warm afternoon breeze through the open window. The pulse of the street comes in with the breeze, competing with the beat of a portable radio.

"We don't have two hundred electives here," he says. "We have math, social studies, religion, science, a language. P.E., too, but only for sophomores. We don't have shop. We don't have arts and crafts. We don't allow any 'Black English.' Black English is bullshit. The people who make you think Black English is okay are making $100,000 a year. Let your kids buy that argument and see how well *they* make it in the real world.

"You don't raise people up by lowering standards. Lowering standards is not a solution, it's an acceptance of getting by. You don't demand less, you demand *more*. It happens here. We raise the standards, they do a little bit more. To pass a course at Verbun Dei you have to make at least an eighty. We used to pass 'em with D's. We were teaching them to be lazy.

"Values have to be qualified. We had open-ended admissions. We put a lid on. We said, 'You can't get in if you don't raise your grades.' They did. In urban schools, teachers and educators tend to believe their students are inferior. Unconsciously, they give that message to the kids, and the kids act it out. It's a self-fulfilling prophecy."

There is no special treatment for athletes at Verbun Dei. No privileges, no excuses to get out of anything. "We don't take for granted that they won't be academically inclined. Some we push, some we talk to, some we kick in the pants — but if they can make it on the basketball court, they can make it in class. We suspended our best athlete for a month last season for horsing around in class."

Verbun Dei takes pride in its toughness. Tuition is $800 a year; there are no scholarships (the budget is tight and the school can't afford them). The waiting list is long. Many of the applicants are outstanding athletes. All incoming ninth-graders are tested. If they read below a fifth-grade level, they have to go to summer school. There are no guarantees even then. "If you can't read, you can't get in. It's too late for you then. That's why it's ridiculous for a college to take a kid who reads at the third-grade level. It's too late."

Verbun Dei discipline is rigid. No braids, no hair nets, no earrings, no corn-rows, no tennis shoes in class, no blue jeans. No alcohol, no smoking, no radios, no tape recorders, no gum chewing or candy or food in class. No fighting, no weapons, no stealing. Everybody wears a tie. "Kids say, 'Why I gotta wear a tie?' 'Because we have external discipline, you can't make these decisions for yourself.'

"Nobody beats on the teachers, nobody gets away with drugs. Seven years ago we kicked out two boys for having some marijuana. I kicked one boy out last year for pulling a knife. There is a five-man disciplinary board and daily monitoring. We make locker checks. We let 'em know we're watching. I tell 'em, 'I love you, but you do something wrong, I'll punish you.' If they have any complaints,

I make them write it out, in 'legible English.' They hate it, but they do it.

"We have a responsibility at Verbun Dei. Black male tradition has had its problems in our society. So we tell 'em, 'Look, you gotta get off your ass. Your mother and daddy might not be together, you might be living with your grandma. That's okay. We can deal with that. But when you go into the classroom, you can't say, 'I want all kinds of attention now.' The hell with that. The teacher can't teach because you want attention? In the classroom you gotta get to them books.

"And we have to keep preaching that and preaching that and preaching that. People have died so these kids can go to school. To not be productive is a sin. The first thing I ask a kid when he comes in as a ninth-grader, 'What do you want to do with your life? Now's the time to start thinking about it, not six years from now when the scholarship has run out and nobody has drafted you.'

"Money has become the big priority. The college people are out to make money, the pros are out to make money. The high schools have fallen into that trap. To make money, you get the best talent. The kids see that early. 'It doesn't matter how smart you are, it's how well you can play.' It's an illusion. I tell 'em all the time. They say, 'I'm gonna make a million.' I say, 'You'll be one in a million if you do.'

"The joy I get from teaching at Verbun Dei isn't seeing a kid get a basketball scholarship; it's knowing when he gets it he can *do* something with it. That he can cope with the college environment — he can read, he can handle himself. David Greenwood got his history degree at UCLA and went on to play for the Chicago Bulls. Ray Hamilton got his degree in speech and drama and is going to work for CBS in New York. Ricky Hawthorne got his in history at Cal. Clarence Richardson made the dean's list at North-western. They were challenged in high school. When Ray Hamilton looked around at UCLA and saw he was the only one not writing, not taking notes, he said, 'Man, I better take notes.'

"You judge a school or a college by the way they help a kid become the person he should be. The school that lets a kid slide and gives him a B-plus isn't helping him. I've seen the Klan. I've seen the dogs. I know what it means to ask for a job and have a guy spit on me. But I'm not bitter, because the situation has changed. Kids have an opportunity today. They can get into college, choose a major, get a scholarship, get financial aid, get a tutor, get a part-time job. They can better the quality of their lives.

"I have no use for athletes who can't stop being 'takers.' I tell them, 'Don't go to schools that offer you anything. Tell 'em you don't want women, or money, or under-the-table stuff. The minute you tie to that, you're dead.' It's been like that throughout history. Voting day comes, we drink the cat's beer and eat his steaks and vote for him. That's the end of free choice. You sell yourself for a hundred dollars, what you gonna do when the hundred dollars is gone?

"I have no use for colleges who 'protect' athletes — keep them from this or that course or this or that professor. People say, 'The experience is enough, just being on campus is enough.' It's not. He needs that piece of paper even if it's for dancing. When one of our kids comes back from a college visit, I ask him, 'Where did the coach take you first, the gym or the sociology department?' If all he's going to see for four years is the gym, it's no good."

Father James swung his legs around and sat up straighter on the floor.

"Not everybody is cut out for college," he said. "Not

everyone can function in that environment. A kid comes to me and says, 'I wanta go to UCLA.' I say, 'Hey, wait a minute. You got a two hundred on the SAT. You can't be a dentist. You're not Muhammed Ali. You gotta go to work.' A kid needs some truth about that. Some guidance. Sometimes the kid who says, 'I got a raw deal in college' isn't telling it straight. He shouldn't have been there in the first place.

"When you get honesty between the schools and the colleges, you got something. We had a boy here, a blue-chipper, named Ken Austin. He wanted to study architecture. Most of the coaches who came in said, 'Architecture? That's too tough. You'll have to study all the time. You can't make it in architecture. We'll help you get something else.' The Rice coach came in. He said, 'I'm going to take your transcript to the dean of the school of architecture. If he can't take you, I won't recruit you. If you want to be an architect, you should get the chance.'

"Ken went to Rice. He said, 'They're giving me a chance to fail. That's all I want.' He wrote me a card from Houston. 'Father, I'm hanging in there.' He might never make it as an architect. He might just be a draftsman. But that's okay. He's getting his shot."

9.

A Shining Example

I HAD been nagged by the thought that at least some of the answers to the problems of college sport might be found right up there on the mantelpiece. In that one most obvious place that best symbolized both its success and its excesses. It was a vague notion, however, like a distant tolling in a fog, and I had no trouble keeping it under control.

Notre Dame held no great charm for me. I know how others were awed by it, but I was never drawn in. Neither Irish nor Catholic, not a fan, not an alumnus, not even especially fond of the Notre Dame victory march ("On Brave Old Army Team" always struck me as a more inspiring number), I had easily resisted. I found it to be a more troubling than compelling presence. Winning was too important to Notre Dame to suit me. Football was too important. Money was too important. The Notre Dame allure was a siren's song and I wasn't having any.

Brief visits over the years on story expeditions did not weaken my prejudice. The place itself is not awesome. There are no splashes of grandeur in the Indiana countryside. The Ursa Major does not shine brighter over the famous golden dome, and, somewhat disconcertingly, the dome itself competes for air space with three ugly smokestacks. Interstate 80 thunders nearby, and the school —

small at 8,500 students next to a Michigan's 35,000 — is
more functional-looking than pretty.

Time, and a unique chance for a closer look, converted
me. I no longer resist. I admit it. I now include myself in
that legion of admirers who hold to the opinion that Notre
Dame really is doing something right. That it possesses
something that, if transmutable, could well deserve par-
celling around. Not a perfect specimen, but a good one.
In such troubled times, intercollegiate sport can use any
help it can get.

Events that led to my conversion are loose in my mind,
but I think it might have begun on a cab ride across Manhattan with a man who, like so many in the thrall, wor-
shipped Notre Dame from afar, like converts to an obscure
Eastern cult. David Cooper is the classic example of what
we heretics used to call Notre Dame's "subway alumni,"
that vast body of communicants who follow Irish teams
beyond good reason or geographical barriers and who,
when the heroes make their inevitable appearance at a
New York arena, cram the subways.

Cooper was fifty years old then, a bony, rumpled-look-
ing man with a toothsome friendliness and absolutely no
inhibitions. The cab was his. I entered into a sanctuary,
a movable shrine of Notre Dame athletic commemora-
tions: pins and ticket stubs and pennants and badges stuck
and pinned on everywhere. For sheer tackiness, I had
never seen anything like it. But it had a certain charm
about it, too, like the inner clutter of a gypsy tea room.

As I settled in, I asked him what had caused the ex-
plosion.

"I'm the greatest Notre Dame fan," Cooper announced.
"I'm a Notre Dame nut." Exercising the right of all New
York cabbies, he pounded his horn. It rang out the first
seven notes of the Notre Dame victory march — "Hail,

hail to old Notre Dame . . ." "It cost me a hunnert fifty bucks, that horn," Cooper said.

I leaned forward so I could see into the front seat. Next to Cooper's side was a pair of dirt-worn drumsticks and a collection of soiled letters. He said the letters were from the Notre Dame giants who had ridden in his cab — Digger Phelps and Dan Devine, Gerry Faust, Father Joyce and Father Hesburgh. "I got a letter from Father Hesburgh!" he cried happily. "*Nobody* gets a letter from Hesburgh!"

At a red light on Fifth Avenue, he grabbed up his drumsticks and began beating a tune on the steering wheel. He said he used these very sticks to play the drums at a Notre Dame pep rally one year after the word got around "what a Notre Dame nut I am." He said people told him "it was the greatest pep rally Notre Dame ever had."

"I never graduated high school, you know?" Dave Cooper said, twisting around to face me. "But Notre Dame, it's in my heart. My for-tay in life is being the greatest Notre Dame fan. What can I say? I never go outside the house without I got a Notre Dame sweater or a jacket or a cap. My interest has grown so big, you know?"

I asked if he could trace this ascent into nutland. "I saw my first game in 1946. I snuck in Yankee Stadium. I live and sleep Notre Dame ever since that day. It is so great, Notre Dame. Finally, in 1967, a guy in my cab had some tickets to the Michigan State game. I drove my cab all the way to South Bend, sixteen hundred miles. What a thrill!

"Now," said Dave Cooper, "I put aside ten bucks a day for my Notre Dame fund. I try to go every year. I drove to the Purdue game and the Navy game. I go to basketball games. It costs me about five grand a year to be a Notre Dame fan."

Blind love, unremitting and unreasonable? I was not so

sure. If Dave Cooper loved Notre Dame so much, and felt so wonderfully appreciated in return, was it not possible that Notre Dame merited his love? It was not as if he were the only one. I had met others who were smitten, and I had seen the same light in their eyes.

It was about that time that I received a challenge I could not refuse. The challenge came by mail, from a valued friend who over the years had favored me with a sporadic correspondence, mainly in the form of gentle but well-aimed critiques on things I had written. This time, apparently, I had gone too far.

He said he had read the things I had done on the recurring failures of intercollegiate sport. Failures to curb the big-money madness. Failures to relieve the pressures which in turn had led to the cheating and the gratuitous violence. And most culpable of all, to the scandalous academic derelictions.

Although granting that such stories call attention to "inexcusable acts," he said he thought it too negative a portrayal, one that would only rally the cynics. Intercollegiate sport had more than its share of those as it was. There was, indeed, another, cleaner side, he said, and he was living it every day. He wrote, "As I read [your words], I say to myself, 'Not the slightest tinge of this scenario is applicable to Notre Dame. It simply doesn't describe the athletic picture as I know it."

Then, taking both sides of a lively little morality skit, he asked rhetorically if Notre Dame might be unique in the high values and integrity it demanded of its athletic program. "I trust not," he answered. He encouraged an appraisal, promising "full access" to records and personnel, and reminded me (unnecessarily) that this was not a self-serving suggestion, that, after all, Notre Dame really didn't need any more publicity. But he thought some good could come from it because college administrators were more troubled than ever that the system might be chronically flawed.

He polished off the challenge with best wishes, and signed it, "Edmund P. Joyce, C.S.C., Executive Vice President."

The letter sat around for some time, but not passively. Like raw dough rising under a baker's towel, it expanded in my interest even as the system's breakdowns made their ugly marks in increasing number on the nation's sports pages and, belatedly, the network television screens.

Shortly after that, I was in the company of a coaching friend, Lee Corso, who I happened to know once lusted for a football job at Notre Dame. A tyrannical pragmatism cured Corso of that itch (needing to eat, he took a job elsewhere and had become the head coach at Indiana), but he was in the general area and I dropped by. I asked him if he thought there were things to "learn" from Notre Dame. That if, in its success in football and resultant rise to almost equal status in academics, there were patterns to be found and followed.

Corso is a combustible conversationalist. When he is into a subject he stomps around and waves his arms. Immediately he was into the verbal equivalent of high gear. "Learn? What's to learn?" he shouted. "That's Utopia! You can't even *compare* Notre Dame with us. Some of us try to run a first-class program within the rules. Some of us succeed, some don't. Notre Dame doesn't worry about it because it doesn't *have* to cheat. Father Joyce brags about not allowing transfer students or junior-college graduates into Notre Dame, and not redshirting players. Notre Dame doesn't *need* to do those things, you get the picture?"

He paused to allow the picture to be gotten.

"Notre Dame doesn't recruit, Notre Dame gathers," he said. "We have to go into the streets. You say 'Notre

Dame' to a high-school football player and it's like saying
'free lunch' to a starving man. Notre Dame could have as
high an academic standard as it wants and it would be the
same. Notre Dame opens its arms and half the top players
in the country tell you they've been *dreaming* about going
there since they were little kids. Nobody tells you they've
been *dreaming* about going to Louisville or to Memphis
State.

"Whata you learn from a place where a coach loses
twelve games in thirteen years? You wanta know that?
Okay. One, tradition. Notre Dame has fantastic tradition.
Two, it has Rockne. He's dead, but he'll live forever. I
just saw his movie again. I cried again. Twelve losses in
thirteen years! Three, it has a great common denominator:
Catholicism. Four, it has a great fight song. Five, it has a
golden dome that blinds you to the fact that in the winter
the campus looks like a penitentiary. But number one it
has great tradition, and you can't get that anymore because college presidents fire you if you don't win, and the
program has to start all over again every time that happens."

(Not long after this conversation, Corso himself was
fired by his president at Indiana. The new coach, starting
over, was Indiana's sixth coach in twenty years. *Sic transit
gloria.*)

"Educationally, I think Notre Dame is overrated," Corso
said, slumping onto a nearby couch. "But for overall pres-
tige in academics *and* athletics, it's in a class by itself. I
think it's great that intercollegiate sport has an example
like Notre Dame. But it's not the real world. It's Utopia."

In time, I took Father Joyce up on his invitation. I was
granted the courtesies he had promised. I have now seen
Notre Dame from all sides, or as much of it as I thought
I needed to see. Prejudices aside, I can assure you that
Joyce's chauvinism is honestly derived at, if not com-

pletely accurate. But neither is Corso's vision of Shangri-La.

Notre Dame *is* special, *but* it is no more the typical American college engaged in big-time sport than Paris is typical of France. And Notre Dame *can* tell us a lot about how to get from Here to There without breaking all the rules, but the message is not nearly as complicated as we would like to believe.

Notre Dame does, indeed, have great football tradition, but other schools have strong traditions. There is no doubt that emerging O. J. Simpsons all over Southern California dream of playing tailback for USC. Like Notre Dame, Southern Cal doesn't "have" to cheat, but it does. Since 1956, the Trojans have been on NCAA probation three times.

Notre Dame had the nonpareil coach of football's emerging years, Rockne, but Alabama had Frank Thomas and Bear Bryant, and Penn State had Joe Paterno. Notre Dame trades handsomely on its Catholicism, but Nebraska and Oklahoma and Texas and a lot of other schools have the religion of statewide football obsessions going for them. In sum, Notre Dame may have more of an encompassing mystique than any other football school, but its lead is nowhere near what a lot of its rivals would have you believe.

Rather, Notre Dame's success in blending big-time football — and basketball — with integrity may be just as easily rooted in far less cosmic factors, factors that other universities *can* copy in one form or another. Joyce himself is the embodiment of perhaps the most significant of these assets: a consistent leadership.

Joyce has been one of Notre Dame's two major influences — the other, of course, being the school's redoubtable president, Father Theodore M. Hesburgh, C.S.C. — for an incredibly long time. Every man or woman hired to a key position at Notre Dame for the last thirty years has been hired by Joyce or Hesburgh — they have been in charge that long. In the harsh realm of higher education, where leaders burn out quickly, or get routed, no other institution has been granted such a golden consistency. None comes close. The national average for time in rank for college presidents is less than seven years.

But when you are intimately tied for so long to an almost mystical quest for glory, as Notre Dame's leaders have been, the achievement tends to dull out what essentially is a painstaking process. A kind of euphoria clouds the view. The abuses of the past (the blatant mixing of faith and football that characterized the early days; the un- seemly acts of expediency that — even at Notre Dame — included firing coaches who fell short of being sublime) are not really sins at all but errors set in motion by cir- cumstances.

The tall, graying, icy-eyed Joyce comes across as a solid and caring administrator, comfortable in his role as a highly visible second banana to Hesburgh. For three decades he has played archconservative to Hesburgh's flamboyant, freewheeling liberalism. "It's Father Joyce," says one of- ficer in the administration, "who keeps Hesburgh from bankrupting the place."

Working companions for thirty-three years with "never a cross word" between them (according to Hesburgh), they make a handsome pair of mitered bookends, and in keeping the monster of Notre Dame football both healthy and under control, they perform a marvelous balancing act. Fiscally, they accommodate to its thundering success even as they keep a tight rein. Philosophically, they accept football's clout as a kind of astral benefit, like a prevailing wind, and refuse to be embarrassed or intimidated by it, although Hesburgh went through an early period of "put- ting it in its place."

At his first off-campus press conference as president, in 1952, Hesburgh was asked to hike his cassock and crouch over a football for photographers. "Would you ask the president of Yale to do that?" Hesburgh replied tartly. He still revels in his in-house victories over Coach Frank Leahy on strict interpretation of eligibility standards that helped establish his power base in the 1950s.

"Intercollegiate athletics are important in the life of an institution, but not *all* important," Hesburgh said at the Notre Dame football banquet in 1982, commemorating, ironically, the Irish's first losing season in nineteen years. He once wrote in *Sports Illustrated* that those who "favor intercollegiate athletics praise them out of all proportion to their merits," but those who deny them "are quite blind to the values" they possess. He told me he would not want to be at a university that did not participate in major competitive sports, as long as those sports were honest.

He said he had compressed his priorities into a two-minute speech he gives new coaches: "The one I gave Gerry Faust is the same one I gave Ara and Digger Phelps and Dan Devine. 'You've got five years. We won't say boo to you if you lose. I think you'll have the tools here to win more than you lose, it seems to work that way, but if you don't you won't hear from me. You *will* hear from me if you cheat. If you cheat, you'll be out of here before midnight.' "

Joyce defends the same hallowed ground in his own speeches and writings. I once heard him wish for the *other* team to win on a Saturday afternoon. He said a victory for that particular underdog "would help their program more than a loss would hurt ours. We've won more than our share." His compassion, he said, usually dissolves with the kickoff, but he "honestly applauded" Georgia's National Championship victory over the Irish in the 1981 Sugar Bowl.

Both men regularly reaffirm their faith that Notre Dame exists not to provide the civilized world with first-rate football teams, but with a place to go for a first-rate Catholic education. The football teams just happen to make it a more attractive place to go. That's what they say. I do not doubt they believe it.

But it is instructive to point out, if only to give schools that run afoul of the rules proof that fanaticism can raise its ugly head in the best of circles, that in the 1920s the late John Francis O'Hara proclaimed Notre Dame football to be "a new crusade" that "kills prejudice and stimulates faith," and blatantly promoted that identification on and off campus. Father O'Hara's letters as president to students and alumni attributed the brilliance of the Four Horsemen and other Irish heroes to "clean living and faith in the sacraments." He encouraged prayer for the team's crusades against Army and other Eastern infidels, and hinted that Mass was a good place to rub elbows with the "grid graph" heroes.

Such extremism may not be cool today, but it is part of the legacy that helps explain Notre Dame. It cannot be severed from the character of the place any more than a man's genes can reject the traces of his grandparents. A Notre Dame faculty member once correlated fifty years of Irish football scores with communion attendance.

And it wasn't *that* long ago that the poor coaches who followed Rockne and Frank Leahy in the royal line that led to Ara Parseghian felt the wrath of the administration and wound up out of a job, just like coaches do at other places when they lose. No matter how beloved their memories, it was no less true of Rockne and Leahy that they spawned academic suspicion at Notre Dame. When they were gone, or going, their detractors moved in hard, and took as much air out of the football as they dared. Their successors had little chance of succeeding. When they didn't, they were doomed.

The difference is that at Notre Dame the taste for a manageable mediocrity has never been a lasting one, at least not in football (other Notre Dame sports are allowed to be mediocre, for reasons I will get to). Losing was only palatable with the reformers when it did not happen too often. But Hunk Anderson (1931–1933), who succeeded Rockne, and Terry Brennan (1954–1958), who followed Leahy, were sacrificed just as surely as they would have been at LSU or Iowa or Texas A&M.

The late Joe Kuharich, who followed Brennan, was given plenty of time to erect his own gallows (as the only losing coach in Notre Dame history), but cheated the noose by resigning. It is all but forgotten now that effigies were burned on Kuharich's lawn in South Bend (his birthplace, incidentally) and his dog was shot and his aged parents harassed. I visited him that last season and was told those things. Kuharich had the slack look of a man eternally put upon. "This insatiable appetite for winning," he said. "It's gotten to be ridiculous." He seemed more bewildered than bitter.

In the Brennan case, it was Hesburgh himself, with Joyce's backing as chairman of the athletic board, who yielded to the dark attraction college administrators seem always to have for firing football coaches.

While bringing Notre Dame into the twentieth century academically, an achievement for which he may well deserve sainthood, Hesburgh had taken on Leahy's victory machine — four national championships and some highly dubious coaching ethics — and by 1953 had cut that eccentric coaching genius down to size with restrictions that, in Leahy's eyes, amounted to deemphasis. Football scholarships were cut from forty to twenty a year, and the football department was made to belly up to strict eligibility rules.

"One afternoon I walked out onto the field and counted only forty-nine players practicing," says Hesburgh. "I went over to Leahy. 'Frank, where are all your men?' He gave me a withering look. 'It's your fault,' he said. 'You're wrecking my team.' Nineteen of his players had been found academically ineligible."

Then, in 1954, Hesburgh helped ease the ailing Leahy, only forty-five but suffering from ileitis, into retirement. "We made no effort to keep him," Joyce admits now. Four years later, Hesburgh had to scuttle Brennan, his personal choice as Leahy's replacement, when it became obvious that Brennan wasn't going to win enough games under those same restrictions. The impression has been that Brennan was the target of deemphasis at Notre Dame. He was not. Deemphasis was already in place.

I met with Brennan in Chicago, where he is now a stockbroker. He recalled an airplane ride with Hesburgh in 1957. Scholarships had been made scarce, and Notre Dame had begun using the College Boards out of Princeton as an entrance criterion.

"We were on the plane and I said, 'Father, you're killing me.' I told him with the boards scores not coming in until April, recruiting marginal kids was impossible. He acted sympathetic, but he didn't change anything. I don't think he intentionally meant to downgrade football [Notre Dame has never admitted deemphasizing], but it had the same effect. He realized his mistake later, but it was too late for me."

Hesburgh and Joyce made Brennan a martyr the likes of which college football has seldom seen. Brennan became more popular *after* his dismissal. It was a bonehead play so roundly rebuked by Notre Dame loyalists that to this day Hesburgh shakes his head at the flak he took. Recalls one Notre Dame alumnus who has been close to the program for forty years: "Fund-raisers were not mad, they were furious."

It is not likely that Hesburgh would make such a mistake again. For one thing, he is too alert to fiscal needs. Notre Dame's endowment was $8.5 million in 1952; it is now over $200 million and in the top twenty nationally. For another, he has a keener appreciation for coaching needs. But he *did* make that one. And it wasn't that long ago.

In recent years, Hesburgh and Joyce have been outspoken critics of those abuses that have fouled the nest of college sport. Hesburgh even threatened to quit scheduling schools that did not maintain comparable academic standards. There is risk in this kind of crusading, knowing as both men do that to paint *any* school playing big-time college sports as beyond reproach is as foolish as trying to paint a moving car. But if you accept the premise that Notre Dame has evolved into something that is good, then certain facts are, indeed, significant.

For example: a private survey made by the National Football League showed that of the thirty-one ex–Notre Damers then playing in the NFL, thirty had their degrees. When he passed on the survey to me, Joyce said that the thirty-first, New York Giant tackle Dave Weston, not wanting to be the lone ranger, had returned to school that very summer to get his. If taken only at face value, thirty of thirty-one NFL players with degrees from *any* college is extraordinary. Only Penn State (thirty-five of thirty-seven) comes close.

The ratio of graduates to nongraduates in the NFL as a whole was a woeful one-in-three when precise counts were discontinued, probably because they shamed too many schools that supposedly took their academics seriously.

UCLA, for example, had twenty-eight players in the NFL at the time, and only five had graduated. Oklahoma had thirty-two, only seven with degrees.

In the eighteen years that Mike De Cicco, the Notre Dame athletic department's liaison with academe who doubles as the Irish fencing coach, has kept such records, only five Notre Dame football players have completed their eligibility without getting their degrees. Since 1971, all forty-one basketball players who have completed their eligibility have their degrees. Every single one.

Moreover, it must be noted that Notre Dame does not offer a "life science" major, or any other apparent means of shielding an athlete from the rigors of scholarship. All schools have a few professors who grade athletes with affection — like the beloved "88 O'Grady" who taught psychology in South Bend from 1926 to 1956 — but there is no such thing as a "jock curriculum" at Notre Dame.

At Notre Dame, a passing grade for all students except scholarship athletes is 70. Athletes must make 77. One bleak winter day Hesburgh happened onto an eligibility list that showed two first-string basketball players below that mark. He put in a phone call to Moose Krause, then the athletic director. "Gee, Father," said Krause, "the team is leaving for the Kentucky game today. They'll be murdered without those two players. If you sent me word by regular mail the way you usually do, I wouldn't get it until Monday morning." Hesburgh said, "Moose, you've got the word now." The two players stayed home. The team got murdered.

There's no athletic dormitory at Notre Dame, either. Notre Dame doesn't believe in segregating athletes. There is no special training table, except during the season of an athlete's sport when he has no choice but to dine late (after practice). Even then he eats the same food as everybody else, in one of the two campus dining halls. The athlete, in sum, benefits from having lived a "complete" college experience, rather than tunneling through a narrow corridor to the pros.

Seventy-five percent of the scholarship athletes in football and basketball are liberal arts or business majors; the other twenty-five percent divide into engineering, pre-med and pre-law. They, like other students involved in extra-curricular activities, are granted one privilege in their academics: a priority in arranging their class schedules so that they can be free by 3 P.M. to practice. But even this isn't always possible, and when laboratories run to 4 or 5 P.M., as they often do, it's the coaches, not the athletes, who must accommodate.

Neither does Notre Dame believe in redshirting (holding players back a year), and allows it only in case of injury, never to "season" a player for later service. It pushes its athletes to graduate in four years. Most do. If one fails or drops a course, he must make it up in summer school. If his grade point average falls below the required 2.0, or if he's lagging in the credits needed (thirty a year) for normal progress toward a degree, same thing — summer school.

The salutary results can be charted: Of the twenty-eight players who were given football scholarships in 1978, twenty-five graduated on time in 1982. Only one dropped out. And there is another benefit to the athletic program under such academic orthodoxy. A subtle bonus. Economics professor William Leahy says the Notre Dame faculty is *"more appreciative"* of its athletes. "They're not privileged characters, and we see it," says Dr. Leahy.

Equally illuminating is Notre Dame's police record with the NCAA. Success naturally attracts debunkers. Great success attracts underminers, trying to bring greatness down. Undermining is tacitly encouraged in the NCAA because its policing process calls for "cooperative enforcement," which means members are encouraged to snitch on each other when rules are believed to be broken.

At last count there were twenty NCAA schools on probation and another thirty or forty under investigation. Since 1952, more than 260 penalties have been meted out. It would seem only natural that with its high profile Notre Dame would get nabbed at one time or another, for one thing or another. And it has. Twice. In 1953, when it was "reprimanded" for illegal tryouts, and in 1971, when it was "reprimanded" for a minor offense involving grant-in-aid forms.

But that's it. Two misdemeanors — "reprimands" are the NCAA equivalant of parking tickets — in sixty-three years of big-time football and basketball. No sanctions (penalties), no lingering stains of dishonor. For a school that attracts so much envy, you would expect it would be defending itself all the time. But nobody points a finger.

The reverse has occurred. Digger Phelps, Notre Dame's basketball coach since 1971, pointed the finger at certain unnamed basketball programs he said were paying star players as much as $10,000 a year under the table. The interesting thing about the charge wasn't that Phelps made it — I have heard him say as much privately for years — but that he aroused no *counter*charges. Not one rival coach was heard to say that Phelps should clean up his own act first. To the contrary. The integrity of Notre Dame's program was never questioned.

But staying clean in an increasingly dirty world is not easy. Over the last couple of decades Hesburgh and Joyce have doggedly avoided the pitfalls that others leap into. For example, Notre Dame does not allow the booster clubs that create so many of the embarrassments (under-the-table payoffs, recruiting scams, etc.). This is not to say that it does not encourage support. It generates millions through the 164 alumni clubs that Hesburgh shamelessly plies for funds. But all the donations go into the university's general fund. No direct influence can be exerted by old grads on the athletic program. Notre Dame alumni clubs are notorious for complaining about Irish football — and consistent in getting nowhere with their complaints.

In athletics, as in anything, there is an endless capacity for self-delusion. When the horror of a bankrupt, amoral education policy first struck intercollegiate sport with the force of a hammer blow two years ago, many administrators were heard to say, "So what's different?" Or, "That'll never happen here." Time proved it *does* happen "here." And there. And almost everywhere. But it does *not* happen at Notre Dame. And that *does* make Notre Dame special.

The winter of Joyce's challenging letter brought a significant change in Notre Dame's athletic family. Joyce hired Gerry Faust from a Catholic high school in Cincinnati to succeed Dan Devine as head football coach, even though Faust had never coached a day at the college level, or ever once had to recruit a college player.

Six months earlier, Joyce had announced that for the first time in Notre Dame history an athletic endowment fund was being established, with a goal of $10 million — to be administered by the office of development, not the athletic department. Joyce cited soaring expenses that had cut the "advantage" football and basketball revenues traditionally gained, as well as the need to expand the athletic program for women. Revenues were at an all-time high ($4.3 million) but expenditures were so large that the net had been only $29,000. By contrast, over a fifty-year period from Rockne's day to 1980, Notre Dame's athletic department showed an average profit of $250,000 a year.

It was easy to make a Katzenjammer connection between the two events — the hiring of a virtual novice to run the vital football program, and the athletic department's shrinking financial cushion. A lapse in good business sense uncommon at Notre Dame. Was it?

What well may be *the* essential ingredient in its rise to glory is Notre Dame's keen eye for business. The power of the profits has neven been lost there. It is a pragmatism that comes directly from Rockne, and is best illustrated by one salient example: In Depression-wracked 1930, when the entire nation seemed on the verge of tumbling down, Notre Dame was *building*. It was building two dormitories, the law school, the engineering school, the commerce building, and the new football stadium.

The Irish were a box-office smash, year after year. And always the profits were pumped back into the general fund. After financing the rest of the athletic program, Rockne's undefeated 1930 team *netted* $689,000. In 1930, you could rebuild a small country for $689,000. Says Francis Jones, class of '29, a South Bend attorney and intimate of his alma mater's administrators and athletes: "Notre Dame has *never* had a depression."

That being the case, what did the hiring of a high-school coach at this critical fiscal juncture represent? One editorialist (no Pollyanna) suggested that it amounted to bringing in a local car dealer to run General Motors.

After a 5–6 season, his first, even Faust was hard put to disagree. He was weeks getting over his disappointment, so beset with doubts and guilt that he moped around the campus like a condemned man. Publicist Roger Valdiserri said he had to chuck Faust under the chin to get him to take his eyes off his shoetops. "I felt like I'd let so many people down," Faust said.

By itself this is not so unusual. Notre Dame coaches have, since Rockne, always felt a grinding pressure. Even the best are subjected. Leahy and Parseghian were basket cases by the end of their careers, although in recent years it is more a self-inflicted burden because the tolerance level of Hesburgh and Joyce grew in direct proportion to their own stature as leaders.

True to his two-minute speech, Hesburgh sent Faust letters of encouragement. One read: "Dear Gerry. Don't get discouraged. Out of adversity comes character, courage, new resolve and, in the end, victory. Devotedly in Notre Dame . . ." Digger Phelps, suffering *his* first losing season, got the same kind of encouragement that winter. Hesburgh thanked Phelps for helping to make Notre Dame a "special" place.

But it struck me that there were other, better ways to look at the chance taken in hiring Faust. One, that it was a gamble not all that inconsistent with the Joyce–Hesburgh rule.

Notre Dame does not subsidize failure, but selecting a football coach is not an exact science. The "commitment to excellence" Hesburgh proclaimed when he hired Kuharich resulted in a descent into mediocrity that was unprecedented. For four years under Kuharich, the juggernaut limped along in the inside lane, losing more often than it won.

Parseghian turned out to be the *beau ideal* of all Notre Dame coaches, but his prior coaching success was limited to several above-average seasons at Northwestern. He was no sure thing.

To this day neither Joyce nor Hesburgh admit to understanding why Dan Devine (1975–1980) was not beloved by Irish faithful. He arrived in South Bend with a distinguished record, and he gave the fans good teams and even a national championship. When he could no longer handle alumni charges that he somehow "didn't fit," Devine quit. He would not have been fired.

Any coaching job carries within itself the seeds of an

abrupt termination, but there was absolutely no movement after that 5–6 year toward curtailing Faust's employment at Notre Dame. The jury of public opinion may
still be out (the Irish were a disappointing 6–5 in 1983),
but Joyce and Hesburgh do not answer to juries. Or alumni clubs. Or anybody else.

Which brings us to the second, or more idealistic, way
of looking at it: that hiring Faust represented a kind of
Dei gratia stand for righteousness — for selecting on the
basis of integrity — at Notre Dame, and never mind the
business risk.

Faust was more than just a successful high-school coach.
He was a devout, stand-up Catholic who made lasting
positive impressions on his players. "We have a short
motto," said Joyce. " 'What's good for the boy is good
for Notre Dame.' I think Gerry Faust will be good for the
boys."

In effect, the Faust hiring made Notre Dame's actions
speak as loudly as its words. This was not always the case.
A South Bend man who was close to Leahy remembers
his installation in 1941: "Leahy asked Father So-and-so,
'What do they want?' Father So-and-so said, 'They want
to win, and they don't care how.' "

Certainly the hiring of Faust was more in line with what
Notre Dame now perceives itself to be, and that is almost
as important as what it is. To be good, you must aspire
to goodness. It does not come naturally.

In answering Joyce's challenge, I heard many voices,
giving many impressions of Notre Dame. Not all the voices
were admiring ones.

One rival coach rebuked Notre Dame's "bullying" ways,
especially at Notre Dame Stadium, and the "smugness"
of its leadership in not taking "certain types of athletes."

O. J. Simpson, he said, was a "type" Notre Dame would not have taken, being a junior-college transfer.

Even some of those who were intimately connected did not necessarily feel sanctified. Alan Page, All-America on the 1966 team, said that the place "never had a mythical effect on me." Allen Sacks, a reserve end on the 1966 team, said for him college football was like "working in a sweat shop," and he found the "intellectual and human needs" of committed young athletes "often sacrificed to the commercial aspects" of "fueling a winning team." Sacks is now a sociology professor at the University of New Haven.

But in a vast accumulation of viewpoints, I found that the majority of those who played there have an unusual affection for Notre Dame, even more deeply felt than I would have imagined. A devotion to Notre Dame *beyond* its Catholicism. Its coaches indicated a similar appreciation, but another thing, too — a staggering awe of the pressures that mashed in on them there. The dark side of Utopia.

I sat at lunch with Parseghian in downtown South Bend, from where he now captains a far-flung business enterprise. He talked of being "a victim of success" at Notre Dame.

He was tanned and looking fit after five years away from a job that has been called, with an ironic appositeness, "the chair." I remembered an earlier time when he was hollow-eyed and ashen, and someone said that starting out on the job at forty, he looked thirty and acted twenty, but at fifty, ten years later, he looked sixty and acted seventy.

"Everything is so far out of proportion to the normal," Parseghian said. "At my first pep rally, I thought, 'My God, I've never seen anything like this.' They introduced me at a basketball game. I thought they'd never stop cheering."

After a while, he said, "You become fearful of letting people down. Two losses is a catastrophe at Notre Dame. In 1966, we won the national championship, but we had to rally to tie Michigan State late in the season. Father Joyce and Father Hesburgh were always supportive, but the complaints poured in. Letters, phone calls, *stories*. People called me 'gutless.' They said I played for a tie. They didn't know what they were talking about, but I was shocked."

He quit, Parseghian said, when he realized there was nothing else to gain by coaching. His Notre Dame teams had gone undefeated, won championships, gone to bowl games, and he felt his job was safe — but he was a physical and psychological wreck. "I got so I was snapping at people. 'How you feeling, Ara?' 'What the hell you asking me that for?' There's no place to hide. I was in Harrod's Department Store in London. A guy came up and wanted to know what kind of season we were going to have."

Hesburgh told me how the pressures battered Frank Leahy. The morning after a 37–0 loss to Michigan State in 1953, he, Hesburgh, "went over to Frank's house in Michigan City to have breakfast. His wife said he was up in his room and wouldn't come down. 'You've wasted a trip, Father,' she said.

"I went upstairs anyway and knocked on the door, and when I didn't get an answer I walked on in. The curtains were drawn, but I could see his silhouette, curled up in the bed. I opened the curtains wide and I went over and shook him. 'Frank?' 'Go away,' he said. 'Look, Frank,' I said. 'The sun came up after all. It's going to be a nice day. The earth didn't stop turning because Notre Dame lost a football game.' "

Hesburgh laughed when he told the story; it had, after all, depicted the teller as an apostle of reason to a confused man. But he knew it was no laughing matter.

By contrast, among ex-players I found very little residue of pressures *they* must have felt. Few talked about being pressured at all; most claimed they never were, certainly not on the ever-amiable Notre Dame campus ("Win or lose, everybody still said 'hello' on Monday mornings," one recalled, "and we lost eight games that year.") They seemed to understand Notre Dame better than the coaches.

Johnny Lujack quarterbacked the national championship teams of 1946 and 1947. He now owns a Chevrolet dealership in Davenport, Iowa. He remembered his first time on the Notre Dame campus, as a high-school senior. "I got to meet the coach [Leahy], to see the Notre Dame team, to be in the locker room after the game. Everything was the way I'd imagined it. Hell, if God had taken me then, I'd have thought I'd had a full life, and I was seventeen years old."

Those whose experience was more recent seemed to see Notre Dame in broader measure, as if in reflection of the greater breadth Hesburgh had brought to virtually all aspects of the university. Michael Oriard, a walk-on (non-scholarship player) who captained the 1969 team, recalled almost defiantly that if a lab was ever in conflict with football practice, "there was never any question which you'd attend. You went to the lab." In his senior year, he was excused from two days of practice before a bowl game so that he could interview for a Rhodes Scholarship.

For others, the experience was richer in more spiritual ways. Jim Lynch captained Parseghian's 1966 championship team. He went on to be an All-Pro linebacker and play ten years for the Kansas City Chiefs, but he said "nothing that ever happened to me in football after Notre

Dame was as important as that captaincy." He said he
"never really enjoyed football as much again." It was, he
said, "the spirit of the place" that got him.

From contemporary players, there was the unmistakable pride in being honorable at a time when honor seems
to be in short supply.

At the Morris Inn, I dined with two articulate black
football players. Rod Bone and Dave Duherson were
brought to me, I suspect, as proof that Notre Dame did
not bow to the academic expediencies of the times. Set
up or not, I was impressed.

Both had been actively recruited. Duherson said one
recruiter in the South told him, "When you take a test
here all you have to do is put your jersey number on top
of the paper." He said the suggestion turned him off. "I
had a 3.75 average in high school. I didn't need any free
passes." He said another school offered him a race horse,
and his choice of a car in "either or both" of the school
colors.

Bone said what annoyed him most was that "the first
place they always took me was the football stadium. I'm
studying electrical engineering. At the other schools, I
never saw the inside of the engineering building. At Notre
Dame, it was the first building I was taken to. I didn't see
the inside of the stadium until my first game."

What these statements of devotion, especially those of
the more recent players, say is that the Notre Dame experience is enhanced by the way football is imbedded into
the very marrow of university life. The larger truth is
tougher to say, but needs to be said nonetheless. It may,
in fact, be the most important thing *to* say:

That Notre Dame would never have made it without
football. Certainly not to where it is today.

The years now describe the university as a venerable

institution, but greater age will not undo that connection. The school is as linked to the game as a man's hand is to his wrist. I think that the majority of those who have to deal with it on a regular basis accept this as a positive. It is not a matter of survival, it is a matter of enrichment. Football has enriched Notre Dame, and continues to do so.

The notion that without football's broad appeal Notre Dame would have grown like other major Catholic universities is a charitable fiction. Catholic education in this country gained its major footholds only around the hives of major urban centers (Marquette in Milwaukee, Georgetown in Washington, Fordham in New York, etc.). Notre Dame was planted in the middle of the Indiana bush 140 years ago by a twenty-eight-year-old priest, the Reverend Edward Sorin, with a cleric loan of $300 to divine a college out of three log cabins. Catholicism was its only sustainer, and though it might easily have survived the years, it would more likely have survived to be another Iona or another St. Joseph's at Rensselaer.

If it is important, therefore, to accept football's part in Notre Dame's life, does doing so not admit that Notre Dame is, after all, a "football factory"? Of course it does. Notre Dame is a place not only where football is played well, but where it is exalted. It is also a place where football makes a positive statement: that under control, it can stir a university, and make it better.

Football brought Notre Dame to prominence, and then to rewards both educational and financial that were beyond its dreams. If Notre Dame has thus benefited from football, it is not only wrong to deny the credit, it is hypocrisy. In a recent banquet speech, Father Hesburgh said that football was "a game, no more, no less." That might be true at Wabash, but it is not true at Notre Dame, and he knew better.

If it were true, I wonder if Hesburgh himself would have been seen running down from the press box to lead the Irish in a victory celebration when they rallied from a twenty-two-point deficit to beat Houston in the Cotton Bowl a few years ago. I doubt it.

According to the most popular myth about Notre Dame, it "got that way," as a kind of national *objet d'art*, because of the unique blending of three factors, number one being the fortuitous arrival on the South Bend campus of a balding little Norwegian immigrant who coached football the way it had never been coached before. That Knute Rockne parlayed football's growing popularity with (2) the passion of American Catholics for anything Catholic, and (3) the pride of the underdog Irish for any Irish achievement at a time in this country when "Irish need not apply" was a real prejudice of the inner-cities, is not denied here. But it is only half the truth.

The deciding factor in the nationalizing of Notre Dame was Rockne's early grasp of a fundamental tenet in sports promotion: that it is better to draw seventy-five thousand paying customers in "neutral" Yankee Stadium than it is to draw eight thousand in a two-thirds-empty arena in South Bend. Notre Dame football has been an export industry ever since Rockne took his 1923 team to Ebbets Field in Brooklyn to play Army and sold out the joint at thirty thousand customers. A light dawned. The little giant-killer from the Midwest could make a buck on the road, just as it was a hard sell at home.

The latter is always missed in the equation. Rockne didn't go east because of a vision; he went because there was money to be made there. Only later would Notre Dame try to sell the myth that the Irish teams "outgrew old Cartier Field" (as current Notre Dame brochures contend). It never happened.

Cartier Field (capacity: thirty thousand) never was in

danger of busting at the seams. In George Gipp's last year, 1920, an unbeaten Notre Dame team played four games at home, and not one drew more than twelve thousand fans. In 1930, the Irish sold out at Pittsburgh, at Penn, at Northwestern, at Southern Cal and against Army at Soldiers Field, averaging seventy-five thousand fans for those games. In the brand new Notre Dame Stadium (capacity: fifty-seven thousand), they played five games and averaged less that twenty-two thousand. They did not fill it until 1931.

Now, of course, they sell out regularly wherever they play. They have become so great a draw at home that management has scheduled more and more games there. And one of the new ironies of practical sports merchandizing has come to pass: opponents who do not draw well at home for the Irish are in jeopardy of being told, "Come to Notre Dame, or get off our schedule." Imports now outnumber exports.

The Notre Dame "ethic" — its virile image, its great integrity — is not a constant, sprung from a bygone miracle, like wine divined from water. It is an evolutionary thing, brought about by a gradual lumping up of beneficial factors (good people doing a good job, mainly). Notre Dame is most of all a product of a strong leadership. To overlook that is to regard the mechanism without praising the mechanics. Notre Dame's special quality is not a superior morality, it is a superior and deeply involved leadership.

For thirty-one years, that leadership has been Hesburgh and Joyce. Notre Dame lives on the hairy edge of overemphasis in sport because these two extraordinary men understand the power and the pitfalls, and do not grow pale when there is a crisis. The integrity of Notre Dame is a reflection of the two.

Hesburgh, of course, is the more spectacular. He has been called "the most powerful priest in America" by the *Manchester Guardian*. He has advised six presidents, and been a United Nations delegate. He has been the architect of Notre Dame's liberalization, from its more lenient conduct code (it used to be said that it was "easier to fornicate under the golden dome than it was to drink beer there"; now both are possible) to its more ecumenical makeup.

When it comes to Notre Dame athletics, however, Joyce is the more influential. This is due in part to Hesburgh's trust in him; it is also because Joyce is so capable. Joyce believes their working agreement is a model of good athletic administration because (1) he has immediate access to the president, and (2) the athletic director and the coaches and staff have immediate access to him.

There is little room for bitter inner conflicts at Notre Dame, or back-street conspiracies. The procedure is too clearcut, and arbitrary. Hesburgh and Joyce set the standards, lay down the rules. Says Hesburgh: "No coach can ever say he was not aware of our policies." Joyce, in turn, "constantly reminds people that integrity is our top priority here. I do that personally, not through an intermediary."

At sixty-four, Joyce is Hesburgh's senior by one year. He matriculated to Notre Dame at age sixteen and graduated *magna cum laude* at twenty, and he cannot remember a time when Notre Dame was not his passion. He shed boyish tears in Spartenburg, South Carolina, when Rockne's plane went down. He told me his one great disappointment in life was that he had never earned a varsity letter. When he retires, the Athletic and Convocation Center, built in 1975 for $8.5 million, will be renamed in his honor.

"Many schools fail in athletics because of a lack of control at the top," Joyce said. "We will never have that here."

Like all human institutions, Notre Dame is not "pure" and never has been. It is not above reproach and never has been. But it strives mightily for those things, and emits from afar a glow of high purpose that does not lose as much color up close as skeptics would like to believe. The heart of the matter is that Notre Dame is proud to be righteous, and this creates a perpetuating kind of morality.

Like a parent whose character has sparkled, Notre Dame's goodness is now *expected*. In one respect this makes it easier. When you build for yourself a glass house, you watch what you wear to the breakfast table.

Ara Parseghian says that he is "proudest" of the fact that he achieved what he did "without ever cheating. People have a need to idolize, to look up to something. Notre Dame provides that."

Notre Dame does not cheat. There is no evidence that it does, anyway, and the prospect of having the top man intervene if it did is surely a reason for not being tempted. Some years ago Hesburgh heard a rumor that a football recruit's mother had been given a fat check by an alumnus. He called in athletic director Krause. "If I don't have that check in my hands torn up by tomorrow noon," he said, "the boy will never graduate from Notre Dame." Krause saw to it.

Joyce rides especially hard on academic matters. He gets monthly progress reports from De Cicco, who gets them from deans and professors. Admissions are gone over with a fine-tooth comb. Notre Dame requires an incoming freshman athlete to score at least 900 on his SATs (200 points higher than the new NCAA standard that has raised such a fuss), rate in the top third of his high-school graduating class, and be credited with sixteen units of English, language, social studies, science and math at a minimum 2.0 average.

There are no special admissions, and Notre Dame does

not take junior-college or transfer athletes. It does not want to appear to be in the business of "prepping" players for pro football or basketball. Neither does it want to risk trusting the entrance criteria or progress standards of other institutions. Circumstances can warrant exceptions, but they are rare.

It would be naïve to believe, however, that Notre Dame does not make academic allowances when competing for top athletes. The halfback who can run a 4.4 40 or the quarterback who can throw a sixty-yard spiral into a water bucket might get in with fourteen credits or a combined SAT of 850 or a "predicted" GPA of 2.0 (the NCAA's minimum), "but never a combination of the three," De Cicco told me. Willie Fry, a defensive end (class of '78), came in with only two years of math, but high grades in other subjects made him a worthwhile risk, and he graduated on schedule.

Halfback Jerome Heavens (class of '79) raised eyebrows at Notre Dame when he was accepted there. His average was barely over 2.0, and he generally didn't have "the numbers" in other areas. In such instances, Notre Dame tries hardest of all. "In Heavens's case, we went on red alert," De Cicco said. "We had him tutored in English, math and science, and we kept waiting for the other shoe to drop. He majored in economics and graduated in three and a half years."

Blacks have remained a small minority on the campus — less than five percent of the student body. "It is something we would like to change, and are trying to, but the requirements make it difficult," says Joyce. Those black athletes who matriculated have, on a whole, done very well. Dick Arrington (class of '63) became commissioner of licenses in Boston. Wayne Edmunds (class of '56), Notre Dame's first black football player, became an administrator with the state of Pennsylvania. The university's first black basketball player, Joe Bertrand, became treasurer of the city of Chicago. And so forth.

Currently, the football team is about twenty-five percent black, the basketball team a little more than half. Those are high percentages for Notre Dame because it will not compromise its entrance standards. The plus side is that the blacks who come in know they will have academic credibility. The minus is that more would be there if they were better prepared. One thing is certain: you would have a hell of a time making a case of black exploitation at Notre Dame. And that *is* exemplary.

Notre Dame has been blessed by many things, but more than anything else it has been blessed by three extraordinary football coaches: Rockne, Leahy, and Parseghian. Rockne's substance bled into Leahy, and Leahy's into Parseghian to create an almost uninterrupted line of sterling leadership.

That's the portrayal anyway. By the Hesburgh–Joyce standards, however, only Parseghian would hold up as sterling today. The ultimate irony of Notre Dame coaching is this: a Protestant, Armenian, Miami of Ohio graduate epitomized all the things Notre Dame coaches are supposed to stand for. The others do not measure up to Parseghian.

Rockne was a football original. He was a brilliant coach, a spellbinding orator, and an entrepreneurial genius. Notre Dame was lucky he came along. But he was also a shameless huckster who played loose with the truth, and there is more than casual evidence that his dedication to the academic side of his players' lives was less than rigorous.

In recollecting Rockne's inspirational talks, former players are hard put to remember whether the "sick kid in the hospital" they beat Army for was really sick, or whether he existed at all. Rockne brought in transfers from other schools, and players with poor grades, and conducted mass tryouts. His greatest player, the immortal Gipp, was a notorious truant, as well as a card and pool shark.

It was said that if Gipp ever wore holes in the knees of his pants it was not from praying, but from rolling dice. At age twenty-five, when he died, he was still an undergraduate. Says Jim Crowley, one of the surviving Four Horsemen: "Rock wanted us to go to class, but he didn't make a big deal out of it."

Frank Leahy had the Irish good looks of a movie idol. He was a man capable of smooth, impassioned speeches, and a football coach of tactical brilliance. He was also a practice field martinet who, one ex-player told me, would croon, "Oh, lads, what a beautiful day for football," and "then put us through the goddamndest workouts you ever saw." Obsessed with winning, Leahy slept in a nearby firehall instead of going home at night, and worried himself sick over teams the Irish would crush by forty points.

Leahy brought more than a casual shame to old Notre Dame with his devious on-field tactics. His sucker shifts and fake injury plays so enraged Big Ten coaches they threatened to quit playing the Irish. In one game three Notre Dame players went down at the same time, faking injury to kill the clock. It looked like a battle scene from Warner Brothers.

Parseghian was Hesburgh and Joyce's triumph, a spotless definition of what a college coach should be. There is no evidence anywhere that he recruited illegally, or that he pampered or paid his athletes, or that he played loose with the rules. He wasn't even paid like a big-time coach, at least at the start. He came to Notre Dame for $20,000 a year, a $2,000 raise from his salary at Northwestern. He did not ask for or get a car or a house. In the end, of course, he became rich and famous. It could be argued that it was justified all around.

In sum, I think Notre Dame makes that one positive statement we need most to hear right now: that big-time sport and meaningful education are compatible. That a university can compete and still have its athletes graduate in four years, and not be segregated in jock dorms, and not be bribed or hustled to matriculate or paid a penny beyond the costs of their education, which, of course, is priceless.

But as long as Notre Dame's leadership clings to the fable that "football is only a game, no more, no less," it will come up short of being an athletic paragon.

The odor of baloney in that statement is evident in any comparison of treatment afforded Notre Dame's football and basketball programs with that of other varsity sports. Football and basketball get a ton of support and attention, not because they are better character builders or better examples of manliness or anything else.

They get it because they represent money and interest.

And the chance to make more money and get more interest.

You do not concoct a $1.9 million budget for a sport that is "only" a sport. The practical consideration is as important as the idealistic one. As long as this is not acknowledged, the inconsistencies will jump out every time the lid is off.

Jake Kline coached baseball at Notre Dame for so long it seemed as if no one else ever had or ever would. Kline was eighty-two when I met him. He remembered Rockne, and Rockne "threatening to leave regularly with offers to go to Columbia, or some other place, if he didn't get his way."

Kline was gassed in World War I. At Notre Dame afterward, he worked three jobs. He taught math, helped coach football, and coached the baseball team without fanfare for forty-one years. Baseball was his baby, but it "lived on a shoestring." He said he "never got anything extra" until the school named the old baseball field after him in 1970. He said he "could have gone other places, but I was easy to please."

Notre Dame supports eighteen varsity sports. Some it supports a lot less than it does others. There are only four full-time head coaches at Notre Dame: in football, basketball, baseball, and women's basketball (as a concession to Title IX legislation). Other head coaches must perform other duties, the way Kline used to. Of the 150-odd athletes on scholarship, 95 are football players (the NCAA limit) and 13 are basketball players. The other sports divide and subdivide the rest — by giving "partials."

The results speak for themselves. The Notre Dame baseball team had eight losing seasons in the ten-year period from 1971 through 1980. Since 1958, swimming is barely over .500. The tennis team won two NCAA titles, but those came over a sixty-year period and it doesn't do very well anymore. Mike De Cicco's fencing team is a notable exception: with its zero scholarships and tiny budget ($45,000), it has achieved a 369–36 record in twenty-one years.

The rationale is practical and tiresomely familiar: football and basketball make money, the others don't. Phelps's teams have sold out every home game for ten years, and the basketball budget benefits accordingly. Football had expenses of $1,900,000 in 1982, including $339,000 in salaries, $651,000 in grants, $148,000 in travel, and $101,000 in recruiting. It spent $36,000 on film, $19,000 on laundry and $18,000 on long-distance telephone calls. And it made a profit of $577,000.

Joyce says he is sympathetic to the idea that increased support could make other sports do better and perhaps make money, but he is careful not to wait too long for it to happen. Hockey was given more scholarships, and it drew nice crowds. But at the end of that one year of "emphasis," it had lost $123,000, and in 1981 its wings were clipped. It competed in a "bus league," where it did not have to fly to the opposition's rinks. In early 1983 it was dropped to club status.

The undermining of support for the Notre Dame hockey program — with scholarship and budgetary cuts — was tantamount to sabotage. It never had a chance. My own feelings are mixed. Club sports are representative of a student body perhaps better than any others because they draw directly from it. They are also the truest expression of a school's love for sport because it cannot possibly derive a profit from them. By the same token, expending huge sums to upgrade a program (with scholarships, with expensive travel, with new facilities) makes no sense at all if the student body does not support the object of this dole.

Joyce is correct, of course, when he says a university can have a "satisfactory athletic program without it being expensive." He is justifiably proud that Notre Dame also supports twenty-eight intramural sports (including a tackle football league) and eleven club sports. These are never revenue producing. Football's profits cover the expense.

The Notre Dame football team has been on national television more than seventy times. It has been the subject of more than fifty books. Its universal appeal has generated the formation of 168 Notre Dame Alumni Clubs, seventeen overseas. It continues to be the catch-net for the entire Notre Dame athletic program, and the centerpiece of the image that makes Notre Dame's endowment drives so much easier.

The sum of the parts? I am somewhat at a loss to come up with that in any brief form. I do remember a full-page ad from *Time* magazine, circa 1970. Taking up half the ad was a picture of a football. Under the football was a caption: "If that's all you know about Notre Dame, you have a lot to learn." This is clearly the truth.

But the greater truth is that Notre Dame football and Notre Dame academics live in harmony, and if we miss that, we miss the real achievement. In one of my last visits there, I sat in on an economics lecture delivered to a packed classroom by Dr. William Leahy, an eminent academician and an implacable Notre Dame football fan. It was a revelation.

Leahy had advanced into middle-age with the slight paunch and the pained look of a man whose logic has foundered once too often on the rocks of youthful ignorance. He sipped from a paper coffee cup as he lectured, skillfully directing the class through the labyrinth of America's urban mortgage practices. A construction project at full volume outside O'Shaughnessy Hall did not distract him, and if it bothered his students they did not show it. Some leaned forward where they sat.

"In 1930, a conventional mortgage in this country was fifty percent down and the balance in five years," said the professor, pacing. "About the only man around here who could afford that kind of financing was, who — ?"

In the front row, a young scholar with the frantic eyes of a born eager-beaver thrust up his hand.

"Knute Rockne," he cried.

"Correct," said Dr. Leahy. "What was Rockne's record that year?"

"Uh, nine and one."

"Unh-unh. Ten and zero. *And* the national championship."

Leahy sampled from his cup, and screwed up his face as though lime had been squeezed on it. He touched his stomach lightly with the fingertips of his free hand and continued.

"The big break for the American family man with limited savings came in 1935, with the Federal Housing Administration. The FHA loan. What else in particular made 1935 a memorable year?"

In the middle of the classroom, a husky black in a letter sweater answered even as he raised his hand.

"Notre Dame over Ohio State."

"What was the score?"

"Eighteen-thirteen."

"Right," said the professor. "The greatest football game in the first half of the twentieth century."

He winked at the class. They loved it. So, in fact, did I.

Epilogue

Having come to the reasonable conclusion that spectator sport needs saving, a more pragmatic consideration arises: what on earth for? The answer would be that if you've never enjoyed it, you wouldn't be convinced either way. And if you have, you don't need to be.

Not long ago, for reasons not entirely evident, I found myself nagged by the impulse to find out why I had endured as a Detroit Tiger fan all those years. Acting on such an impulse can be a tricky business, like following up on the urge to see an old flame. But I thought it might be necessary, if only to satisfy the curiosity. I do not know how I became a Detroit Tiger fan. I cannot even pinpoint in time the onset of the malady, only that I was quite young and that in the redolent, sizzling-sweet summers of those earliest days, my ball-playing buddies in Miami and Key West worried about catching polio and I worried about catching the Yankees. But none of the obvious reasons apply.

As a boy I never saw the Tigers play, not even on television (an experience that, come to think of it, might have cured me). Newsreels were the closest thing. Neither had I ever been to Detroit. I couldn't have without a financial windfall, living poor and two thousand miles away. Detroit (the city) did not interest me until very recently. In my adulthood I had been to Africa more times than I had been to Detroit. Detroit for me had the aura of a place perpetually on the defensive, like a public service commissioner, and was dominated by labor goons, factories the size of Rhode Island and skies the color of crankcase oil. It was hardly coincidental, I felt, that the last Detroit entry into the World Series (in 1968, when I was out of the country) followed closely on the heels of the last Detroit race riot.

Once, on vacation, I passed into Detroit from Canada, beating my way south, and because I was exhausted stopped at a motel on the edge of the downtown area. The motel billboard promised "free TV" and I went in to check the rates. The proprietor was a burly man in an olive-drab undershirt, which identified him as an army veteran, and a three-day beard, which identified him as an ex-sergeant. He said a double room with free TV cost $15. I asked him how much *without* free TV. He said $12. I figured that to be the Detroit mentality, and asked him how far it was to Akron.

It would be reasonable to think that my interest might have filtered down from someone else's, but it didn't. As a boy I never met a Tiger fan I liked. Or one that I didn't like. I never met a Tiger fan, period. For a very long time, even after I reached the age of reason, I figured I was alone in the world — the only Tiger fan alive outside Detroit itself. This isolation did not trouble me. I accepted it as a fluke, like having one brown eye and one blue one. My closest friends were fans of the Cardinals and the Dodgers, and ran in packs. None of us were Yankee fans, a discrimination I attribute to an unusually high IQ among the group.

I was reminded recently that Tom Selleck, the television detective, wears a navy blue Tiger cap with the familiar Old English D on the peak when he is out and around bashing thugs. The D is distinctive (for decades the only adornment allowed on the Tigers' creamy-white home uniforms) and may be at the root of some of my feelings. When first smitten, at about age ten, I cut with painstaking precision an Old English D from a scrap of white felt and glued it to the peak of my already well-broken-in baseball cap. A team of blacks we played regularly in the projects of Key West saw it and, hearing me called "Johnny" by my teammates, took to calling me "Johnny Groth," after a Detroit outfielder who had ears that stuck out like twin spinnakers.

I wore that hat until the felt disengaged at the edges and the D looked like three earthworms wrestling. I don't know, but I saw Selleck on television the other night and his D looked factory-made to me. Selleck looked factory-made, too. I checked him out and sure enough he was born in Detroit, which, of course, meant he didn't count. Anybody who is born in Detroit *has* to be a Tiger fan. There's nothing else.

Groth was not my hero, as it developed. Hal Newhouser was my hero, and that made about as much sense as any of it. Newhouser had won twenty-nine games in 1944 and pitched the Tigers to a World Series victory over the Cubs in 1945, and then won twenty-six games when all the great players were back from the war in 1946, but I was not aware of that or of him at the time.

My appreciation came later, as I was advancing fitfully toward puberty and the Tigers had the runner-up concession in the American League, finishing consistently behind the gluttonous Yankees. Newhouser was the ace of the staff, a prima donna everybody called "Prince Hal." In the pre–Don Larsen era, he had one of the smoothest pump-handle deliveries you ever saw, and I cursed the luck that made me right-handed. Prince Hal was a lefty. When he pitched against Bob Feller, the Cleveland ace, it was an event.

There was a drugstore at the corner of Duval and South-ard streets in Key West then that had a Western Union sports ticker in the window and an illegal book operation in the back room. In the afternoons I would round up a friend of mine, a tops and marbles expert named Donnie Williams who was exquisitely gifted at making up rainy-day sports games with dice and cards, and we would walk the mile downtown and press our noses against the glass to check the progress of the games.

If Donnie wasn't agreeable, I'd hike it alone, and hang around the drugstore for what seemed like hours, awaiting fragments of news: "AL, DET 000, CLE 000." I would leave, ostensibly to inventory the toy counter at the nearby Kress but actually to concentrate harder for a Tiger victory (had I been older I might have just repaired to the back room), and then I would return to the window. "AL, DET 000 010, CLE 000 000. MOSSI PTG., CLE, 7TH." Ahh.

My support undoubtedly reached Detroit in diminishing waves, coming from so great a distance, but I practiced a number of other rituals I knew to be helpful. If I looked at the box scores first before reading the morning head-lines, the Tigers had a better chance of winning, as though newspapers came with alterable type. If the Tigers made Gordon McLendon's national radio broadcasts on Mutual, which were actually recreations from a Western Union wire (Gordon described the players vividly, but I could see them as well as he), it was vital that I hear the first pitch. A hair late tuning in was the kiss of death. I helped the Tigers out in many ways like this, expecting nothing in return.

I knew in those days what every Tiger looked like. In the private gallery of my mind they hung like royalty. I could count the missing hairs on Vic Wertz's head, and knew within a millimeter the wingspan of Groth's ears. Wertz wore a steel plate over his right foot to protect his toes from his prodigious foul tips. Charlie (Paw Paw) Maxwell hit home runs only on Sunday. I lulled myself to sleep at night imagining George Kell scurrying around third base in his baggy pants, and Hoot Evers chasing flies in center to partisan cries of "Hoot! Hoot! Hoot!" I later substituted Kuenn and Kaline for these recitals, and traced the lines of ascension at each position as I drifted happily off to sleep. With all their other attributes, the Tigers saved me from becoming an insomniac.

But it was the Tiger pitchers I loved most. Once, while in the service, I hitched a ride from West Point to Yankee Stadium and watched Frank Lary and Jim Bunning shut out the Yankees in a doubleheader. I had lifted up my head in Paradise. My companion, who had a mind to review the jazz centers of Harlem on the way back, was annoyed that I insisted on sticking the entire eighteen innings, and kept tossing peanut shells in my lap. I was oblivious. When we finally got up to go, the shells cascading onto the concrete sounded like I'd hit three gold bars at Vegas and was late getting the cup under the spigot.

Had I been given some say in my looks at the formative stage, I would have looked like Newhouser. I thought him to be the classic Teuton, lean and intense and handsomely scarred under the right eye. The scar looked as if it might have been acquired in a trench or a parking lot and helped give Prince Hal a menacing image. According to stories, in his early years his managers couldn't *drag* him off the mound. Years later, Ted Williams told me the image was no lie. "Jeezus, I'd get a hit off him and he'd *stare* at me," Williams said. "*Nobody* was supposed to get a hit off Newhouser."

"How good was he?" I asked Williams. He did not know of my partisanship, and I wanted him to say "the best," but he drew a line. Newhouser, he said, "was the best left-hander in the game for four or five years there."

"What happened?"

"He hurt his arm. He pitched hurt for years."

I did not remember that. Gordon McLendon's wire must not have acknowledged sore arms.

In time, the ultimate influence that was moving me out of my youth also got its bony fingers on the gullet of the Tigers and as they began to fade the front office made a series of spectacularly daffy trades for a grabbag of minor talents. Newhouser had wound up in Cleveland, where he flamed briefly in a World Series, then retired and became a Detroit banker. In the late 1950s and early '60s, the Tigers went nowhere at the same pace. Writing, then, had become my real passion, and although I never wrote for print about the Tigers (Heaven knows they could have used me), I kept this as my lament for the period:

> By June every year now, the notions of success that are born in April are well out of the Tigers' system. By June, their early foot has developed the pennant-race equivalent of the gout, and they have settled comfortably into place down in the standings, like an aging ship at its moorings. They are in what might be called a chronic state of dis-ascension.

So I banked the fire and let it grow inward, like an old man occupied with his infirmities. With nothing to talk about, I didn't talk. The rituals were private, consisting mainly of reading the box scores. It was an exercise in suffering, but I still did it. The box scores are a baseball fan's life support, as addicting as chocolate bars or garage sales. When the Tigers made brief revivals, as they did in 1967 and '68, my support continued on anonymously.

But then, more recently, I became aware of a new estrangement. Before, when I ran down the names in the boxes, I could match all but a few with at least a foggy 60-line-screen image of a face. With the years, however, a disturbing number of phantoms had cracked the lineup. I first laid this to my reading habits. I had lost my appetite for clichés and no longer bought the baseball publications. A more sobering conclusion was that expansion had led to more and more trades and defections, and a depressing cross-pollination of rosters. Free agency's advent made matters worse. It was like trying to keep tabs on a salmon run.

The Detroit front office seemed to try harder than anyone to hold on to the big fish it had, but just when I got used to the idea of Jason Thompson being a Tiger star, he was a Pirate star. I gave up trying to figure out who Reggie Jackson was starring for (if he was no longer a Yankee, why hate him anyway?). Once, long ago, I had read that Newhouser "lived and breathed" to be a Tiger. It was his only wish from childhood. I could appreciate that. Nobody seemed to "live and breath" to be a Tiger anymore, only to be richer than the other guy. But whatever the reason, the Tigers were slipping from me.

But then, when the Tigers moved out smartly in 1983 and showed no hint of thrombosis, I instinctively began reassessing their chances — and discovered a startling thing. I had no idea what any of the heroes looked like. Not one. Even Parrish, the catcher, and presumably the team's best player, I knew only from his All-Star appearances. He was white. And I knew Whitaker, the second baseman, a rising star, was black. The brilliant shortstop, Trammel, could have served me breakfast and I wouldn't have recognized him.

The only name whose face I could vouch for was that of the manager, Sparky Anderson. His silver hair looked like it had been riveted into his scalp and his eyes were the eyes of a man who has spent eighteen months in a mine shaft — a consequence, I assume, of managing several decades in the big leagues. How ironic, I thought, that in an age of million-dollar ballplayers and dollar-ninety-eight managers, I knew the manager and didn't know the players.

The folly of mentally romancing a team I no longer knew — *never* knew — finally hit me in June as the Tigers flirted with the lead in the American League East. I decided, with some uneasiness, that the romance was at a turning point. I decided some form of action was imperative. Under such conviction, I did what a man of action always does. I called for a second opinion.

Jerry Green, the sports columnist for the *Detroit News,* is an old friend. Green said he didn't think it odd I was a Tiger fan at-a-distance at all, even though he never suspected. He made it sound as if I was admitting to being brilliant. He said Detroit was the "best sports city in America" and that he himself had broken off a long affair with the Dodgers to come there. He said the thing about Detroit was that the fans loved the players and the players loved the fans, a perfect marriage. He said I should come see for myself.

So I did. In July, I spent the weekend there, centered on a four-game series with the Orioles. I stayed at the Westin Hotel in the Renaissance Center, a geometry of stores and restaurants and office space in five podlike structures that hug the Detroit River and jut into the sky like giant cleanser cans. The Westin is the central jewel, at seventy-three stories a world leader in attenuated hotels. It is a beautiful place. Its ubiquitous, sharply dressed hotel staffers give the impression they wouldn't be caught dead in an olive-drab undershirt.

I was there for every game, seeing each one through to the end. The Tiger Stadium I had cherished in my mind's eye was more impressive than I had imagined. It was being refurbished at the time and its contents sparkled with fresh makeup, mostly in the bright blue they used to paint porcelain horses on carousels. The new seats, the steel pillars, the padded fences — everything was carousel blue. The decorator must have come upon a terrific paint sale. Like most parks built exclusively for baseball (as *all* baseball parks should be), Tiger Stadium was slightly asymmetrical, presumably made to conform to the irregularities of the old neighborhood, like Fenway Park in Boston. I could see why Ted Williams liked it so much. The right field fence was a cozy 325 feet from home plate.

The Tiger fans, moreover, seemed to me an exceptionally bright, amiable group that knew when and at what volume to applaud the subtleties of play. They seemed the type that could take a loss in stride (as they had proven capable of doing often enough), and in any case were there, like me, for the duration, getting the most out of their sports dollar. In dead centerfield, a mostly shirtless group of sun-worshipers enlivened the dead spots by bouncing two huge beach balls overhead, section to section.

Each day I changed my seat location, moving around to audit the heroes from all angles. Wherever I went, I encountered neighbors more than willing to fill me in on which Tigers were worth the extravagant salaries they got and which were burning the candle at both ends instead of setting the world on fire. At one point I found I had paid $8.50 to sit behind a steel post, and when I leaned too precipitously to follow a double play, I hit the arm and spilled the beer of the man on my left. And *he* apologized.

We exchanged first names. The man said he had been a Tiger fan since his father took him to the 1934 World Series, and the Tigers thereafter were "simply a matter of life and death to me." In 1968, he said, when he was "still in the factories," he slept in his car to be in line to buy Series tickets. He said it was getting so he couldn't go much anymore, though. "It used to be a buck-fifty, these seats," he said. "I can't afford it like I used to."

None of the games was particularly well played. The Tigers looked like they had been climbing mountains instead of sleeping at night and were blown out in the first two, but they rallied to win the third. By then I was able to cheer them by name. It hadn't taken long to match the names in the box scores with the new (to me) faces.

Whitaker was handsome and whip lean and an obvious talent, and whenever he did anything at all, the fans chanted "Lou! Lou! Lou!" Kirk Gibson, an outfielder, had more of a strut than a walk and blond hair that stuck out of his cap like straw. During batting practice he seemed to concentrate much of his attention on the girls in tight pants who camped near the third base boxes. Jerry Green had told me that Parrish, the catcher, was the team's catalyst, and I could see why. He was built like an upright freezer.

The Tiger publicity department had authorized me to freeload in the Tiger Club before the games. There I ran into Kell and Kaline. They were quintessential Tigers to me, stars of past teams who stayed after their great careers were over and now did the Tiger broadcasts. Kaline told me how much he loved the Tiger fans. I told Kell about following him by tickertape as a boy, circa 1950. He said the 1950 Detroit team that blew the pennant to "the lucky Yankees" the last week of the season was one he could never forget. I told him 1950 had been a low point in my life because of that. "You, too?" he said.

The next day, on arrangement, I met Newhouser. He came to the park in the early afternoon, driving up in an Oldsmobile that had some miles on it, and when I saw him the years rolled away. He was in his sixties, but looked fifty and he moved with the unmistakable grace of a great athlete. He led me into the stadium and we sat down behind the first base dugout. The grounds crew was primping the infield for the night's game.

Newhouser said he had "about twenty minutes." We talked two hours. I asked him if he really was the hothead everybody used to say he was. "Definitely," he said. "I was my own worst enemy. I couldn't stand to lose." I said I didn't blame him. He said he was still that way, and that his grandson blamed him for *his* fits and tirades. "He tells me it's a blood trait."

I told him I hadn't known about his arm injury. He said he still didn't know how it happened. A ball came off his fingertips as he pitched in a game in 1949 and the pain shot through his arm. "No damage you could see in X-rays, but I never pitched again without pain."

I asked if he'd enjoyed pitching in Cleveland. He said yes, but he always considered himself a Tiger. I was relieved. He said he once thought he would have pitched for the Tigers for nothing, and had. At sixteen, he was so good they let him pitch batting practice.

As we walked out, the sun had waned and in the softer light the old scar under his right eye stood out. With some reluctance, I asked how he got it. He said his mother squeezed a pimple and caused an infection.

The final game of the series left my curiosity banked but not entirely satisfied. A visit is not a homecoming, but it can be fun, and this visit was. In any case, after the game, feeling the urge to linger, I let myself get caught up in one of the chutes where the crowd exits and rode the current across Trumball Avenue and into Hoot Robinson's place for a closer.

Jerry Green had touted me on Hoot's. He said it was the place to go to sop up Tiger culture after a game and to see the young hedonists on the club — Gibson was supposed to be one — who were regulars there. It was an

ancient one-design cinderblock building with a faded sign
that promised "good food" on one line and "fine food"
on another. Apparently you got a choice.

The drinking trough inside stretched from front to back
and there were three rows of tables. A color television
dominated the view at one end. The place was packed but
the atmosphere subdued, the Tiger fans more reflective
than festive. I stayed almost an hour, and never once
checked to see if any of the current Tigers showed up. To
my surprise I found I had no interest whatsoever in getting
to know them. I had enjoyed watching them play, but my
interest simply did not extend beyond their abilities on
the field. I knew it was not always that way, so I attributed
it to maturity, and decided it was the best way to feel. Or
at least the most practical. The Tigers I really loved were
all those Tigers of my memory and not these wealthy
transients in Tiger clothes. I would like to have felt differently, but could not, and I suspect such emotional shifts
are irrevocable.

A man with a gray crewcut and a face like a fist was
settled in on my right, apparently for some time. He had
one of those pinched, ageless looks I have seen in men of
the sea, which, of course, was unlikely in his case, and his
bright little spaniel's eyes begged for attention. I asked if
he'd seen the game.

"Yeah. Six innings. Friend of mine gimme a ticket," he
said. He went on unencouraged. "I used to go more. I
foller'd 'em for thirty years. I'd play hooky from the Ford
plant on Saturdays and come out. I played hooky even
when it was time-and-a-half for overtime. My wife didn't
even know I did that. She'da divorced me. I foller'd 'em,
you know what I mean?"

I said I knew, and asked if he had thought of stopping
completely.

"I dunno. They wear me out. I can't love 'em as much

now when they wear me out. I don't mind all the money they make, I guess, but jeeze, you'd think they'd play harder for it. Or stick around." He drained his beer. "And the management, *they* wear me out. I get the feeling they don't care about baseball so much, it's can they get their hand deeper in my pocket, that's what they care about. You know what I mean?"

I said yes, I knew what he meant.

I bought him another beer. But I didn't wait for him to finish it.